D1590914

This book is a lively memoir of growing up with the charismatic American astronomer and science impresario, Harlow Shapley (1885-1972), written in the 1960s by his daughter, the late Mildred Shapley Matthews (1915-2016). Shapley remains widely regarded as one of the most unusual, interesting, and noteworthy American astronomers, internationalists, and humanitarians of the 20th Century. The "round table" refers to a large rotating wooden desk mounted on a central spindle, which graced the Director's Office at the Harvard College Observatory from 1906 through the mid-1950s.

Harlow and his twin brother Horace were born in rural southwest Missouri. Their futures diverged in a spectacular manner — Horace remained on the farm, and Harlow, after an initial foray into journalism, studied at Princeton University under the Dean of American astronomers, Henry Norris Russell, and became the Director of the Harvard College Observatory at age 36. Scientifically, he is best known for correctly placing our Sun near the periphery of the Milky Way Galaxy, in much the same fashion that almost 400 years earlier Copernicus displaced the Earth from the center of the solar system.

Harlow Shapley was also an outspoken political progressive who openly espoused his ideas and actively supported his political and social causes. He was one of the "suspected communists" named by Senator Joseph McCarthy, and in 1946 was called before the House Un-American Activities Committee.

Shapley retired as Director of the Harvard Observatory in 1952. Over the next 20 years he wrote several books and lectured extensively on college campuses across the country, sharing his enthusiasm for the wonders of science, and his witty disdain for humankind's hubris, with a generation of future thinkers.

This book will appeal to all who are interested in the development of astronomy, Americana in the first half of the 20th Century, and the "red scare" that gripped the United States in the 1940s and 1950s.

Shapley's
ROUND TABLE

Mildred Louise Shapley, Age 20

Shapley's
ROUND TABLE

A Memoir by the Astronomer's Daughter

edited by
June L. Matthews and Thomas J. Bogdan

Contents

FOREWORD

Mildred Shapley Matthews was not just any astronomer's daughter. Her father Harlow Shapley was one of the founders of the field of cosmology in the early 20th century, and was known as the "golden boy of astronomy" in his younger years. He not only discovered that our Milky Way galaxy was far larger than anyone had previously imagined, he revealed that our solar system was located off in the suburbs of its spiraling disk, not in its central core. As Shapley liked to put it, "The solar system is off-center and consequently Man is too."

Mildred completed her biography of her father Harlow Shapley in the early 1960s, after several years of working closely with him and collecting material. She circulated the manuscript, in near-final draft form, among family and close friends. She fully intended the manuscript to be published, but by the end of the decade had essentially abandoned this goal. There were three principal reasons. First, she had received little or no encouragement (and even some active discouragement) from her brothers. The reasons for this are not known, but perhaps they felt that her account was too informal to represent the renown of the Shapley name. Second, Mildred's own career had taken a new and increasingly demanding path when she began working at the Lunar and Planetary Laboratory at the University of Arizona and became editor of their *Space Science Series* -- eventually some 30-odd volumes. Third, in 1969 Shapley published his quasi-autobiography *Through Rugged Ways to the Stars* which contained a fair amount of the same material as in Mildred's manuscript. From time to time during the succeeding decades the manuscript would re-surface at various family gatherings, and several of us would say "We really should work with Mildred to bring this to light," but higher-priority projects always intervened, and Mildred herself seemed quite content for it to remain as a family reminiscence. Late in her life she put together a final version of the manuscript and again distributed it to family and other interested persons. It took a new reading by a fresh pair of eyes, those of science writer and historian Thomas J. Bogdan, to convince me that this work was indeed worthy of publication, despite the existence of *Through Rugged Ways to the Stars* and other published material dealing with Harlow Shapley's life and career.

Mildred's story presents a unique viewpoint, and in editing the manuscript I have made only a few minor emendations. The words are all hers, apart from the quotations of Shapley's (and others), which she transcribed either from her interviews with him or written material provided by him. Several of his essays or extracts from essays which she included subsequently appeared in published form, *e.g.* in Shapley's books *The View from a Distant Star* (1963) and *Beyond the Observatory* (1967); these have been omitted. Notes have been added, researched by Tom Bogdan, to identify the Shapley family members and some of the prominent scientists and other people who appear in the story, plus in a few instances where we felt that correction or clarification was needed. We have retained Mildred's use of present-tense verbs, so that readers may be transported in their imaginations back to the time in which her story was written.

Shapley's Round Table, referring to the large rotating desk that her father inherited from his predecessor Pickering, was the title chosen by Mildred for her book, which we have retained.

June L. Matthews (2021)

CHAPTER ONE

I Meet My Father

Eleven long miles to Pasadena down Mt. Wilson,[1] taking all the short-cuts! In the afternoon, my father had hiked with care-free strides up to the Observatory. He wore his usual hiking outfit which consisted of a pair of old trousers, old shoes, flannel shirt and a battered old hat. He enjoyed the exercise and the climb gave him, as well, the opportunity of inspecting various plants and ant hills on the way. He had arrived at the top well ahead of the Observatory auto which made the daily trip up the mountain at dusk. By hiking he would have more time to prepare for the night's observing.

But my father and the stars did not meet that night. On the mountain top a telephone message awaited him which sent him hurrying back down the trail in the semi-darkness to the Pasadena hospital. As luck would have it, I had arrived inconsiderately ahead of time, and my birth certificate still reads "Baby Shapley" with an X after the female, because my parents weren't ready with a name for the records. Later my father named both me and a newly discovered asteroid[2] Mildred; and so, I began my revolutions around the Sun from a beautiful spot on the planet Earth, Pasadena, California.

My earliest memory, unaided later by "do-you-remember-when"s was one of terror. In an empty lot located catty-cornered across the street from our house a field of grass caught fire. From my low vantage point being young and, as the saying goes, only knee high to a grasshopper, the wall of flames seemed to reach the sky and my screams told everyone how I felt. But I have other memories, very pleasant, of my tender years in California. There was a grape arbor, pronounced in those years the "gray barber," in our back yard, and there was Onychophora our Greek (was he?) cat who sat on top of the gray barber. He sat there, or in an equally inaccessible spot to avoid the teasing Shapley children, for there came, at two-year intervals and without asteroids, Willis Shapley,[3] and Alan Shapley.[4] I remember us all rolling on the floor and thinking to myself, "I am really too old for this" but all the same taking part happily in the game. "Now I must put on my rubbers," my father would say in false gruff tones and he would proceed to put one foot lightly onto one ticklish stomach. "Wrong size!" and then to another, "No good!" and another, "too old! I'll have to get some new ones." And all of this would produce squeals of glee from the floor. "Do it again!" we would shout.

I remember trips in our old brown Overland, a rattly open touring car, which would go downhill with great glee. Once we took my Kansas City aunts for a picnic in the Arroyo Seco canyon. The picnic was surely a success because I don't remember it, but the going home was not. Our brown auto refused to make the grade, and all of us but my mother, who was elected to be at the wheel, had to get out and push it out of the canyon. Then there was the time we were motoring out in the country and my mother and the same aunts complained to my father, "All these tempting road-side stands selling fruits and vegetables and other interesting things and you never stop." Later in the drive the car came to a standstill in the middle of nowhere and my mother and aunts who were chattering in the back seat wanted to know, "Why are we stopping here?" My father pointed to a sign which advertised COW FOR SALE.

"Little girl," some friendly passer-by said to me as I collected dandelions in our front yard, "How are you?" "Fine," I replied going on with my work without looking up. "Is that your brother in the carriage?" "Yes," I said, "and I've got another in the house." "How nice! How nice for you. What does your father do?" I looked up and said importantly, "He's an astronomer." "Oh, how interesting! Then someday perhaps he could tell me my future. I was born under Aquarius." "I don't think so," I replied, "he's a very *serious* astronomer and he has no time for silly things, and if he does, he plays with us." She murmured, "Oh, well, goodbye, perhaps you're right." She didn't trouble to chat with me again. But I didn't care. My father *was* an astronomer and he was busy, and that lady should know that the stars aren't working for her future. Nevertheless, when I went back in the house, I received a lecture on being more polite another time.

My father was short, slim, and "boyish looking," people always said. He had a large forehead, and blond hair, with a forelock and a thinning spot on top which he tried to hide. His blue eyes were full of good humor and enthusiasm. His voice and manner were energetic. And this description still holds today, some forty-five years later, except that he is not so slim, and the boyish look has changed to one of mature alertness that still belies his true age.

Harlow Shapley and Martha Betz on their wedding day, April 14, 1914

My mother was petite and lively.[5] She wore her long hair piled on top of her head and fastened with combs. Her shyness she conquered by force

3

and her judgment was always sound. And this description fits her well today except for her hair arrangement and combs which are no longer the fashion.

Four generations: (R to L) Martha Betz Shapley Mildred Shapley, Annette Wittig, Louise Wittig Betz

We children just looked like children. My brothers had Dutch haircuts, with bangs – boys were treated this way then – and I had the same with a hair bow added. I was blond and looked a little like my father, people told me, patting me on the head. Willis was dark and resembled his mother. Alan was blond and resembled his father. And so, the pattern of the Shapley children began.

Our big brown house in Pasadena on Los Robles Street was the scene of much noise and growing up. It still stands today painted white and modernized but surrounded by the city in place of the vacant lots and fields we knew. One of the nicest parts of the house was the big upstairs screened-in porch where we played and slept. There were rolldown curtains to keep out the rain and which didn't work because they flapped in the wind. There was an upstairs guest room usually without guest, where the roof leaked when it rained hard. I remember helping to carry up all the pans that the kitchen could spare to catch the scattered drips and what a variety of tones the plink-plop-plunks made in the containers! I would stand there in the doorway listening to the strange music and be glad it was raining.

It was here in this house that my mother, who had German-speaking parents, tried her German experiment on us. She spoke no English to us in those first years of our home life. My father brushed up on his German and cooperated with her. It was a painless way to learn a foreign language. But when I started kindergarten. I picked up English, brought it as well as the measles back home to the younger brothers, and in this way lessened the effect of the experiment on them. The German had only a few disadvantages. When visitors came to see us, we appeared more stupid and open-mouthed than normal for children of our age. My mother was mortified once when Willis inquired in all seriousness before a group of visitors, "Mama, *was ist ein* BATH?" Alan who was the most confused bilinguist is credited with asking, "Mama, do I like spinach?"

My "remembers" could go on and on but to reminisce is not the purpose of my tale. To illuminate the figure of my father I must speak of his colleagues and others who knew him and remembered him well. He helps me with some reminiscences of his own, of what he calls the early care-free days, and which only now he finds time to tell me.

One day I found in an old scrap book a snapshot of him and another man in aviation suits posing by an old-fashioned biplane. "What about this?" I asked him. "Who is the man with you? What are you up to? Trying to observe the stars above the clouds?"

"In the office next to mine was a young Spanish astronomer, the Reverend Luis Rodés of Barcelona who was visiting Mt. Wilson for a year," my father's story began. "He took a lot of ribbing from the rest of us because his research was on Venus. In fact, this Catholic holy man was a real expert on that planet. A rich widow befriended the Reverend, and one day she took us both to a Los Angeles suburb where for five dollars a commercial flier would take us for a ride out over the ocean. This plane resembled more a box kite than today's airplanes; it was a breezy one engine craft. Father Rodés and I bundled up in flying suits, helmets, and goggles. The widow snapped our picture and we went. Neither of us had ever flown before. "Don't be nervous," Rodés said, "for if anything goes wrong, I'll take care of you. I have a special contact on high." We got aloft – perhaps a thousand feet – and the single engine sputtered. Rodés crossed himself and went into prayerful action, scared to death. The engine died and the aviator Swede made a crash landing without damaging us, thanks to the Lord (and the priest). A few days later we went back, bundled up again, said goodbye to the widow, and safely flew to the ocean and back. Then we went home and boasted. For years Rodés showed the pictures of us in costume, next to the box kite, at astronomical meetings telling how scared I was. Of course, he was the scared one. Rodés survived the Spanish war and the anti-clerical craze in Spain but eventually, sad to say, starved to death, or maybe it is better to say, died of privation."

These, my father says, were the dangerous years, and often to save my mother's nerves he told her only afterwards about the adventures. But often when a courageous sitter could be found for us, she resolutely went along. One afternoon my mother and father, the widow and Father Rodés went to the Riverside Mission together. In the courtyard up on a balcony there was a one-octave assembly of bells on which my mother played *Silent Night*, impressing everyone. My mother was also an enthusiastic mountain climber. She tells me of the time she killed a coiled rattle snake with a big stone. "Weren't you afraid?" I asked her. "Oh no," she replied, "Your father was right behind me with a big stick." The trophy (rattles) long graced the library mantle shelf. Another time they and other astronomers went to the top of Mt. Baldy and hiked down. The plan was to signal across to Mt. Wilson with pocket mirrors, but Mt. Wilson evidently hadn't been forewarned. They aroused no reply. On these expeditions my father who caught poison oak very easily would rub soda and water all over his face and hands and as the solution dried, he would turn a deathly white. I imagine that he was a frightening sight.

"Tell me about this other picture," I asked, showing one taken of him and another man on a mountain trail, each in hiking attire, carrying large knapsacks.

"This man was a visiting Japanese physicist," my father began. "Toshio Takamine was his name. One day I invited him to lunch. 'So sorry, so sorry,' he replied, pointing at the shelf in his office, 'but I have my sandwich lunch here, so sorry.' But you can this time let it go, I said, and he agreed. Precisely at the appointed time he knocked on the door of our house, came in and handed us the sandwiches. He thought that I had meant let them go along."

"I suppose you cut up his sandwiches, ate them, and complimented him."

"Something like that. But getting back to the snapshot, Takamine and I went on various mountain climbs. One was unforgettable because it was so expensive. This Japanese gentleman was a tense sort of person. It wasn't enough for him to go on a hike, study the geology, the insects, and the plant life of the mountains. 'What is the meaning of the universe?' he wanted to know; 'Why is man? Which is what?' So forth and so on. I looked at the mountains. He followed in my cliff side steps and searched his soul and mine. We were at a delicate place on the trail, canyon to the left of us, mountain to the right, and the damn gnats were gnawing me. One got in between my eye and my pince-nez just when Takamine called out: 'Dr. Shapley please, do you think there is a God?' It was hot, sweaty, and gnatty. What's that? I asked. 'A God – is there one?' I took an irritated swat at the imprisoned bug, hit the glasses, which took off into the canyon. Whatever my momentary religious beliefs," my father chuckled, "I'm sure I made use of the terminology. But Toshio Takamine was OK," he concluded. "He worked on the Stark Effect and was an expert in the analysis of that feature of stellar spectra."

Dr. Seth Nicholson was my father's closest friend at Mt. Wilson. It was with him that my father unintentionally found the asteroid, Mildred, while searching for new satellites of Jupiter. In those days newly discovered asteroids were often named, not numbered, and astronomers had fun giving some strange or personal labels to some of them. Our two families were also close; both had daughters of nearly the same age and younger sons. Dr. Nicholson and my father occasionally "herded the daughters" to Pasadena's Brookside Park Sunday mornings to give their wives and baby sons a rest. While the daughters played with delicious freedom, the astronomers would lie on the grass, talk, and write astronomy. Most of a joint technical paper concerning the spectra of pulsating stars was written at Brookside Park.

In these "carefree years" my father had more time to enjoy his young family, and to pursue his serious hobby. Milton Humason tells of the staff meeting at the Observatory when all were assembled awaiting Shapley. He, however, didn't make his appearance until fifteen minutes later. He walked in admitting sheepishly that he had been detained by a fascinating ant hill, a large mound in a vacant lot which he passes each day from home to office. Then there was the time my mother discovered a lively ant trail that came in the kitchen window, went up the wall, crossed over the ceiling, down the other wall and into a jam pot. She was on the verge of annihilating them when my father stepped in to defend them. He wanted to perform an experiment on the ants before eliminating them and the jam. It was common knowledge that in hotter weather ants ran faster. On this hot summer's day, he fired up our furnace, raising the temperature of the already warm kitchen to an unbearable degree. My mother and I fled the house to escape being baked alive, but my father remained, stripped to the skin, and succeeded in discovering the temperature above which the ants began to slow down. It was 102 degrees Fahrenheit.

Up on Mt. Wilson were the great 100-inch and 60-inch telescopes. There also were interesting ants for daytime observing. There on the windowpanes of the laboratory building my father discovered a species of ants that hunt flies and other winged insects. He spent many hours watching them in action.

Dr. Benioff, who spent some summers on the mountain with my father, tells me, "He wasn't all stars and ants; he was also boy." It seems the seventeen-year-old Hugo Benioff constructed a single rope swing which he attached to a branch of a large pine tree situated next to the porch of the recreation room. The porch was perched over a mountain side that fell away steeply to the canyon below. One would pull the rope to the back side of the porch and swing out over the canyon. "One afternoon shortly after the swing was installed," he tells me, "Dr. Nicholson and your father accompanied me to my swing site and all three of us had a hilarious time swinging out over the canyon. It took considerable skill to return face-to to the porch and frequently we would hit the banister backside-to. This game went on most of the afternoon and when evening came, and it was time for your father to begin his observing at the telescope he was so battered and exhausted he had to go to bed instead."

My father's ant activities were less exhausting but also led to some amusing incidents. Once, as the story goes, he was observed sitting all morning on the curb of Los Robles Street, holding something in each hand and staring at the sidewalk. He had discovered an ant trail traveling along the crack in the sidewalk in front of our house. He marked off a measured length of the groove and then timed the passage of a given ant over this length, thus determining its speed. At the same time, he noted the temperature of the air above the sidewalk. So, there he was, with thermometer in one hand and stopwatch in the other. However, the bus driver going back and forth on his route couldn't see the ants and became more and more suspicious and finally called the police, who, my father remembers, "inquired kindly if I were well."

Several valuable technical papers resulted from my father's painstaking observations. One unusual result was that by using his graphs of ant speeds versus temperature, it was now possible to determine the temperature of the day by measuring the speed of a particular type of ant.

One of my father's most rewarding moments in his ant studies was his discovery of freak *Pogonomyrex* ants. On a vacant lot at the corner of Lake and East Orange Grove, which was *en route* to his Pasadena office, lived several vigorous colonies of the Harvester ant (technically known as *Pogonomyrex californicus*). From day to day he watched their hopeless fight against another species, the Argentine ant. One afternoon, upon closer inspection, he noted that in one of the nests there was a colony of Harvesters that was different from the rest. The workers that ran in and out of the entrance to the nest, in the service of their egg-laying queen far below, had little spots or knots or feathery protuberances on their backs where normally they should have been smooth and shiny. My father sent a few specimens from this strange nest to the leading American authority, William Morton Wheeler, at Harvard University, who reported that three of the submitted specimens were indeed pterergates (which means "winged workers"). At that time only six other pterergates were known in the world: three collected in New York, one in England, one in Belgium and one in Mexico. And now here in Pasadena was a whole nest full, seven hundred or more pterergates.

The ant society, as we know it today, has one small aristocratic fertile caste, passing on the inheritance from one generation to the next, and another caste, comprising the overwhelming majority (the common ant), with its individual sterile females that have little directly to do with the genetic development. Only the queen mother temporarily possesses wings that she can use on her nuptial flight. For the past forty or fifty million years the common worker ant has been wingless and effectually sexless, and totally dependent (with a few exceptions) on her community for food and shelter. The ants had discovered adopted and developed society millions of years before man tried it. But, some hundred million years ago the forerunners of the ants all had wings and probably all were fertile.

Here, in front of his eyes, my father was watching a fossil society. He was witnessing a scene that should have been possible only in the age of the mighty reptiles when ants were yielding gradually their independence as individuals, abandoning their ability to fly, and adopting colonial advantages and restrictions. "Could this mean," my father mused, "that after fifty million years of experience this particular ant society in Pasadena would now tend toward the non-social family rites of the Mesozoic Era?" Unfortunately, the question goes unanswered. Fate and the warring Argentine ants did not permit the survival of this unique nest of the Harvester ant. Years later my father and other scientists tried in vain to find descendants of these strange ants in the sandy lot where now a billboard and gas station stand.

There was always ant or insect experiments going on at our house. I remember years later in Cambridge Massachusetts, coming upon a glass jar containing graham crackers in a filing cabinet in my father's study. "Oh," he told me, "not a forgotten lunch! Beetles used to be in there with the graham crackers. This special kind is alleged to synthesize its own H2O. I was testing to see how long they would live without moisture." The fate of those beetles I never learned but the word *graham crackers* in connection with my father always brings to mind not bugs, but how surprised we children were to catch my father spreading butter on graham crackers! We thought butter should go on bread. He remembers our laughing at him, for we reminded him continually of this *faux pas*.

His enthusiasm for ants, for his family and the sunny California life was even then surpassed by his enthusiasm for exploring the universe. I was too young to appreciate what my father was doing in addition to being our parent, but evidently it was enough to award him the important post of Director of the Harvard College Observatory. He has now told me how this came about.

"One morning in 1919 the news came that the great Edward Pickering,[6] director of the Harvard Observatory, had died. Walking home to lunch I came to a halt on a street corner and mused to myself, 'the new director of the Harvard Observatory, the third or fourth largest in America and historically the most famous, could it be I?' Right on that street corner I decided, I was going to try for it. A crazy ambition maybe – I was only 34 – but in 1912 when I, a Princeton student, was visiting the Harvard Observatory, the famous astronomer Miss Cannon[7] predicted that I would someday become Harvard's director. Yes, I'm going to try for it."

"I wrote to my friend and teacher at Princeton Observatory, Professor Henry Norris Russell.[8] Might I aspire? 'Good heavens, no!' Russell replied, 'It's for big people.' True, I reflected, I am something of a pip-squeak on Mt. Wilson, but I've had seven good years from which have come many papers and theories, although not enough gray hairs perhaps. I let it be suspected that I was available but didn't let the people at Mt. Wilson know of my unholy ambition. They wouldn't understand why I would wish to leave the large tele-scopes and my globular clusters. Then Russell's advice was sought by Harvard. Russell could have had the job, but he didn't want it. He knew he couldn't happily run such a complex show as the directorship at Harvard – too hard on the nerves. It was probably at this time that he mentioned me as a possibility."

"This year of 1919," my father goes on to say, "the Harvard football team was making history, as it seldom does, and in January as champions of the East it went to Pasadena to play in the Rose Bowl. Along with the team and the coaches went an official representing A. Lawrence Lowell, President of Harvard. This man was instructed to interview Shapley. The football game was a success for Harvard, as was also the interview for me. I was offered the title 'observer.' It was at this point that Mt. Wilson's shrewd director, Dr. George Ellery Hale,[9] got into the act. A clever letter writer, he wrote to Harvard, 'If Shapley is the man you think he is and we think he is, you will not want him there in second place.' This bold move seemed rather risky to me, but Hale had skill. He raised my salary so that Harvard would have a target. Harvard considered."

At this point my mother comes into the story. Professor Duncan of Wellesley who happened to be on the west coast at the time, came to call on her. (It seems that a Harvard Professor must have among other things an acceptable wife.) When my father came home from the office that day she said, "You can pin a blue ribbon on me! I feel like the prize cow at the County Fair. We discussed Harvard and the formal life in Cambridge. I had the strange suspicion the purpose of his call was to look me over to see whether I would fit into the Harvard social menagerie." Her suspicions were right.

Harvard continued its investigation. Two men of the Harvard Adminis-tration, George Agassiz[10] and Theodore Lyman,[11] went to Washington where the National Academy of Sciences was staging a debate between Shapley and H. D. Curtis on the dimensions of the universe, which was stirring up interest among astronomers everywhere. The inspectors were sufficiently impressed. Harvard took the gamble.

CHAPTER TWO

Young Life in an Observatory

T he director's residence of the Harvard Observatory was an old and elegant mansion built with much grace and imagination in the eighteen-forties and enlarged with even more talent sixty years later. To the regret of those who lived and visited there, soon after my father's directorship came to an end, the house was torn down. Each year crying for more attention, the old house was deemed too expensive to preserve and maintain. This great gray structure was built on a hillside making possible an intricate design full of curious details that took years of exploration before all the surprises were exhausted. Not counting the bathrooms and the wide hallways, there were something like twenty rooms in the house. The three of us children counted them many times, never coming up with the same number twice. As to fireplaces, we all agreed; there were eleven. For a game, while we were still imprisoned in bed with chicken pox, my father drew us rough floor plans of the house and had the idea of assigning numbers to all the rooms as was done in the adjacent office buildings A, B, and C of the observatory.

"Shall we use R for residence or H for house?" he asked us. We favored residence – more dignified, we thought. On our floor plan the rooms on the first floor began with ten; twenty and over were assigned to the second floor, thirties and forties to the third and fourth floors. It was a fine idea, but in the end, it proved impractical, because nobody could remember what number was assigned to what room. Nevertheless, for many years the R survived and was used in one particular case. When our parents said to us "go to R" it meant stop wiggling around, go to the bathroom! It was fortunate we had chosen the letter R and not H.

The Harvard College Observatory, with the Director's Residence
in the foreground, as it looked in Pickering's time.

On the first floor, besides various closed-off storerooms and the house furnace, there was a large square room with a beamed ceiling, the reception hall, which you entered by the great front door. If you did not know that you must *pull* at the brass knob to ring the bell, and tried the ornamental door knocker, you might still be there, for the front door was far away from the ears and the living part of the house. But, if you did pull the knob, our maid would eventually arrive to open the door, or if she was busy, one of us would come thumping down the stairs three or four steps at a time to see who was there. Along one side of this room was a long wood box which served also as a bench where you could lay down your coat, and above this was a Gilbert Stuart portrait of George Washington who watched your coat while you were upstairs. On the wall opposite the front door was a large floor-length mirror flanked by draperies. If your eyesight were poor, you would walk up and find yourself trying to shake hands with yourself. Then you would retreat and take the grand staircase decorated by a beautifully carved banister to the right. On the first landing there was another draped mirror but now, you would be more wary and just eye yourself in an approving or otherwise manner. On a wide ledge high above this stairway stood three large Chinese vases, each differently shaped. You then approached the true reception hall where my mother and father greeted their guests and led them into the handsome and spacious drawing room. From this hallway opened, in addition to the drawing room, a small music room (with an ornate balcony over the front door) where the Shapley Symphony Orchestra held sway in later years. Also, off this hall was the large library which my father made larger by raising the bookshelves to the ceiling, and the staircase that led to the upper floors. Next to these stairs you entered the dining room from which spread the kitchen wing, back doors and stairs, and the maid's quarters. Because the house was built on a slope, this floor was also a ground floor. Glass doors from the drawing room opened onto a big terrace and lawns, the scene in summertime of pleasant luncheons, picnics, and tea parties.

The drawing room had a grand piano with great lion-claw legs; beautiful to see but sorry to hear. My mother, soon after we arrived and were settled, engaged a highly recommended Viennese piano tuner to tune both this and the upright piano in the music room on which we children were later to practice. He tackled the upright first, singing as he worked, and trying out the piano with sweeping arpeggios and scales. We stood in the doorway without making a sound, watching the happy little man work. Nevertheless, he kept saying, "Little children, don't bother me," over and over until my mother happened to hear, and suggested that we go outside to play. Later at dinner she was explaining to my father, "He finished the upright and then went to inspect the piano in the drawing room. He took one look at the museum piece and shook his head. Then he played a chord, threw up his hands, covered his face and began to cry." My mother had tears of laughter in her eyes.

Along one side of the drawing room was a long window seat on which twelve people could sit in a row. A beautiful fireplace with a carved mantel

15

stood at the end of the room with a pair of ionic columns on each side. The arches that they supported framed two large windows with a view of the dense lilac bushes bordering the south lawn. The furniture was dark and ornate in the Victorian style. There was one piece, a fragile looking, fragile-really settee that was a constant worry for my mother. It was nick-named "the professor-holder," because invariably one or two large professors elected to sit on this delicate seat. After a party, my mother could be heard saying, "we really must get the professor-holder re-enforced."

The library could be entered from either the drawing room or the hall. A dark portrait of Galileo hung over the library fireplace and this mantel was set with colorful tiles. At one end of the room hung a gilt-framed mirror doubling the count of my father's books. This was another of my mother's worries; this mirror and one in the music room were periodically taken down so she could re-gild their frames, and when she did this, the whole house smelled of banana oil for hours. On a marble table in front of the library mirror was an old-fashioned music box, with a beautiful inlaid case – fun to play but tedious to operate. The main spring was broken so we would have to stand by, holding down the lever to make it play. We could make it sound sonorous or staccato at will by setting a clamp. In those days I often wondered why our parents wanted us to take piano lessons when this little music box so obviously sounded better.

The dining room was impressive mainly for its ten high-backed chairs, each as tall as a man. A new dinner guest had to be warned before he rose from the table, because the chairs were extremely top heavy and could easily fall back and crash against the glass doors of the ceiling-high silver chest or china cupboard. It was a festive sight when we had guests, at Thanksgiving for instance, and all the chairs surrounded the mahogany table. My father would stand at the head of the table and begin to carve the turkey as we all applauded. The maid would be waiting behind him with an empty plate to exchange for the one he was loading with white meat and dark; she'd then place it before the first guest while our mouths waited and watered. I remember once on such an occasion the turkey skidded slightly, causing a small grease spot to appear on the lace tablecloth. This prompted me later to ask him, "What would you do if the whole thing slid off onto the floor?"

"No problem at all," my father answered. "I'd simply say to the maid, 'Mary, pick up that bird, take it back to the kitchen and bring in the other one.'"

"Oh, but suppose there isn't another turkey in the kitchen," I persisted.

"Mary is an expert, she'd dust off the fallen bird and bring it back for another try," he replied.

In the main hallway there stood a grandfather clock which was usually working but never chimed. It was a conversation piece, detaining guests who seemed to enjoy discussing its various extra dials. One that didn't move we called the century indicator, but I don't suppose it really was. Opposite the silent grandfather was a two-foot square floor register, the warm air from which made my skirts balloon out in a pleasing fashion and gave me a cozy feeling. Willis and Alan also liked to feel the warmth, and while I was nearly always there first, they were continually trying to stand on the register too and crowd me off. It was here just outside the dining room doors that we waited with powerful appetites for the dinner call.

Up the stairs to the third floor, on the first landing there was a door that led to A-17, the first room of the observatory offices. The third floor of our house consisted of a T shaped hallway, two spacious bedrooms, a sitting room, and a study containing bookshelves and a massive ten-foot desk with one side for my father and one side for my mother. There was also a very small, screened-in, porch where we sometimes slept on hot nights, if we were willing to fight clever mosquitoes.

In the hallway next to the door of the sitting room stood the white table, a little inconspicuous oval table that was the nerve center of the house. "On the white table" was a common phrase used in our household. All kinds of important things could be found on the white table: important keys, memos, lost buttons, shopping lists, our Saturday job lists, the day's menus, the money for the cleaning woman. Things accumulated. It was a major job clearing it

off when guests were expected. In the sitting room nobody sat; it was practically filled with my mother's plants – an enormous number of different varieties which gave a green glow to the whole room. The staircase continued to
a fourth floor which was the children's domain – four small bedrooms, each
with its own fireplace.

Surrounding the house and observatory buildings and telescopes were
six acres of private grounds, including a narrow, wooded section, for us to
trail blaze, giant trees to climb (some easy, some hard), bushes for bandit
hide-outs, and slopes with tall grass for playing. There were gardens and
walks, and close to the house were terraces to somersault and roll down. It
was our country estate, cached away in the noisy city of Cambridge.

In 1921, after the first summer and fall went by, came our first experience with winter, and the snowy pictures in our old story books took on new
meaning. The snows came, soft floating flakes, hard swirling flurries, wet
snow, slush, and ice. The wind whistled in through the window cracks and
disrespectfully rattled and shook the old house. On the top floor where we
slept it was particularly frightening on stormy nights and I often had dreams
of catastrophe. I would imagine that the fourth floor became disengaged
from the rest of the house and sailed away through the air. I did not think my
bedroom would crash to bits when it hit the ground but that it would land in
some populated square of the city with curious people peering about while
I sat upright in my bed in my not too beautiful pajamas.

But the next morning all would be well – the house firm, intact and quiet,
and outside the unspoiled snow waited for our footprints and sled marks.
Bundled up from head to foot till we were round as balls, we would go out
into our winter wonderland. Perhaps the snow would be moist so we could
roll great balls and make snow forts. We tried the conventional snowman
too and once had the ambitious idea to build a great snow telescope for the
whole observatory to admire. But this, when finished turned out to look more
like a short-legged giraffe. Willis and I set Alan on top of it for a ride and the
whole thing collapsed. Alan got snow down his back of his neck, and to his

further distress we found it was impossible to take snow out from a warm neck without putting more in.

Overnight the snow might freeze hard and the next day would be a sledding day. We'd speed down the various hillsides so fast that our runners would make sparks on the protruding pebbles. Sometimes we would string several sleds together and then we would fight to ride on the end sled which would swerve and sway, giving a thrilling sensation. Occasionally on Sunday my father would join us. We would pile three or four high on a sled and fly down the hill with screams of joy and excitement. When the sled came to a standstill, we would all roll off into the snow. Maybe Alan would play dead. My father would poke him with a stick and say, "yes, he's dead. We might as well leave him here." And Alan would then jump up crying delightedly "I fooled you, I fooled you!" and climb back on the sled for a free ride up the hill. Coasting was most fun at the end of the day when it was almost dark. We knew that in a few minutes we would be called in for supper and bed, and instinctively our gay shouts became stage whispers. The lights of our tall house looked pretty from the outside. We could see the streetlights and automobile lights blinking through the trees and periodically a trolley car would roar up or down the hill of Concord Avenue beyond our woods. Only the snow seemed to stay light in the dusk around us. Wouldn't it be fun, I said to my brothers, if we each had a flashlight installed on our sled; we planned to work on this project the next day. At this moment, the expected call came from an upstairs window – "*essen ist fertig!*" So, we trudged up the steps to the kitchen entrance with our sleds, and standing them up on the back porch, we would bring inside all the snow sticking to our clothing. Sometimes Willis and I would cooperate to pull off our boots. Sitting on the floor each taking hold of the other's boot, we'd have a tug-o-war and with a jerk land on our backs. Willis's shoes always came off with his boots and mine never did. Alan of course being little didn't have to do anything but stand and sit when he was told; my mother or the maid helped him. After putting our snowy wet wraps on the back-hall radiator to sizzle dry for tomorrow's winter adventure, we would hurry into the kitchen for supper.

Supper in those first years we ate early at a large table in the center of the warm kitchen because we talked too much. Breakfast and the noon meal we ate in the dining room with our parents, in spite of this defect. One by one, as we became older and our table manners improved, we joined them for the evening meal. But surely it was our father who talked too much and whose manners were questionable. When Willis very politely said, "Please, pass the cookie plate" (he wanted to choose for himself), my father let all the cookies slide off and handed him the empty plate. But we had our jokes, too. Once when I got to the breakfast table early, I took a banana, carefully hollowed out the fruit and place the empty skin, good as new, back in the fruit bowl in a tempting position certain that our father would reach for it. He did and tossed the skins at Willis's head. I was capable of looking innocent. My brothers were giggling too hard.

One summer day in 1925, soon after Alan had fallen out of a tree, a truck arrived delivering a Jungle-Gym that was to substitute for tree climbing until we were older and wiser. This, plus a pair of rings and a tree swing of great amplitude which our father installed, kept us happily playing on the south lawn closer to the house for the rest of the summer. When that novelty wore off, we turned to another of our favorite pastimes – watching Michael, the old observatory gardener. He didn't talk much but he was always pleasant and friendly and busy doing something interesting. We gladly tagged along wherever his duties took him. One day he would be mowing the south lawn and we'd gather the fresh green grass cuttings into piles and have a great grass battle. Another day he'd be weeding the flower beds in front of Building C next to the rhododendron bush and we would collect weeds putting them in his wheelbarrow for him. "This is the biggest rhododendron bush in Cambridge," Michael told us. "Be careful not to break the branches when you play there." He knew it was one of our favorite places to play house, because it divided itself into many natural rooms some of which even had flexible branches that we used as doors. Michael's tool house was full of almost everything that could ever be useful. If my father needed a screw driver or a file or a stiff wire to open the locked filing cabinet in the study whose key had been safely put away somewhere, one of us would be sent out to find Michael to see what he could do.

The best time to be friends with Michael was when winter was near and it was time for him to put down the boardwalks – 150 yards of them – over the maze of dirt paths. They were all lettered and numbered and thus not hard to arrange in their proper places, but it was a long process, with usually a few loose sections to repair and rotten boards to replace. Michael always seemed to guess well. As soon as he had finished laying down the boardwalks, the snow came and the season of shoveling and sanding began. At the end of the winter the reverse happened. We'd watch him re-label the sections, disassemble them and stack them away. When the job was completed, spring would promptly arrive. Michael never failed.

We children were curious about and fascinated by the observatory telephone system, whose bells could be heard throughout the house as well as in the observatory buildings. My father's call was one-three; his secretary Miss Walker's[1] was two-two; my mother's was three. The observatory staff each had a number. We children would be allowed to call our father to dinner. Using the little button on the base of the old-fashioned telephone, we'd carefully tap out the signal, and then, "dinner time," we'd shout into the telephone when he answered. "All right, right away," he would say, which usually meant five to twenty-five minutes later.

My father invariably brought some letters and work from his office to the table. Mealtimes were his opportunity to talk and discuss things with my mother. But when we had guests, things were different. His routine cliché was "children are to be seen and not heard," and accordingly he would monopolize the conversation with jokes and interesting stories. Sometimes even the maid would be caught holding a steaming platter, so engrossed that she was forgetting to serve the dish.

Over the years a long parade of great and lesser people of many nationalities came to our table and our receptions. In the early days one of our favorite guests was Professor Henry Norris Russell, who had been my father's teacher and guiding light at Princeton University. He was a tall, erect man giving the appearance of being stiff and dignified but he always bent over to give the Shapley children special attention. With his crisp dry voice, he was a fine storyteller with an excellent sense of humor. He had a talent for composing or collecting limericks, my favorite one being the following:

> *There was an old woman of Clyde*
> *Who ate green apples and died.*
> *The apples fermented*
> *Inside the lamented,*
> *And made cider inside her inside.*

When Professor Russell was at our table my mother gave instructions to the maid to set a full pitcher of water by his place. As Professor Russell told his stories and matched his wit with my father's during the course of the meal, he would drink glass after glass of water as if he were trying, in vain, to wet down his dry cracking voice. After dinner was over, he would call to one of us for sheets of white paper and scissors, and our game would begin. The scissors were used only for making the paper perfectly square. Then, by series of intricate folding, he would make from the paper squares, little pigs of various sizes with twisted snouts and tails, and birds that flapped their wings when you pulled up their tails. And he could make, from a single sheet, a ball that could actually be blown up. In later years, he used to tease my brother Alan about the time he was four years old and came with a ball that had just been made for him, saying "Please, Professor Russell, blow down my ball." This was the ritual that Professor Russell went through while coffee was being served and the candy passed in the library. Afterwards we children left the library with our paper treasures, glad to leave the grownups to their serious conversations.

Professor Russell wasn't the only favorite we had those first years. Right in our own Harvard Observatory there was Miss Annie J. Cannon – the J stood for Jump which was surely something Miss Cannon could not do. She was an ageless woman of large and shapeless form. She had large features and her hair piled and twisted about concealing in part the earphones she wore to aid her hearing. But nobody cared what Miss Cannon looked like. She was Miss Cannon, loved by old and young, one and all. No party was really complete without her. We children knew her well and loved her infectious laugh. We often ran to her when shyness overcame us at a tea party. She would hug and kiss us in her special way on the back of our necks and always had something nice to say to us. She was an excellent conversationalist in spite of her hearing defect. She relied more on her lip-reading talent than her batteries and seldom failed to understand. She enjoyed a good joke and often told stories and jokes on herself. At a Wellesley College reunion, she overheard two women speaking about her. One was saying with surprise, "You mean that big fat girl could do astronomy?" "Oh my, yes," the other woman answered, "she even has received an honorary degree from Oxford University."

Annie Jump Cannon celebrating her Oxford degree with Helen
Howarth and Mildred, Willis, and Alan Shapley

I remember years later Miss Cannon telling me the first impression of my father as the new director of the Harvard Observatory. "At first, we thought he was a visiting college student," she said, "before we were introduced. He seemed so young and boyish; such a contrast to the sober and dignified Professor Pickering who preceded him. But we immediately liked him because he was so friendly and enthusiastic, and really interested in our work."

From the time I was six until I was a married woman of twenty-five, Miss Cannon was my friend and I can't remember that she changed at all in all those years. She was always the same jolly person, in love with life and dedicated to her research. Miss Cannon's great contribution to modern astronomy was the *Henry Draper Catalogue*. She classified some 300,000 stars according to the type of spectrum they exhibit, a long exacting task examining with her eyepiece one spectrum after another. This classification, filling ten quarto volumes, is a tribute to her remarkable eyesight, her memory for numbers, her patience, and her perseverance.

During the summer of 1939, I did some semi-artistic work for her, labeling the stars on large star charts. These were then to be scaled down and photographed for publication. She was a glutton for work. Setting a photographic plate covered with stellar spectra on a frame that had behind it diffuse lighting to make examination easier, she would pick up her eyepiece and begin. Margaret Mayall, her long-time assistant, would sit beside her to record. Miss Cannon would call out "71 G5, 72 AO, 73 K2." After a while there would be a short pause while she rested her eyes. She'd exchange a few pleasantries, accompanied perhaps by her inimitable good-natured laugh, and then she'd begin again. Young as I was, I felt privileged to be a part of her team that summer.

She lived alone in a little house across Bond Street from the observatory grounds; she named it Star Cottage. It was I and my baby daughter who were the last of the Shapleys to see her. She had recently returned from the hospital partially recovered from a stomach disorder, dangerous because of hardened arteries. My call at Star Cottage lasted only five minutes or so. I could see that she suffered much, and we didn't want to tire her. My little daughter June gave her a moment of pleasure – the characteristic kiss on the back of the neck. "Tell me," she asked, "how was your trip with your mother and your baby to Kansas City?" I told her about our visit to my grandmothers and about the birthday party for my one-hundred-year-old great-grandmother. "Five generations of daughters[2]," she exclaimed. "And your great-grandmother, is she really in sound health still?" I caught a momentary glimpse of a sad and envious Miss Cannon that I had never seen before, one who still loved life and her work and didn't want to leave it. That evening she was forced to return to the hospital and the next day she died. For a long time afterwards, the observatory family did not seem the same. That peal of merry laughter was gone.

Five generations of daughters (1940). From L to R: June Matthews, Martha Betz Shapley, Annette SchurmannWittig, Mildred Shapley Matthews, Louise Wittig Betz

The residence and the main buildings of the observatory were all connected. From our house you could walk directly into Building A which, in addition to offices and a rotunda library, housed two telescopes, a 15-inch visual refractor and a strange stationary Coudé telescope with a fixed lens and movable mirror. This telescope pointed earthward from a second story office window. Building A, in turn, was connected by a covered bridge to Building C, a three-story brick structure that contained many more offices and the valuable photographic plate collection.

As we children were growing accustomed to our new home and environment, our father was doing the same, with his new career as leader of a leading observatory. Sometimes on Sundays we would go over to his office in Building C for a ride on his merry-go-round desk,[3] a huge circular revolving table with space to spread out twelve different jobs. With a slight spin of his desk he could go from one piece of work to another without disturbing any job. In the center of this remarkable table was a cylindrically shaped bookshelf that also revolved. In addition, he had a revolving chair so that he could turn his back on his desk and its twelve projects and face a conventional table which was covered with even more work. Next to his chair stood his Dictaphone and the inside and outside telephones. But there was always space made amidst the piles of papers large enough for one of us to sit happily while he spun the merry-goround.

Harlow Shapley's round table

One summer my brother Lloyd[4] arrived. It was in 1923, and I was eight and now had three brothers under me. I don't know much about Lloyd's arrival in our midst except that I didn't think much of his looks when I first saw him. Until he was walking and talking, he couldn't be a part of our gang and so we mostly ignored him. We ignored him for many months. One day when my father was dictating on his machine at home in his study, my mother brought Lloyd in to show off a tooth. The rest of us had lots of teeth but Lloyd's one tooth was more important because it had made him ill. Lloyd was awfully angry and making lots of noise. My father called us all to come around him. "Let's record Lloyd's remarks on the Dictaphone and play it back to him. Maybe he will be ashamed of himself." We helped push the start and stop buttons and to hold the microphone to Lloyd's big noisy mouth.

The following day at dinner my father arrived at the table with as usual a handful of letters and papers. "Anything of special interest today?" my mother asked.

"Just this," he replied and showed her and us a beautifully typewritten letter with carbon copy starting "*oooh wahwaah ooh wah ooh wah ooh waaah.*" Miss Walker had typed all the day's letters she found on the Dictaphone cylinder and handed them without comment to my father for inspection and signature. He had forgotten to erase Lloyd's remarks from the cylinder.

Miss Walker, as we have mentioned, was my father's secretary and receptionist throughout the whole of his complicated career as director. In all situations, whether commonplace or small emergencies, she maintained a calm and solemn face. I may be wrong, but I have always had the impression that her life was made interesting for her mostly through her association with my father. The contents of his letters were often startling and amusing. His interests and projects reached far beyond his scientific and administrative work. She never showed her excitement, but this may have been because she was a devoted Christian Scientist. If some big shot should walk into her office and ask to see my father, she wouldn't raise an eyebrow but simply tell him to be seated for a moment. I, on the other hand, was always easily impressed and excitable over anything out of the ordinary, and I remember later asking Miss Walker, "weren't you just a little surprised when you came to my baby brother's recording, and wasn't it difficult to spell out?"

"Well," she answered, "I had to play back the recording two or three times to get it exactly right, but I wasn't really too surprised. Your father is always full of surprises."

But life in general was full of surprises in those years. There was the case of the eggbeater and let's call her, Mrs. Beacon Hill. An aristocratic Boston blueblood she was, who had much time for formal calls, and she had come to pay her respects to my mother who had little time for callers but nevertheless pretended politely. Mrs. Beacon Hill sat gracefully down upon an eggbeater which was concealed in the cushions of the drawing room sofa. My mother had difficulty explaining the presence of this eggbeater, but I easily can. On maid's night out, we children often did the supper dishes. I would wash by preference, Willis would dry, and Alan was supposed to put away. But the eggbeater, like some other gadgets, was hard to dry. Willis would be walking all around the house in a bored manner humming a tune, drying a dish or utensil, and Alan would have to follow him around to take over the things and return them to their places in the kitchen. Somehow the eggbeater was overlooked, left behind, and forgotten until Mrs. Hill sat on it.

We had other visitors more annoying than Mrs. Hill, namely Gwendolyn and Hyacinth. They managed to fall down a light well and became imprisoned under the house, and there they gave off the perfume characteristic of angry skunks. We were unpopular until they were rescued. Then, there was the case of the hop-toads in the laundry yard. There were thousands of them in that small enclosure where the clothes were hung. The ground was fairly alive with them. Willis and Alan found it great sport to collect large quantities of them in a wastebasket. I pretended to like them too because if my brothers knew that I didn't, they might find a way to make use of that information. I convinced them so well my love of toads, that one evening they brought a whole basket full up to my room where I was doing arithmetic. I wasn't especially glad to stay in the room after a few high jumpers escaped and began hopping around. And I had a hard time getting to sleep that night, even though Willis and Alan thought they had all of them accounted for.

Another time we nearly gave Marianna, our young German governess, heart failure. Our parents were out; we were alone with Marianna in charge. Willis and I were doing something constructive in the pantry. We had a row of twenty or more bottles filled with water, each to a different level. By blowing across the top we could make musical tones. While we were busily adjusting the water level to improve the pitch, Alan was pacing the floor behind us with nothing to do but watch us. This pantry was connected to the kitchen by an enclosed cylindrical turntable. The cook was supposed to put the hot dish in the turntable and give it a spin; the butler in the pantry was to take the dish out and carry it into the dining room. But we didn't use this system because we didn't have a cook and butler. We had a maid who simply walked out of the kitchen into the dining room with the food. When Alan was younger, he could squeeze into this revolving cylinder, eighteen inches high and two feet in diameter, and with his body folded up tightly, he could go for a ride. He hadn't tried this form of amusement for many months, but with his hands in his pockets and nothing to do, once again he eyed the turntable. While Willis and I were trying to play *Jingle Bells* on our bottle organ, Alan got into his private cylinder to take a spin. Then, when he was finished, he found he couldn't get out! In his painfully cramped position, he simply stayed there and screamed. We all tried to help and give advice. Marianna tried to unfold him. We didn't know what to do. Willis suggested that maybe we had better get Michael and an ax to chop him free. Marianna ran for Michael, but then Alan made one last effort and wiggled himself out into freedom.

But usually we three played together harmoniously. Lake City was a good example. Off the dining room was a series of storerooms, under the offices of Building A, that my father named the *Unterwelt*, and beyond them were the dungeons – true dungeons with dusty dirt floors, massive stone walls and no windows. The main dungeon was doughnut shaped – like the observatory library above it. The large foundation pier for the 15-inch telescope with its green dome, a Cambridge landmark, filled the center. But in those years the dungeons were too frightening to explore even with lanterns and flashlights. We never ventured beyond the windowed storage rooms. It was in these rooms that we built Lake City and played happily many days in a row. Our parents would have preferred that we played out of doors more, because the air in Lake City was stale and damp and the sun never reached us. Each of us had an elaborate homemade doll house that we decorated and furnished. I was Mrs. Anderson, Willis was Mrs. Shephard, and Alan, for want of more imagination, Mrs. Shapley. Besides operating our various households with much realism, we each had piers beside our houses with many flat-bottomed ocean liners and tugboats. All kinds of trucks and cars were available, and an electric train made the circuit around the city. There was also a well-equipped fire station; make-believe fires were numerous and exciting in Lake City.

Each birthday and Christmas, Lake City gained equipment and grew more elaborate. We built harbors and parks and a school. There was a fine grocery store; there was milk delivery and garbage service. In our eyes it was the most wonderful game imaginable, and our own creation besides. What grown-ups really thought when they were allowed to come in and praise Lake City, I'm not sure. The maid once remarked that it was an impossible place to clean. But this did not disturb us; we had our own street sweeper, and anyway we didn't want outsiders poking around in Lake City. It was too crowded for big people; just we could carefully move around in the midst of the set up.

In later years Lake City was gradually abandoned and eventually it became a ghost town. Then we were old enough to appreciate the now, not so frightening dungeons. One Halloween my father helped us have a big children's party using the dungeons as the main attraction. He rigged up spooky red and green lights, floating ghosts and witches riding on broom sticks. Some of our girl guests were really scared and everyone got dirty. However, my mother's refreshments were ample and good; that made the party a success.

But the evening grown-up parties which we were still too young to attend seemed even more fascinating. My parents gave big parties; often all the people of the observatory would be there. A notice on the observatory bulletin board would appear "Tonight at 8:30 in the house, come one, come all to celebrate XXX." I remember we used to lean over the banister at the top of the stairwell on the fourth floor. We would be clad in our flannel pajamas (the kind with feet), looking two floors down upon people's heads. They moved about with such good party manners completely unaware of all the monkey shines, mimicking, and giggling that went on above them. It was fun to guess who was there and what they were doing. Often, we could distinguish the ringing laugh of Miss Cannon and occasionally the voices of our parents would stand out above the rest. One unfortunate time Lloyd let go of his Teddy bear which usually he held with an iron grip. The luckless animal fell down the two floors assuredly aimed for some guest's head. We didn't wait to see; this time by mute consent, we scurried off each to his room before our designated bedtime. We didn't want to meet what might be coming up the stairs to see why Teddy had gone down.

With December came Christmas. And Christmas meant many things. It meant that my mother went more often to Boston to shop. It meant a Sunday afternoon in the kitchen with the whole family helping to make thin, decorative Christmas cookies. It meant the observatory Christmas Tea in the residence. For this, the rooms downstairs were decorated profusely with sprays of evergreen and holly. Red and green candles were placed on the various mantels. There'd be a large wreath for the front door and a smaller one in the front window of the drawing room – everything but a Christmas tree! My mother was firm about this. The Christmas tree was for the Shapley children, not for the observatory party, and it must never be visible until the actual family celebration on Christmas Eve.

Later in the afternoon of the 24th we would be banished to the fourth floor while my mother and father prepared for the Christmas Eve celebration. Where the celebration was to be was a secret. Each year a beautiful tree appeared in a different room, sometimes on the second, sometimes on the third floor. My mother's singing or playing *O Tannenbaum* was the signal for us to emerge from the fourth-floor confinement and hunt for the tree. We would explode down the stairs (sounding, my father said, like a thundering herd of buffalo) and then we'd begin tiptoeing around the pitch-dark house. The light of the night sky from a window would finally give the secret away. One of us would spot a black feathery form in the corner of one of the darkened rooms and shout, "I've found it!" We'd all converge on the point and at that moment the tree would blaze into light, with my father crouched under it, his hands still on the main switch. We'd stand there spellbound for a moment and then all together we'd sing *O Tannenbaum*. Then the magic time arrived, the opening of the mountain of gift packages under the tree. My father was the master of ceremonies, of course. A Santa Claus without costume, he would sit on the floor beside the tree, reach at random for a package, call out a name, and the lucky one would jump up to claim it. After a while there would be an intermission. We'd troop to the dining room for a buffet supper, but no food of any description really interested us. We were impatient to return to the celebration and the dazzling tree that by tradition always touched the ceiling.

But, at the Observatory Tea, that my parents gave each year a few days before Christmas, food was of prime importance. There would be a colorful fruit punch in a cut glass bowl served in the library; red sherbet at a table in the hallway; the tea table was in the drawing room; and in the dining room coffee was served. My mother would invite a hostess to sit and serve at each refreshment table and extra maids, engaged for the occasion, kept the tables supplied with sandwiches, ornamental cakes, Christmas cookies, salted nuts, green mints and sugar-rolled dates. The little thin sandwiches were one of my mother's specialties. She sliced the fresh soft bread herself because no one could make it thin enough. Four or five volunteers from the observatory would be invited to the kitchen to help make the sandwiches. The butter would be creamed soft so it wouldn't tear the delicate slices and various unusual and delicious spreads were ready for application. The crust edges would be cut away and saved for a future bread pudding. Some sandwiches would be made into Christmas shapes with a cookie cutter. Then the sandwiches would be piled onto plates with a moist cloth covering them, waiting for the hundred or so tea guests to arrive.

Toward the end of the party, when everyone had had all they could eat, my father would encourage a group to the piano where they would begin to sing Christmas carols. Song books would be passed around, and the group would grow and soon the rooms would ring with song after song. "Now we'll have *Jingle Bells*," my father finally called out. "All those over twelve keep quiet and listen." It was the children's favorite; the children of the observatory family were invited too so *Jingle Bells* was loudly sung. My father's favorite was *Deck the Halls*. Mine – I could never decide. There would be some special voices in the crowd, and these would be urged to the front to do the solos in *Good King Wenceslas* and *We Three Kings*. The house always seemed very quiet when the last guest had departed and the decorated rooms were empty; only scattered cups and napkins, and we were left. Another traditional Christmas tea party had come to an end.

Only three degrees above zero, and pitch dark! Our feet squeaked on the snow as we walked to the street. I rubbed the sleep out of my eyes and asked Willis, "How do you feel?" He was stamping his feet in the snow like a nervous horse, and yawning.

"The streetcar will come around the corner in three minutes," said my mother, looking at her watch.

"I wish I had eaten that second piece of toast," Willis finally answered me.

"Oh, I've brought mine with me," Alan announced, pulling the buttery mess from his pocket and proceeding to eat it. Fortunately, my mother was occupied in checking her purse for money, train tickets, and streetcar tokens and didn't notice. She was pleasantly excited over our adventure, and so were we. It was 4 AM of a winter's morning (January 24, 1925, to be exact) and we were on our way to Connecticut to see a total solar eclipse.

"Here comes the Huron car!" My mother was the first to see it because we were all facing the other way, kicking holes in the high snowbank against the mailbox. It screeched to a stop. The motorman hadn't expected early customers at the corner of Buckingham and Concord. We clambered aboard. The streetcar roared down the hill of Concord Avenue, found its way to Harvard Square with reckless speed – for in the dead hours it had no traffic competition – and dove into the subway hole. We walked down the drafty ramp to where the Boston subway train loaded. Now, there was a small knot of people here and there. We even spotted Miss Walker some distance away. "Hi!" we called out. She replied with a friendly nod. Many of these early risers were headed, as we were, for South Station to take the special Eclipse trains that were going to various sites in Connecticut, the only place in New England where the entire disk of the sun would be covered by the moon. Not until we were on the special train eating sandwiches did the day begin to show itself. We were lucky, very lucky this January morning – not a cloud in the sky to give us momentary worry. On top of a barren hill, we watched the eclipse begin, happen, finish. It was inspiring, mysterious, wonderful. These were the words I heard people around me use. Immediately after it was over, we were hungry. On the train riding back, we finished off the sack of sandwiches.

"You've got jelly on your face," Willis informed me.

"Mind your own business," I told him, but then countered brightly, so as not to appear tired, "weren't we lucky with the weather – too bad papa couldn't have been with us." After all, a family adventure was not really complete without his participation.

"He is observing the eclipse in Buffalo, New York" my mother reminded us. But he wasn't. It was cloudy and he saw nothing.

The spring of 1926 Onychophora II had kittens and we discovered that we were all going on a big ocean liner to Europe for five months. My father had been invited by the Belgian-American Education Foundation to give a series of lectures in various universities in Belgium. Preparations for the trip were not very interesting. I remember my mother hiring a dressmaker to remodel some of her old party dresses into newer styles, and that she was crossing items off a long list as she put our things into a steamer trunk, and that we each had five new pairs of shoes. Onychophora's kittens, on the other hand, were much fun. It seemed that any cat named Onychophora was destined to think Shapley children were nuisances. She was always moving her kittens and in this big house it was really a big job to locate them. Once she found an opening in the wall of Lloyd's room that went in under a roof over a part of the third floor. We could look in and see two big mama cat eyes, but we couldn't reach in far enough to rescue the kittens that still had their eyes closed. But while Ony was busy eating a plate of raw liver, my father shone a flashlight on the kittens. Hungry, squeaking, and unhappy, they crawled instinctively towards the glaring light until we could reach them and pull them out. They were so dirty we had to clean them up in the foot tub in the bathroom. Onychophora, who had by that time finished her liver, didn't appreciate our intervention. She washed them all over again.

In the meantime, our plans for Europe proceeded and at last we were on the way. I was eleven. I had a party dress, all white with ruffles, and I had a fancy-dress costume. My mother made me a red cape with a hood to go over this white dress and she packed a straw basket in our trunk. And so, I became Little Red Riding Hood for the ship's fancy dress ball. This, I think, was the first grown-up evening party I attended. I remember a great storm and that the dance floor tipped first to one side and then the other. Everybody was screaming with excitement, pretending to be frightened. The floor was terribly slippery, and the dancers were sliding with the ship's motion more than they were dancing. During a calmer moment I danced with my father (lucky for him I had been to dancing school that winter), and with the ship's friendly doctor. I might have danced with the captain, but the ship started tipping so badly that he had to leave the party and go up on the bridge to see what the first mate was doing. I had watched him dance with my mother and others, noticing that he did so always sporting a stiff right leg. Did he have a wooden leg, I wondered? But later, I noticed him running down some stairs, lickety-split, bending both knees. It must have been his dancing style as a sea captain.

Much of the time my mother was busy with Lloyd who everyone told her was really much too young to take abroad. But Willis, Alan, and I had a jolly time running all over the ship. We were energetic and disgustingly healthy while many of the passengers sat around worrying about the storms. One evening when it was too rough to dance, my father agreed to give an informal talk on astronomy. "Can you get me a few balloons? I need white, blue, yellow, and red ones," my father said. The officer in charge of entertainment thought he could. "I also will need," my father added, "some grapefruit, a few round-as-possible potatoes of various sizes and oranges." I went with the officer to gather the stage props for the show, and by that evening everything was assembled.

My father stood in front of the audience beside a small table on which were piled these fruits and vegetables and the colored balloons in various stages of inflation. All that was missing was the tall silk hat and the rabbit; but he was able to make astronomy as entertaining as sleight-of-hand. The three of us children sat cross-legged on the floor right down in front and laughed along with the audience. It was fun.

He paced off the floor space at his disposal, and proceeded to arrange the various fruits and vegetables into a make-shift solar system as much according to scale as possible, describing each planet as he put it in its place. Uranus and Neptune were overboard in the ocean. The nearest star was on the moon. And then he explained the evolution of the stars, using the balloons, showing how new stars such as the red and yellow giant stars contract and as they shrink the temperature rises so that they become sometimes explosive blue and white stars. Eventually they exhaust their energy, becoming cool red dwarfs that have no hope but to die. He assured his audience that our sun will go through these same stages but advised them not to curtail their travel plans. "The sun will stay comfortably constant for another ten billion years," he concluded optimistically.[5]

For three months the four of us were left at a school in Switzerland while my father was busy giving the lectures in Brussels and my mother watched. I don't remember that we liked the school very much. It rained every day and every day we went out for a walk in that rain. (The day we left they began filling the school swimming pool.)

After Switzerland we rejoined our parents and went to the coast of Brittany, and here we had a better time. The broad beaches were wonderful. At low tide we went shrimping and explored the rock piles that were under water at high tide. One great rock was shaped like the prow of a ship, and the high-tide waves rocked and splashed against it. There was a harbor with fishermen about, and many sail boats with brick-red sails. At very low tide, one could wade across to a long and narrow island. And behind the hotel, up over the hill was the small village of Trébeurden where an old woman, wearing the characteristic head-dress of the region, had a charcoal burner on wheels and made sweet *crêpes-chauds* for tourists and natives alike.

It was this summer on the firm sands of the beaches that I learned to ride a bicycle and only here that I was allowed to pursue this dangerous occupation. For miles around there was no obstacle that could collide with me except a few limber people who would move, and some giant stationary rock piles that I could swing around.

Even though we never tired of playing on the beaches of Brittany, we were even happier to return home to our house, our yard, and our playthings. Now the music lessons began again in earnest. I had had some piano and now I got used to violin lessons, as well. My violin teacher was a fat jolly lady; she bore my scrapings admirably, and so did my parents because they were paying for it. Willis followed my example – a little piano and then the flute. Alan got the same treatment ending up with the cello. A peculiar thing about the music business was that all our teachers had the first name of Alice. Maybe we improved or maybe our parents became more indulgent, but eventually we began playing together, and the Shapley Symphony Orchestra was formed. Lloyd, who was only three and too young to play anything at this time, was our conductor. He had a podium not much bigger than a postage stamp, but when he lifted his baton, he looked very professional. There are pictures in the family album to prove it. My mother and father and a few well chosen, indulgent or tone-deaf guest would applaud after our various pieces and then my father would say, "now we will have *the* request number," putting special emphasis on the *the*. *The* request was silence. But we performers didn't mind our father's joke – he joked a lot – and since the exertion had been considerable, silence was fine with us, and the cookies that followed.

My father, who couldn't carry a tune, or maybe he could but wouldn't, was continually encouraging music. We went to the opera and to symphony concerts at an early age. My mother played the piano well, although she was too busy most of the time to do so. On Sundays, often there was a chamber-music concert in our drawing room. Good amateurs would gather together to play for their own pleasure, and anyone from the observatory who was a good listener was invited to drop in. The Shapley Symphony Orchestra was later replaced by the Observatory Philharmonic Orchestra.

When my father discovered that Miss Frances Wright, besides being a dedicated research worker in the variable star field, also played the piano like a house on fire and that Miss Jenka Mohr, one of his able assistants in the galaxy hunt, was also a fine violinist, and among the students there was this one that played the clarinet and that one some other instrument, and that there were various others who wished they could play, he felt that surely this interested group should come together. Since Haydn was dead, why not try his *Toy Symphony*, which required all kinds of extra instruments (bird whistles, bells, rattles) in the percussion department? After Haydn, other composers suffered. Even now, though many changes have come with my father's retirement, this Philharmonic society under Miss Wright's enthusiastic direction still plays. My daughter, now twenty-three years old and an M.I.T. graduate student, brings her cello to these rehearsals. One of the most interesting members of the orchestra is George. George came into being many years ago when one astronomy student mentioned that he could play the string bass and would be glad to if an instrument could be found. Various enterprising members proceeded to build George, who sounds much more like a string bass than he looks. Through the years, there has always been someone willing to try to play George.[6]

My father also encouraged sports, and in these he participated. Summer evenings, after dinner he would go out on the south lawn with a ball and bat and pop flies for Willis and Alan to catch, or to chase after in the inconvenient woods behind. Observatory picnics always included a baseball game. My father was good at hitting home runs. He also made a good ump, using the lingo he had learned when he was a teen-age sports reporter on the Chanute, Kansas newspaper. The spectators, made up of elders and ladies who wished to remain so, would have as good a time watching the semi-comical show as the players.

Then there was deck-tennis, which my father brought off the ocean liners to our lawn. It was easy to construct the small court necessary – simply stretch a net between two trees – and he encouraged the staff and students to take a half hour or so of exercise. I would often look out of my window on the top floor and see two or four at play with the rubber ring on the deck-tennis court next to the woods. Bart Bok,[7] Fred Whipple,[8] Subrahmanyan Chandrasekhar, Martin Schwarzschild, to name only a few, tried their skill at this game while they were at or visiting the Harvard Observatory. For many years, my father was a champion player, both because he was agile and because he used psychology. He'd look abruptly in one direction and toss the ring in another. My mother could almost but never quite beat him. At a crucial moment he would contort his face into such an expression that she would be overcome with laughter and confusion and lose the game. We children could never beat him; he always tossed the ring where we weren't, and we invariably tossed it right to his outstretched hand. On a hot July afternoon, we would finish a game, panting and perspiring, and throw ourselves down in the grass in the shade of an ash tree. We'd look up to a sign nailed to it that warned winter visitors, NO COASTING PERMITTED ON THE TERRACES, and feel a little cooler. In later years one of the wealthy patrons and a personal friend of my father gave the observatory a genuine tennis court and so the sporting life persisted.

Each fall Mr. Johnson from the maintenance department of the Harvard University came to visit my mother to see what had to be done to modernize or redecorate our house. The budget was sorely limited. Nevertheless, each year more rooms were electrified, and the dangerous gas lighting went out. Some rooms got new wallpaper, some got paint. It was a great occasion when it came our turn on the fourth floor for new wallpaper. From huge sample books we chose our own paper with no suggestions or restrictions from our parents or Harvard University. I wanted my room to be beautiful, so I chose as carefully and as adult-like as possible, but my brothers were less concerned. They chose the brightest and the wildest they could find and apparently lived with their choices for many years with no feeling of discomfort.

Some winters the water pipes would freeze and burst in the night and the plumber's arrival was awaited as anxiously as one would wait for a doctor. This sleepy plumber would be as calm as a doctor too. "This is not so bad. You should see what happened at the president's house. I'll go get my helper and the rest of my tools and we'll have this fixed before you can say John Harvard," he'd say. But I could have said hundreds of John Harvards before he returned and fixed the pipe. And it would be a waste of time to say John Harvards while waiting for the plasterers to show up to repair the water damage to a ceiling below; they might be two weeks coming. It would be lucky indeed if all were put to rights before a certain scheduled reception took place.

My mother had a tremendous job and many responsibilities: raising a large family, running a large house with almost no help, being a hostess to the observatory, planning and giving my father's parties, some of them spur-of-the-moment ones. He loved parties! I once heard him say, "I'm a selfish person, I like to see people enjoying themselves." Surely, my mother was always busy and seldom had any time to herself. It was remarkable how she could see to all the details of a clean house, proper choice and quantity of refreshments, extra maids to serve them, and appear rested and as eager for the party as the guests were. It took expert management and she always succeeded. In addition to all this, Carl Shapley[9] came, four years after Lloyd's arrival. We were alternating blond, dark, blond, dark, blond but if our parents were also trying to alternate the sexes, in this they didn't succeed. I now had four brothers.

About this time my father became Pop and my mother, Mom. He often complained that all he got out of the change was a noise; but papa sounded too childish, and mama also. Pop called Mom Gretchen because her name was Martha – this I can't explain better. Mom called Pop nothing. She had a peculiar whistle she used if she thought he was within whistling range. To us she would ask, "Have you seen Papa?" and she would speak of herself as Mama. Stubborn she was, but so were all five of us. To this day we write "Dear Mom" and "Dear Pop." I have heard my mother say the name Harlow when she is speaking about him with other people, but never have I heard her call out his name. And this also I cannot explain.

What was Carl like when he was young? Very much like my large doll, which I had discarded years before. In fact, at one point my father photographed the two together to prove the similarity. But Carl was more alive (dolls then were not as clever or realistic as they are today) and he was more fun for me. Now I was thirteen and old enough to play mother to him. I helped give him his daily bath (although why daily I could not understand) and I was good at feeding him his cereal. Also, I could make him laugh when nobody else could. Lloyd too was more interesting now that he was five and would do anything that I suggested. Willis and Alan had become boys, and at eleven and nine, they had minds of their own. I had to abandon my domination over them.

The five Shapley children. From left to right: Mildred, Lloyd, Willis, Carl, Alan

Some summers, as a family group, we evacuated from hot mosquitoey Cambridge (there was a mosquito egg-laying pond in the Harvard Botanical Gardens across the street) to try the heat and mosquitoes somewhere in the country. We went to Woods Hole one year, to New Hampshire another, and still another year to Nantucket Island. I remember especially Nantucket because there we met the Gilbreth[10] family which, to use their own words, came "cheaper by the dozen." We had various friendly encounters that summer even though we were outnumbered, five to eleven. We lived in an ordinary house. The Gilbreths lived in a converted lighthouse that had a spiral staircase and a bed on every landing. We were there once for dinner. I'm sure there were other foods besides green peas, but the green peas are all I remember of that meal. My father told an old horse chestnut in connection with discussing children and table manners (at this table there were plenty of children and all kinds of table manners) that went something like this: "Pa, an old self-esteemed gent was so startled at Ma's table manners that all the peas rolled off his knife." I sat there wondering if the telling of this joke was a coincidence or whether my father had noticed that Willis had a lap full of peas which he was picking up one at a time as inconspicuously as possible and putting them in his mouth.

I was growing older and felt the need of proving it. I dreamt of achievements that would impress my parents. I was a little tired of my life as it was, and of my parents who seemed so accustomed to me. First, I thought I wanted to go to Sunday school. I thought I would be able to prove something to my non-church-going parents. Then I thought of writing a book – a book explaining astronomy to children – but after the first few pages that seemed too much work. Next, I fell headlong into the realms of music appreciation. With my clothes allowance I bought symphony records and decided that the best way to happiness was to be curled up in front of a phonograph with the volume turned up. While this method served me for many years, and still does, I gladly abandoned it in a quest for adventure. Eventually I had a plan. Next summer (1930) – no one knew of this yet – I was going to travel by myself to Kansas City to visit my relatives. All fall and winter I hoarded practically all of my clothes allowance until I had enough for my train ticket. Finally, I became so accustomed to the idea of traveling a thousand miles to Kansas City that it didn't seem adventurous any more. I became braver in my imagination. What would be really startling would be to take my two favorite brothers with me. Now, my secret really excited me. Carl was still too young to consult. Anyway, he would say yes to anything. But Lloyd I asked in utmost secrecy if he would like to go on a train ride with me to visit *Grossmama* – that's what we called our Betz grandmother – in Kansas City. His big eyes fairly popped with excitement (everyone commented about his big eyes) and I was afraid that he could not hold the secret for long. I decided that now was the time to have a conference with my parents and explain my plan. I took my money out of its hiding place to show them, and they were immediately impressed and approved of my going to Kansas City. About my taking Lloyd and Carl along, they hesitated a little. But they agreed and I was happy that they had confidence in me and could see that I was as capable and as grownup as I knew I was.

Eventually the big day came. My memory becomes evasive when it comes to the actual train ride. I remember we all slept together in a lower berth. I remember my brothers were easily manageable but that I had a unique head-ache probably caused by the new responsibility on my shoulders. In Chicago I had to change trains. My uncle John Shapley[11] was there in the station to help me, but he wasn't much help. I felt like a somewhat harassed mother with my two children aged two and six meeting a relative whom she was glad to see, and vice-versa, but who couldn't possibly understand her tiredness and the great burden on her shoulders. I wrote a telegram to send to my parents cleverly using up the maximum number of words, telling them that we were alright. But Western Union kindly informed me that I could not spell alright as one word, suggesting I use OK instead. It was embarrassing. Even today I am a poor speller and if all the words in this book are spelled correctly it is only through the diligence of the editor. My father once suggested that I should learn shorthand. That would provide an excuse for my poor spelling.

John Shapley viewing the official Observatory portrait of his brother (December, 1972)

At the station in Kansas City, neither my grandmother Betz nor my aunts were there to meet us. It was through no fault of theirs; they simply didn't know I was coming. I had begged my parents not to tell them because I wanted to surprise them, so they said nothing beyond the plan for the Shapleys to drive out to Kansas City and Jasper Missouri in July. And this was June.

The doorbell at 300 West 51st Street Terrace had rung, and at the door stood a young lady dressed in a black summer coat and black broad-brimmed straw hat. (Black was all the rage, and fashionable that spring.) She had two small children with her, and a taxi waited out front. *Grossmama* looked startled when the lady simply said "hello."

"You must be looking for the McDonalds who live next door," she said. The tired young lady looked dismayed.

"*Grossmama*, don't you recognize us? I'm Mildred; this is Lloyd and –"

All of a sudden, *Grossmama* did recognize us. She and all the aunts welcomed us with tears and laughter and open arms, a welcome which I thought was going to last all day. But finally, the taxi driver came up the walk to the door and asked if we would like him to bring the bags in. My adventure was successfully concluded.

CHAPTER THREE
It Began With A

"They've come!" I shouted for the whole house to hear. Our blue Buick was pulling up to the curb having completed the 1500-mile trip from the Cambridge house to Kansas City, Missouri. My brothers tumbled out as soon as the car stopped; my mother and father sat there a moment longer with a well-we-made-it look on their faces. They looked a little travel-worn and dusty, I thought; probably Willis and Alan were too, though on them it didn't show. But my parents were smiling and so were the Kansas City folks, and there we all were, all talking at once and hugging each other right there on the sidewalk. We were all together again.

After a week's visit with *Grossmama*, and *Tante* Nettie, *Tante* Alma and *Tante* Louise, we moved on to visit our relatives in Jasper, Missouri. In spite of the good time we were having in Kansas City, we were all eager to see new places. Traveling was fun. The baggage fitted well in the big Buick and after the baggage all seven of us squeezed in. We chattered about the Shapley farm, we played the alphabet game with the road signs, we took turns sitting in the front seat. We stopped two times and had lunch twice. At the end of the day we arrived in Jasper at the Shapley farm.

This farm had one feature that distinguished it from the other farms surrounding it. The large meadow in front of the house had been made into a beautiful lawn where another owner might have put a hay field. Hay was the main crop, even so, with plenty of haystacks to show for it. Willis,

Alan, and Lloyd wasted no time in running about and exploring the fields, the barn with its animals, and the creek. Because I was wearing fashionable summer black, I stayed behind to talk with the grown-ups. I was feeling old and sophisticated after my traveling adventure, and they welcomed me in their circle. We had tea and discussed the fly epidemic and how best to make wild blackberry pie while my brothers jumped off the tops of haystacks and played in the barn. I was momentarily a little sorry I had grown up, but still I was proud to be treated as an adult.

In Jasper, I remember, we were eating good things continually. There were elaborate picnics where you couldn't possibly eat a sandwich, for there were too many tempting concoctions both hot and cold to fill you up before you got to the sandwich platter. At these large outdoor gatherings were people of all ages and descriptions, all somewhat related to us. In the front yard near the house there was a hammock stretched between two trees where I would occasionally retreat to swing and dream. When I was tired of doing something or nothing, I would lie there trying to imagine my father's life when he was a little boy. There was my jolly Aunt Lillian,[1] his older sister; there was my friendly Uncle Horace,[2] so similar in looks to my father. There was my Uncle John, his tall younger brother who was seldom in Jasper. There was my energetic little grandmother, his stronger-than-she-looked mother. But I didn't know any particulars about my father when he was young, so my daydreams didn't flower into any stories. There was only one sad event I had somehow heard which was no fun to muse upon. My Grandfather Shapley had lost his life through a stroke of lightning in a great hay barn many years before.

My father never talked much about his boyhood, even when I displayed interest in it during that summer of 1930, nor does he now thirty years later. But by persistent questioning, I have managed to gather a few recollections of this part of his life for my story.

"Concerning this project of yours, I am somewhat embarrassed," my father began, as I settled myself in the chair he offered before the fire in the Sharon, New Hampshire living room. "This place won't be too hot for you," he said, by way of changing the subject. "I remember you belonged to the some-like-it-hot clan."

"Yes, I'm rarely too warm," I replied, "and I remember you said, years ago, that I was preparing for the wrong place! But I'm not prepared to discuss heaven and hell with you. Let's go back to the days when boys were boys. Tell me, why are you so reluctant to reminisce?"

"It isn't that I'm so damned modest – just embarrassed and skeptical about my being worth all the labor and fuss."

Nevertheless, I was able to convince him that this would be a sad chapter if I had little to go on besides the encyclopedia and *Who's Who*. "By the way," I said, "I got a bit of a shock reading that you were born in Nashville, Missouri. How long has this been true? I was under the impression it was Jasper."

"No, Nashville – Jasper never figured in it!" my father insisted.

"Strange, this fixation," I went on. "You weren't born on the town line to justify my error? For twenty-five years I have filled out forms – you know the kind – father's name, Harlow Shapley; father's birthplace, Jasper, Missouri. I've messed up a lot of people's files."

"You're still running around free," my father laughed.

"Very well," I continued, "now I've got you born in Nashville, Missouri – a little town then, an almost ghost town now (isn't it?), on November 2 of 1885, the day after that famous supernova exploded in the Andromeda Nebula.[3] Couldn't you have been born on November first? The story would have been much better if you and the star could have used the same day. You see, I am neither satisfied with your birthplace or your birthdate!"

"That would have been an interesting coincidence – it could have explained how I happened to stumble into astronomy. As it was, I had no excuse." My father reached for a cigar. It had been a year at least since I had seen him. It felt good to be here now in his New Hampshire home and to be having this long overdue conversation. To me he seemed no older although he insisted he was.

"Still smoking cigars, I see," I remarked.

"Less work than keeping a pipe cleaned and going. You know the reason I took up this vice some ten years ago, don't you?"

"Yes, I remember the young daughter of one of your research assistants needed empty cigar boxes for a rock collection or something of the sort. By the way, I met that young lady in Switzerland this summer just before she left to enter college. She told me to 'tell Dr. Shapley he can stop smoking those awful cigars now.' She doesn't need any more boxes."

"Gretchen," my father called in the direction of the kitchen, "don't you need cigar boxes?"

My mother came to the door, "I'll be joining you in a moment with coffee. What's this about cigar boxes?"

"I thought perhaps you had a need for empty cigar boxes."

"But we're getting too far ahead of our story," I interrupted. "You can't smoke cigars yet – you've just been born."

"All right, if you really want it, here goes. I was born with a full head of hair and probably squawking, but not alone. As you know I had a playmate with me; your efficient mother has always envied the super efficiency of my mother in producing twins."

As if on cue, my mother returned with the promised coffee. "I am satisfied with our production," she put in.

"Sit down Gretchen and join our pow-wow of sorts by the fire. Help me satisfy this offspring of ours," my father urged. But she begged off, promising to return in a few minutes. She was occupied in the kitchen watching the toll-house cookies. My mother's toll-house cookies with their chocolate bits and chopped nuts are famous with all the Shapley clan and their friends. She considers it her duty to see that the cookie jars are always full, and this is a major job when there are sweet-toothed grandchildren visiting.

My father continued with the story. I learned that his father, Willis Shapley, was a small-town hotel keeper for a while, a small-town schoolteacher, and a farmer. He was not educated except for some self-teaching, for he was in frontier country with small opportunities either in Missouri, or in northern Illinois where he was born and lived until he was about fourteen. My father's mother, Sarah Stowell, was educated in a girl's seminary in New York State where she was born and grew up. She got to Missouri as a visitor of her sister in the 1870s. She had some money and bought land, married Willis Shapley and lived most of her life in one farmhouse. The marriage, it seems, was not very happy, for life was rather hard and one parent was ambitious, the other not. His father was widely read for those times and places, but the home library was rather trivial. The *St. Louis Globe Democrat*, and the *Youth's Companion*, and some schoolbooks were about all that was available until my father was seventeen and left home for various schools.

When he was ten, they lived a year in his grandfather Stowell's house, a lovely place near Hamilton, New York, now labeled by the New York Historical Association as a landmark. Presumably in civil war days it was a station on the Underground Railway, its function the smuggling of run-away slaves bound for Canada. This grandfather Stowell was the stamina of the family. He lived to be over 95. He was a farmer, and a citizen of some renown, a Baptist, an abolitionist, and the inspirer of grandsons. The Stowells arrived in America from England in about 1641, and the Shapleys in about 1650. There is more to be found about these early settlers in the *Stowell Genealogy*, a book three inches thick, but that belongs in another story.

Coming back to the present, I asked my father, "You and Horace – you're not identical twins, are you? I remember Horace as similar but not the same."

"Yes, he's a healthy country man, a successful farmer and landowner. I'm a pale city boy, successful in other ways. My older sister, Lillian and my younger brother, John and I have been rather close over the years. With Horace it has been quite otherwise. I do not want to go into his feelings and our long lack of contact. It is sufficient to say simply that Horace is a retired landowner, without keen interest in science." My father got up to poke the fire. He is a sensitive man, intensely unhappy when there cannot be understanding and cooperation in the family and elsewhere.

"Those logs are burning well in spite of their dampness," I said in an effort to distract him from his sober thoughts. "Tell me more about your boyhood."

His boyhood, he told me was quite ordinary. He remembers saving two boys from drowning, although he was not an enduring swimmer – just solicitous, as he puts it. Somebody had to do it. Like all boys they were alternately kind to animals and stern, but mostly kind, even to the dog that put scars on his back and arm that still faintly remain. "The poor dog most likely had been awakened too suddenly from a dream of ancient fights," he commented.

In those early days, imagination was his strong asset, and the making up of wild tales and talking them to his brothers engaged many an hour in the hayloft or in the field. He was, he confessed, for a long time rather ashamed of this secret vice; but lately he has come across others who have confided that they too were secret daydreamers, practicing their tales on a less imaginative companion. His inventions were not erotic tales – mostly westerns or local heroism. This operation, over three or four years, surely was the forerunner of his later intense interest in the stories that rocks, bugs, and the stars could tell.

"Then, during those years began your interest in journalism," I asked, "but not yet astronomy, isn't that true?"

"No, not astronomy," my father admitted. "I remember that in 1900 our father encouraged our staying up late to see the predicted shower of meteors; we simply gazed with full ignorance at the slim phenomenon."

"It's amazing how little I know about your early life," I insisted. At that point, my mother entered the room with samples of freshly baked cookies, and I asked her, "Are you better informed about him?"

"Yes," she admitted, "I was curious and asked questions from the start because I planned to marry him."

"Gosh, I thought it was my idea!" he interrupted. "One morning I looked in the mirror, saw that I was getting a little bald and ran out and got married quick!"

The next morning was a beautiful Indian summer day, crisp without being cold, and clear. The leaves were putting on a spectacular autumn show. My father and I agreed that this morning we should talk outside, and so we turned to the woods.

"Shall we head for the Yachting Basin?" he suggested. We started down a steep grade, the beginning of the Tough Ladies Trail, a rather rugged path, as the name implies, not to be attempted in high heels, and then to a new, easier short-cut trail, Tough Ladies Reformed, that branches into the conventionally named Deer Trail. My father has 117 acres of wooded land, both high and low ground, with two active brooks running through it. The land is a naturalist's paradise, and as he regretfully points out, we have not bred any naturalists in the family. Yet certainly he can be called one. For over forty years he has been a member of the New England Botanical Club and here in Sharon he has been very busy out of doors. In recent years he has planted about 2500 trees. Perhaps 500 were lost in a drought but he has pampered the survivors by carrying pails of water to the most suffering. He mentioned, as we walked down the trails, that he has identified 121 different flowers and shrubs on his land.

"It's a disease with me," he explained. "When, as a Princeton student in 1913, I wandered alone all over Europe; I carried with me a German Botanical guide to the wild plants of Europe. I identified flowers on the way and wrote the date and place in the book. As a result, my plant vocabulary is largely in German and Latin."

Of course, he also visited observatories and astronomers on that European trip – Paris, Greenwich, and Cambridge observatories in particular, but he told me he was too shy to get much out of them. What he remembers most vividly now about that extensive trip was the news of his father's tragic death – news that caught up with him in Paris.

We arrived at the Yachting Basin – no yachts, however. This is a yachting basin in name only – simply a wide place in a pretty bubbling brook. Once, years ago, we could float a raft here, but the beavers have been busier and more numerous than we. They dam where they please and all we have left is a wading basin. We settled ourselves beside the water in the weak and welcome sunlight and he began the story of his schooling.

"I had a dreamy ambition of becoming a newspaper reporter or something of the sort," he recalled. But actually it was his sister Lillian who had much to do with getting two of her brothers somewhat educated. It was she, he told me, rather than the parents, who encouraged their ambitions. True, his mother, who was ambitious in all ways, acquiesced and hoped her sons would become famous someday. But both he and his brother, John worked for most of their educational expenses; there was not much available money at home, just a lot of land. Lillian taught a year or so in the local Shapley school, a quarter of a mile away; and in later years, after much intermediate experience with country bumpkins (as my father puts it), she claimed that her brother Harlow was the brightest student of her career. Lillian was rich in friends because of her keen interest in the achievements and troubles of others. In her career as a teacher she taught in Missouri, Kansas, Washington, and Montana. Her influence on people is illustrated by the fact that during her last painful sickness she was receiving chatty letters from the children of students she had taught. She was a great letter writer – one could always count on her to answer. It is a great loss to me that I don't have her here now to help me tell about the old Jasper days. She remembered so many things long forgotten by others.

Even with Lillian's encouragement my father's education got a rather late start. He was seventeen when he left home to try for an education. First, he went to Warrensburg (Missouri) Normal School, but that was only for one term. Then came the Pittsburg, Kansas Business College – pretty nearly a total loss for one year. Next, he spent two years as a newspaper reporter in Chanute, Kansas and Joplin, Missouri, towns not far from the homestead. Both Chanute and Joplin were tough mining regions, oil in one, zinc in the other. He saw some things that were not pleasant – shooting, fighting, bums, racketeers. It was in Chanute, he told me, that he was incited to go to college by the charm of the college-boys home for Christmas. But he had not gone to high school (academically neither the few weeks at Warrensburg nor the business school experience counted much, and, he reminded me, a reporter saves no money).

But he followed his ambition to make a career in journalism. The University of Missouri was talking of installing a School of Journalism but to get to Columbia, Missouri, for a four-year college course was a vain dream. Reporting had helped to make him glib and perhaps bold, notwithstanding a natural shyness that has lasted a lifetime. So he made a plan. With his five-year younger brother, John, he enrolled in Carthage Academy (a college prep school somewhat under the protection of the Presbyterian Church). Tuition was low, food was cheap, clothes not good or expensive. A little help from the parents made it possible for one term and then he stayed home for a half year so that the younger brother could stay in school – but really because he thought he could do well enough by self-teaching. He learned his geometry in a hay field, also Latin and English literature. He took the Academy examinations and passed all right. This Carthage Academy was a small school – later bankrupt – but had four very good teachers, all of whom helped him enough so that after about one year of this high school he was admitted to the freshman class of the University of Missouri, with one or two conditions readily disposed of when he got to Columbia.

Recently the small city of Carthage, Missouri, where my father went to high school paid a unique tribute to their renowned native son. May 3, 1963 was designated Harlow Shapley Day. A homecoming celebration was planned by E.L. Dale, publisher of the *Carthage Evening Press*, with the help of his staff member Marvin Van Gilder and a committee of thirty citizens. Jasper, Nashville, Lamar, Joplin, and other surrounding communities joined in this effort, a celebration which my father considers perhaps his greatest honor. It was the kind of welcome given a figure such as a Channel swimmer or Olympic athlete. Possibly it is the first time that a scientist and humanitarian has had this type of public recognition. On the appointed day Missouri's Governor Dalton and other state officials, various representatives from the University of Missouri and nearby colleges, joined the influx of twenty thousand visitors and Carthage momentarily tripled in population.

Greeted by cheers and bouquets, my mother and father arrived at the Joplin airport to be the stars of this homecoming show. The big day began at the Mark Twain School in Carthage which stands on the site once occupied by the Carthage Collegiate Institute. Here in the front hallway a portrait of Harlow Shapley and a picture of the old Academy building were unveiled at a ceremony conducted by the Board of Education. A press conference followed, and a luncheon presented in the Shapleys' honor by the Chamber of Commerce.

The highlight of the day was the 87-unit Shapley Day Parade. Much the biggest that Carthage has ever had, it included 20 marching units (one of which was the drill team from the Richards-Gebaur Air Force Base), 50 majorettes, 12 marching bands, and 27 floats. The floats depicted parts of Shapley's life and work, and the Age of Space. One elaborate float showed Mt. Wilson and a telescope discovering Cepheid variable stars in a sky of flowers. Another labeled *Harlow's Dream* represented his boyhood on the Jasper farm. A small boy, as Shapley, sat beside a haystack daydreaming his future. My mother and father and other honored guests sat in a reviewing stand while the parade passed and saluted Harlow Shapley. Afterward, there was a reception at the Civic Center where all the citizens of Carthage and visitors could meet him. My parents greeted relatives and friends some of whom they hadn't seen for more than fifty years, and my father had an opportunity to talk with young students of the area, always a special pleasure for him.

Another more impressive event later at the dinner was the presentation of a framed copy of the *Resolutions* voted by the House of Representatives of the Missouri State legislature and forwarded to the President of the United States, saluting a great Missourian. Following the dinner my father gave an address to which the public was invited. He took his fellow townsfolk on a journey among the galaxies and concluded the evening with a partial show-ing of the film based upon his book *Of Stars and Men*. The whole day, filled with emotional experiences and memories as it was, caught my father both with tears and laughter. Letters and telegrams came from many admirers who could not be present. Nathan M. Pusey, President of Harvard University, wrote:

> *"It is disappointing to me not to be able to attend the celebration in honor of Professor Harlow Shapley. But to remedy this deficiency I should like at least to send a message of hearty congratulations to this distinguished son of Carthage at a time when all his old friends and fellow townsmen gather to pay him tribute. Harlow Shapley was a notable member of the Harvard faculty for thirty-five years, and he continues his interest in Harvard and Cambridge. I suspect, however, that some of him has always been in Missouri. Thus, our university is especially grateful to Carthage both for its part in nurturing a noted American scientist and then sharing him with us. Harvard sends greetings to Professor Shapley and best wishes for a happy day."*

So, he had left the *Chanute Sun* and the *Joplin Times* in order to seek a college experience hoping that a university degree would help him go up in the field of journalism. He could write with some dramatic skill when permit-ted. He remembers it was a thrill of a boyish type to have his little stories from the oil fields around Chanute accepted by the famous and presumably judi-cious *Kansas City Star*. Also, he could kick (operate) a Gordon press and set type slowly by hand. But the part he didn't like very much was the catering in his news stories to the advertisers. "Could one be fair and honest and a journalist?" he mused.

"I dreamt that someday I would have a country newspaper of my own," he continued his story. Missouri's school of journalism was my goal, and in this ambition, at the age of twenty, I was encouraged by my sister, and by Mr.

Knight and Miss Ross of Carthage Academy; they probably touched up my class-room records when writing to the University Admissions Committee."

"But what happened?" I asked him. "You haven't succeeded in owning a newspaper. You're still buying them daily."

"Journalism and a surrounding general education was my goal," my father went on, "Science I would avoid. But the best laid plans certainly went wrong. When I showed up at Columbia, Missouri, to be a freshman in Journalism, I discovered that they had decided to postpone for one year the starting of the school (which later was to become the most effective school of journalism in the country, and perhaps the first – I don't remember)."

"I see; so, you tried something else and liked it better," I said.

"Don't spoil my story with your impatience," he reprimanded me. "Let me tell it." I smiled to remember how many times he had had to tell us when we were children to listen and not interrupt.

"So, what to do," he went on. "One could elect almost anything in those rather loose curriculum days. Latin seemed attractive, and English and history. But just what? I got ahold of the big catalogue of courses, alphabetically listed, and started at the beginning. Here in first place was the word a-r-c-h-e-o-l-o-g-y. Sounds good but how do you pronounce it? Is the c-h- hard or soft? In southwest Missouri we did not have that word, and I was too vain or shy to ask."

"So, you became an astronomer because it began with A!" I couldn't resist getting ahead of the story.

"So, I turned the page and thereby turned my life. For the next category in the catalogue was a-s-t-r-o-n-o-m-y, and I could pronounce it, even though I knew nothing about the subject; nor did I have more than an average curiosity about the sun, stars, planets, and the like."

(Incidentally, his younger brother came up to the university the next year; he could pronounce that long word, and before long he was a professor of art and archaeology at Brown University, and went on to teach at New York, Chicago, Harvard, Johns Hopkins, Baghdad, and the Catholic University of America.)

Some people question this story of how it happened that he became an astronomer, but they do credit his statement that Professor F.H. Seares[4] soon spotted him; he became an assistant in astronomy at a thousand dollars a year, and never got around to the study of art and archaeology.

"I never regretted leaving journalism," my father continued. "My Chanute boss came over to Columbia and offered me (fabulously) a third interest in the *Sun* if I would quit the college glamour and come back. I said no. Maybe I made the wrong choice – my chief Latin teacher thought so."

"How come?" I asked. "Teacher's pet?"

"Well," he said, "he had the wry duty only a few years ago to invest me with an honorary degree. It was a local-boy-makes-good recognition from my alma mater, because I was then the new director of the Harvard Observatory. While the president of the University of Missouri was telling the assembled commencement thousands about my carryings-on, Dean Jones, the Latin head, whispered to me 'you know, Shapley, I think you were wrong not to go on as a Latin scholar, for I remember you could correctly write poetry and you made that translation of Catullus.' The president finished eulogizing with a gesture, and up rose the Dean and I, he still muttering about my error as he hung the orange and black hood over my mistaken shoulders in recognition of my trivial operations in a scientific field."

Surprised that he had this Latin streak in him, I asked if he still composed Latin poetry for mental exercise or relaxation. It seems that he has forgotten all his Latin except a couple of Horatian odes. Back in his college days, however, one of his first published papers had to do with Lucretius and his lunar theory, and there was also an undergraduate essay on the subject of meteors and the poet Horace.

It didn't take long for astronomy to win him over from his older loves, Latin and Journalism. After the first few weeks in the elementary course of astronomy he had no doubt but that he should become a professional astronomer. Offered a small job at the observatory by his professor, doing computing and typing for him, he was assigned a desk – and he has never left it; the subject was so varied, so remote, so fascinating. He liked figures and he didn't mind the routine so long as there was a reasonable goal in sight. Even the pointing out of the constellations, he admitted, had its charm for this older-than-average freshman.

"Maybe we should be heading back," my father said, interrupting his reminiscing, "to see what Gretchen and the seven cats are up to. We can talk as we walk."

I should explain that my brother Carl was and is the cat lover of the family. My father enjoys playing with kittens; my mother tolerates them as long as they aren't underfoot. As a result, practically every summer Carl arrives in New Hampshire with either an expectant mother or a carload of homeless kittens bound for some country experience.

As I followed my father up the trail, I asked him if it was all clear sailing in college once he had discovered his major interest. Money-wise, he explained, he was not an impoverished student, for after the first year he was an employee of the department of astronomy. In his junior year (he skipped the sophomore year) he reduced variable star measures at something like thirty-five cents an hour which in those days was enough to keep one going. In his senior year he taught a semester of elementary astronomy to freshmen and others. "I was horribly scared of the ten or so girls in the class and they knew it!" my father exclaimed.

"Judging from your battery of female research assistants through the years at Harvard, you seem to have overcome your fear of girls," I laughed.

"I tried a foolish thing at the first meeting of the Missouri class – handing out, to the thirty or forty students, slips of paper on which they were to write useful information about themselves. It was foolish because my hands and voice trembled so that I dropped the slips and stuttered. But my willpower came to my rescue and by the next class meeting, I had them eating out of my hand. Three years ago, I met one of those frightening coeds who admitted that she and her pals had deliberately baited and tormented the fair-haired youth!"

"Did you have any difficulties in your courses?"

"Well, there's one further episode in my rather loose and sloppy career at the university (things tightened up when I got to Princeton). For some reason I started my study of physics not with the elementary course but with a harder second or third year dose. Professor O.M. Stewart was an excellent lecturer, but the lab assistants were not inspiring. Near the end of the first semester came an uninteresting examination. I did less than well and was called in and advised to drop physics. It shocked me! I was getting high marks elsewhere. I declined to drop out; I was able to show Professor Stewart that some of the questions I had answered almost correctly. Damned if I would be defeated just because I had not been thrilled by the course. I stayed with it, got an A at the end of the year, and two years later got the highest honors in physics and mathematics ever given by the University. In my senior year I was awarded the Laws Medal for outstanding achievement in astronomy. With these recognitions it was easy to get the Thaw Fellowship at Princeton for three years of graduate work and the Ph.D.; and easy to build a considerable astronomical bibliography."

University of Missouri graduates (1913) Alma (L) and Martha (R) Betz with Harlow Shapley

I asked him to tell me about the teachers who inspired him at the university. I learned that Professor Oliver Kellogg of the Department of Mathematics was perhaps his most influential teacher at Columbia, Missouri. He advised the Princeton move, and effectuated it. My father did an original job on Fourier Series which he guided, but it was never finished or published; later Kellogg himself finished it off. Kellogg went to Harvard soon after my father left Missouri; and years later he was involved in Shapley's coming to Harvard. It was an unhappy day for my father when Kellogg – a superb teacher and friend – died on a mountain climb in Maine. Professor Seares, the astronomy head at Missouri also was a great help to my father. He left for Mt. Wilson in my father's senior year and was influential in getting Shapley later from Princeton to Mt. Wilson. Seares preached and practiced precision, reviewing and checking. The two were in adjacent offices in the Mt. Wilson headquarters on Santa Barbara Street, Pasadena, seven years working together in photometry. Both of them were haunted by the uncertainties of photometry when carried on with photographic emulsions. Later Shapley turned to globular clusters and Seares to observatory administration.

"But, of course, my major influence was Henry Norris Russell of Princeton – but let's talk about that next time." We were coming out of the woods to the meadow and the clearing where the white frame house stood, "I'm stopping to inspect an ant mound, *Formica exsectoides*," he said.

"And I'll go in and see if Mom needs help with getting lunch," I replied. I found her in the small dining room, busy sorting the morning mail. The dining room has a wall of windows and glass doors making it possible to view the woods, the canyon, and the hills beyond in fair weather and foul. The blue dining room table was strewn with letters, papers, and books.

She greeted me and asked me how far we had progressed this morning.

"Almost to Princeton," I told her. "But there are a few holes here and there. Tell me, when was the first time you saw Pop, and where, and what did you think?"

"That's a long time ago," she said evasively. "I'll tell you sometime, but now it is time for lunch. Do you think it is too chilly to eat out on the porch?" Being heartily in favor of eating outside, I carried a stack of dishes out to the long picnic table on the open veranda, just outside the glass doors of the dining room. "Papa should be coming in soon; I think we are ready."

A sudden irrelevant thought struck me. "Mom, why don't you ever say Harlow to him?"

She smiled. "There he is now," she said. The slamming of the front screen door had announced his arrival.

"The ant colony is bedding down for the winter," my father reported, walking into the kitchen. "They show little interest in yesterday's steak."

"I don't blame them. Yesterday's steak sounds a little uninteresting even to me," I remarked.

"They had it yesterday," he mumbled as we sat down to lunch.

"Doesn't this warm weather excite them a little," I wanted to know.

"Some, but they feel the temperature drop these frosty nights and know it's time to slow down and go underground for the winter."

"How deep do they go?"

"Oh," about five feet in this case. It varies according to how dry the terrain is. It's less deep in damp soil."

I decided to change the subject. "Just before you came in, I was asking Mom when, where, how, and why she first met you, but she didn't seem too eager to give me any details."

"She probably doesn't remember," my father remarked, giving her a special look.

My mother has never liked to talk about herself, or about things sentimental. My father, I found out later, had met her in a mathematics class at the university. She sat in the front row, an alert, eager student. He sat somewhere in the back and watched her. "I thought she was wonderful," he told me.

And from her, I eventually learned about her college career. Wonderful fun, she called it, although not, perhaps, in the way one might think. Almost entirely college was such a serious affair for her that she could not waste time in frivolity or relaxation. Or at least, she thought she couldn't. Her interest and joy in college were the courses, of which she took as many as were allowed at a time, and the fascinating fields of knowledge that they opened up. Two of her sisters went to college to become teachers, but she never had the desire to teach, except to earn money so as to be able to study more. She could hardly wait to get to the frontier of knowledge and have a chance to add a little to what is known. Research is what she wanted and, strangely enough, in what field really didn't matter. There were so many interesting ones, it was hard for her to choose. Her chief interests were mathematics and languages. The reason she chose languages and started towards the doctor's degree in philology instead of mathematics was simply because a graduate scholarship was offered to her at the University of Missouri that helped her get her master's degree, and later a scholarship was available at Bryn Mawr in that field. If similar aid had been available in mathematics, she might have preferred it, but in those days, scholarships were few and far between. One semester she obtained special permission to carry five courses instead of the usual four, and then proceeded to get a grade of 97% or better in all five. As my father had discovered, she was wonderful!

"What about astronomy," I asked her.

"I never took a course in college," she replied. "I had a private extracurricular tutor."

"Of course! And I can imagine the whole routine." I turned to my father. "You let it slip out that as a freshman you liked pointing out the constellations."

"It wasn't so easy," he remarked. "Even though I was a glib talker in those days, I had to be especially interesting to keep the Betz sisters listening to me as we all stood there on the front porch. I once had a private bet with myself that I could keep them up until midnight, listening to this idle freshman tell his stories. I won, but it took some tall talking."

"Oh yes," I said. "I've heard *Tante* Nettie and *Tante* Alma mention this. Suddenly in the middle of a really exciting story you stopped and took out your watch and said, 'Ha, midnight! I wanted to see if I could keep you up to this hour. Now I must go home!'"

"We never did hear the other half of that story!" my mother recalled.

Serious as my mother was, she did more at the university than go to classes, do homework, and squander some evenings getting acquainted with astronomy. She was a star basketball player, for one thing. We have a victory picture of her and a group of girls all wearing middy blouses and dark pleated bloomers posed with a basketball. In those days one did not need to be tall to play basketball. If one was agile enough to elude the opposing players and, while in the clear, had a quick eye for putting the ball in the basket, it made a perfectly good score, and so her team won. She also played field hockey and was runner-up in the graduate tennis tournament at Bryn Mawr. She liked sports, probably due to the influence of her father, Carl Betz.[5] He was a pioneer in introducing physical education into the public school system in Kansas City and elsewhere. It is too bad that he could not have lived to enjoy her many successes at the university.

She finished college at the age of nineteen, and her master's degree she received when she was twenty-two. Then in 1913 she went to Bryn Mawr to begin work on the Ph.D. in philology. But she didn't finish. Astronomy became more and more interesting, and, as she explains it, "your father still tells some pretty good stories!"

We had finished our lunch. "If you will give me a reprieve this afternoon," my father said, getting up, "I'll go help the Red Sox beat the Yankees." He is a loyal radio fan of Boston's baseball team. That was agreeable to me as I had a great deal of information to digest before asking for more. My mother mentioned a trip to Peterborough for groceries, as well as letter writing to the boys, as her afternoon activities.

The next morning, I emerged from my room and found my father already at work in the upstairs hallway. His custom-made knotty-pine desk stands before a picture window from which he had a wide view of the sloping meadow and the barn. After I'd helped myself to some breakfast, I was back to resume yesterday's conversation.

"Do you have much to do?" I asked.

"I'm making work for Gretchen, writing some letters for her to type."

"Hmmm, shorthand," I noticed. "I'm safe. I never learned."

My father has written shorthand nimbly ever since early school days, and it has helped him turn out great volumes of work otherwise impossible. His notes at lectures and meetings, his first drafts of manuscripts, his letters home, his records of hunches are practically all first in shorthand.

"I wrote a shorthand letter once," my father continued, "to Mr. Gregg, the inventor of the system I use. He replied in longhand! And when I was a student at Princeton, there was a small brunette, 50 miles away at Bryn Mawr, to whom I said, 'if you want to hear from me, which is not likely, you will have to write in my shorthand, for I am too busy and illegible for long-hand.' Damned if she didn't take me up, (I was stuck) and for half a century the correspondence between us has been only in shorthand."

"That must make writing to your children, not skilled in this art, a bit of a chore," I said, as I sat down opposite him at his crowded desk. "You were going to tell me today about your friend Henry Norris Russell."

"My great friend, but my first meeting with Professor Russell at Princeton was horrendous. He was shy, and I was embarrassed. He was not sure whether this Missourian would be bearable. I felt that he considered me a servant on trial. 'Mr. Shapley, you might close the door,' was Russell's first remark. For some reason that supercilious remark and manner stung me into remembering the occasion. But for the next forty years we were the closest of friends, personal and scientific. His astronomical interests covered all fields except, strange to say, galaxies (the specialty of Shapley) and the structure of the Milky Way. His health had to be watched; otherwise he would have used his genius brain more hours per day and made all my own contributions look trivial by comparison."

"I agree Professor Russell was surely a genius, a great and also a likeable man. Remember his paper pigs?"

"Yes, and as a genius, at times pretty hard going for many of us followers who think and talk slowly and raggedly. As one of his first graduate students, I quickly learned to use monosyllables: yes, no, yes? so? how's that? and ummm. That drawling ummm concealed more careful ignorance than any other in the Queen's English. But I doubt if I fooled him. We would walk on the Princeton campus, he, waving his cane to shoo inconsequential students off the walk – he, calculating and scintillating – I, listening, guessing, wondering, trying to de-confuse myself. You may remember that I claim to be the original Russell Mixture."

"Yes, I have heard you say so, but what exactly do you mean?"

"That's my wise-crack: the effect of his rapid talk and thought on me." The textbooks say the Russell Mixture is a theoretical composition of the atmosphere of stars; it gives the possible proportions of various chemical elements.

Russell's informal role over three decades as National Astronomical Consultant was a fortunate assignment. He visited all the important American observatories and the assistance he gave everywhere was immense – criticisms, hunches, and much more computational labor. He liked to play around with numbers. One of his colleagues once remarked "Russell will spend much more time hunting for ingenious short cuts than would be required to take the long cut."

In 1912 Russell and my father began their joint work on the orbital theory and practice of eclipsing binary stars. My father's doctoral thesis was on the subject of eclipsing binaries. I told him that I was planning to read it so that I could talk a little about it in the next chapter in words of one syllable. "You can try," he commented, "and if you succeed, I'll hand you my Princeton diploma."

At Princeton, my father was supported by the Thaw Fellowship. In those days, this thousand dollars was quite a triumph – a big bonanza, he called it, and more than he needed, living frugally in rooms at the Prospect Street observatory. The second of the three Princeton years he was supported by an equally large Proctor Fellowship that had just been created. A few years ago, my brother Lloyd, then a graduate student at Princeton, reminded his father of his Proctor Fellowship priority and announced that he had just been awarded a Proctor Fellowship, 40 years separating their appointments. "It was in the blood," as my father put it. And there is more to the coincidence. Lloyd and he were son-and-father getters of Ph.Ds. That had never happened at Princeton before. And, again, they were separated by exactly 40 years.

Perhaps at this point I should interrupt to check up on a few dates. In 1905 and 1906 my father was at Carthage (and home), Missouri; in 1907 he went to the University of Missouri, receiving an A.B. in 1910, and an A.M. in 1911. He went to Princeton in the fall of 1911, and to Europe in the spring of 1913, getting his Ph.D. in absentia, and then he had one post-doctorate year at Princeton. In 1913 he was offered the job at Mt. Wilson.

"I took it the next year," my father explains, "going to Pasadena by way of an evening wedding in Kansas City. The job paid ninety dollars a month! Of course, there was soon a raise.

The low offer to this Princeton whiz (with a formidable bibliography already) was sort of a slip; it included free room and board on Mt. Wilson, but from the first I lived down in Pasadena. Then followed seven years of many papers and theories, and three kids. And in 1921 came the shift to the Harvard Observatory."

"You were twenty when you started high school and fifteen years later you were a Harvard professor and director of one of the largest observatories in the world. Rather a Young Man in a Hurry! I'd like to know, before we go on, a little more about Princeton, about your wedding, and about your first days in Pasadena."

"I did nearly one full year in research on eclipsing binaries at Princeton after my degree. There was much to do. In fact, Gretchen and I were computing orbits on the train, April 15th, 1914, as we headed west from the wedding in Kansas City. We set ourselves a goal of trying to finish certain computations before we hit the Rockies, and of course we did!"

"And this was your wedding trip! I'd like one of you to tell me a little something about the wedding itself."

"I doubt if Gretchen would care to talk about the wedding. I made a mess of the formalities, declined to drink the celebrating champagne, and with cousin, Ralph, as best man, I marched to the guillotine eagerly – that is, at double the customary speed. Nobody had told me "notting," and I had never seen a wedding ceremony. It was a quiet homey affair, in vast contrast to a top-hatted wedding you may remember, that I took part in a couple of decades later. Gosh! What a binge that one was!"

"Mine," I admitted, "but I don't recall the top hats. I also declined the champagne; that I do remember."

We looked out of the picture window and saw my mother walking up the front path. The shopping bag she carried suggested she had been to the mailbox, a quarter of a mile down the road. "Here comes more work," my father remarked, groaning good-naturedly.

"Anyway, we're about through with this interview I think," my father said.

"Only a little something more about your arrival in Pasadena?" I asked hopefully.

"Maybe Gretchen won't mind if I tell you the poisonous ant story. Although I've told it various times, I have never written up my observations of the Amazons, the kind of slave-making ants that must be fed by slaves or perish. Some eastern slave makers (*Formica sanguinea*) can have slaves or not as conditions warrant, but the *Polyergus* has a mouth suited to warfare but not to self-feeding. Wonderfully beautiful is this genus, *Polyergus* – I longed to see them sometimes outside the books. One day, nature provided the opportunity. Gretchen and I were hiking down West Fork Canyon above Pasadena. Suddenly the trail was covered with the reddish *Polyergus*, far from where one would expect to find them – northern California, yes, but not southern. It was obviously a slave raid – hundreds of ants crossing the trail from their home nest, which was guarded by slaves, to some unfortunate nest of the rather cowardly *Formica fusca*."

"I got busy with notebook and magnifier, keeping out of reach of the biting slave-makers. I wonder if they are poisonous. Ummm, I have an idea. 'Here, Gretchen, take this vial and pick up a few for later study. Don't mind their kicks and bites; get them while I watch the attack on the *Formica*.' Of course, she did pick them up, with squeals and squawks. It was getting late. The camp was a mile or so away, and off we went, with me curious about the effect of the martyrdom.

'Hands hurting?'

'No, why do you ask?'

'Just curious.' Another half mile and again I inquired, 'Hands aching a bit from swinging as we walk?'

'Why no; why are you so solicitous?' And into my little record book went the notation 'bite of *Polyergus rufescens* apparently not toxic to large mammals.' Another use, I tell my audience, for wives."

"That story is good for laughs but not for wives!"

"Gretchen will vouch for its validity. Well, I'm going out to inspect my *Formica exsectoides*."

I could hear my mother typing downstairs. "I'll begin collecting my notes, since I can't help Mom with the shorthand and I'm skeptical about helping you inspect your ants!"

CHAPTER FOUR

The Universe Explored and Debated

Take a large grapefruit and a small lemon – or rather take two lemons, one of them slightly green. This is not the beginning, as you might think, of a recipe for a new drink. My father sometimes used fruit when he explained astronomy to us. Following his example, I am attempting to illustrate the astronomical subject of eclipsing binaries. This was my father's first major work under the guidance of Henry Norris Russell at Princeton.

So we take these two lemons, connect them with each other by an invisible knitting needle, suspend the pair in space and start them revolving around an imaginary central point. Now, look edge-on at the circle they describe. At one instant the dull green lemon will pass in front of and hide a part of, or all of, the bright yellow lemon. If the lemons were self-luminous and you were in a darkened room, you would notice a marked decrease in the light coming your way. Half a revolution farther around the yellow lemon would hide the green one and this time you would notice only a slight decrease in light, because the green lemon is, we shall say, less bright. At other times both lemons are completely visible to you and during this interval you would get the maximum light from these fruits – still supposing they were self-luminous.

If instead of fruit, we deal with balls of gas, that is, two stars revolving around each other, we have what we call a binary system and we would see a periodic variation of light as each star goes into and comes out of eclipse.

Usually these two stars will be too close together, comparatively speaking, and too far away from us for our telescope to show them as two separate stars. It is by studying the light variation that astronomers can deduce what is going on.

The first job for the astronomer is to make many and frequent observations of the star(s) in question, recording the brightness at each observed time. Perhaps for a long interval the stars' light may remain constant; this is the interval during which the star and its companion are both sending us full light without interruption. Then the light will be observed to decrease to a minimum indicating, for instance, that the brighter star is being eclipsed by the fainter; then the light will recover to its maximum brightness. Again, both stars are sending us light. Then after another equally long interval there will be a second decrease in light perhaps less pronounced than the first indicating the eclipse of the fainter star by the brighter companion. Then back to maximum light. This is the cycle, and the cycle repeats and keeps repeating in this manner for as long as we wish to observe it.

The diagrams that astronomers make of these observations, hour by hour, of what are called eclipsing binaries, are known as light curves. Without becoming too involved in technicalities, let us attempt to understand the various deductions that astronomers make from the study of the shapes of these typical light curves, A, B, and C.

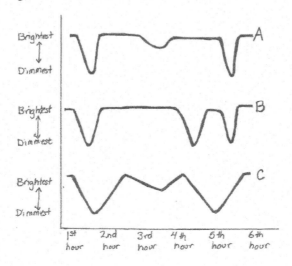

But first let us go back to that grapefruit and that lemon. If they are revolving around each other in a plane containing your line of sight – that is, you see the orbit exactly edge on, the grapefruit at one time will eclipse the lemon, and, the lemon being small, this *total* eclipse will last a considerable period. When it comes time for the lemon to eclipse the grapefruit, it is unable to hide all of the big grapefruit behind it. This eclipse is called an *annular* eclipse, where a ring of the larger disk is left showing. If the lemon and the grapefruit are revolving in a plane at a slight tilt, the eclipses will be called *partial* – neither total nor annular.

Return now to examine the light curves. From light curve A (call it a coconut-orange combination) we can tell that one star is large and dim, the other bright and smaller. Their orbits are in our line of sight making alternating total and annular eclipses possible.

From light curve B (a two-grapefruit combination) we can tell that we have two stars of the same size and brightness because the dips are similar in shape and depth. The pointed minima tell us that the eclipses are only partial and so the plane of the orbits of this binary system is slightly tilted from our line of sight. Notice also that the dips in this case are not evenly spaced. From this we can deduce that the orbits are elliptical, not precisely circular.

Light curve C (two elongated lemons, one bright, the other less so) illustrates another type of eclipsing binary system. From the curve, near maximum light, we can tell that the stars are not spherical but ellipsoidal, because here there are no flat maxima of the light curve. These revolving lemons are continually changing brightness even when both are shining at us. Some of the time the two stars are seen nearly edge-on and at other times broad-side to us; the more surface they show us the more light we see. These ellipsoidal stars are often very close or even in contact with each other. It is the mutual gravitational forces that pull them out of spherical shape. The more widely separated binaries are more nearly spherical.

This subject of eclipsing binaries I have boiled down to very little in my effort to simplify it. Yet it is still anything but simple. It was perhaps a vain hope to succeed in explaining my father's doctoral thesis in ordinary words. I was born of astronomers, but it hasn't made me one. Nevertheless, I have inherited an enthusiasm for astronomy and it is my hope to impart some of it to you. Perhaps you can see what a wonderful universe of mysteries the astronomical inquirer has. His laboratory is spacious and even though, as yet, he cannot walk around in it, he knows a great deal about his heavenly specimens from his observation post on Earth.

It isn't all smooth going even for those who do understand the subject. There are many complications that haunt the experts when a new theory or method is being born. Several of my father's papers had to do with limb darkening. In deciphering these light-curves it is convenient to assume that the disks of the stars are uniformly bright. It simplifies matters. However, we know from the Sun, the only star near enough to give us a disk to study, that the center part of the disk is brighter than the edges, or limbs. Stars also have limb darkening and allowances must be made for it. Mathematical formulas were developed to deal with this problem, and others, that we cannot take time to mention here.

We should not feel dismayed if the subject goes beyond our comprehension. Even the greatest scientists have made observations that they could not fully explain. For example, Professor Henry Norris Russell's name is permanently linked with that of Professor Ejnar Hertzsprung because each independently discovered a relation between the luminosities and the temperatures of stars. This Hertzsprung-Russell diagram, more simply called the H-R diagram, is the most used plot in current astronomical research. But when urged by some of his eager students to explain more fully the why of this relationship, Professor Russell confessed that he did not know exactly its meaning. Later he read with much amusement in the student humor magazine that the H-R diagram is a plot of H against R.

But we have got away from our eclipsing stars and we are not quite finished with them. In addition to studying the characteristics of the light curves of these binary systems it is important to study their spectra. Most of us have seen what a glass prism will do when sunlight shines on it. The white sunlight is separated into a rainbow of colors, the longer wavelengths (red) shading into the intermediate (yellow) and then into the shorter wavelengths (violet). By attaching a prism and camera to a telescope, astronomers can also photograph the spectra of stars. From the study of the spectrum they can learn the composition of the starlight, that is, the amount of the various chemical elements in the burning gases. They can also learn the radial velocity of the star (the component of its motion in the line of sight) and whether it is approaching or receding from us. This they do by observing the Doppler Effect.

If the words Doppler Effect worry you, take a piece of stiff wire and make a series of kinks in it like an endless W. You are at one end, the star in question is at the other, and the wire represents the starlight traveling in waves. If the star is coming your way, it will push your W and squash it a little. The succession of peaks and valleys will be closer together. If the star is moving away from you, it will stretch your W and the peaks and valleys will be spread farther apart. When the wavelength (the distance between two adjacent peaks) is shorter, the light is bluer. When the wavelength is stretched, the spectrum is reddened. This stretching or shrinking of the light waves is called the Doppler Effect after the 19th century physicist who first observed the phenomenon. If a series of spectral photographs of a variable star shows the light alternately bluer than normal and redder than normal, the astronomer deduces that the star is a member of a double star system, revolving around a companion, moving first towards us and then away. The amount of the shift to the blue and to the red carefully measured tells just how fast the star is approaching or receding.

And so the study of the light-curves and spectra of eclipsing binaries tells much about the nature of the stars: dimensions, orbital characteristics, temperature, luminosities and for some of them the distances; also they give at least rough values of age, mean densities and shapes. Some are closely spherical; others are lemon shaped. For a few we can get the distribution of the light over the surface, that is, the darkening at the edges, and the speed of rotation. And for a few we can get the rotation of the line of apsides, that is, the twisting of their eccentric orbits in space.

My father's doctoral thesis dealt with the orbits of ninety eclipsing binaries, a quarto treatment, published as *Princeton Contribution No. 3* (1915). It was epochal for that branch of astronomy, thanks to the interest and advice of Henry Norris Russell. Their method, in essentials, remains the standard procedure even today. They did the theory together, but the student, Shapley, did the laborious observations and calculations. There was much observing of these stars with the Princeton telescope, a 23-inch refractor, much harmonizing and standardizing of measures, their own and those of others. Russell liked to give credit where due and used to tell how it happened: He, being a pious man, said "I worked on the theory, looked at the observational mess in which the eclipsing binaries were tangled, and then the Lord sent me Harlow Shapley."

It is not my plan to cover many aspects of astronomy in these chapters. I shall choose various topics of my father's researches and expose just enough to associate his name with particular astronomical achievements.

So, let us go to another of his studies, that of Cepheid variable stars in the globular clusters. The eclipsing binary idea succeeded in explaining the light variation of many stars, but for one found in the constellation Cepheus, and thus called a Cepheid variable (or simply a Cepheid), it did not work well at all. Astronomers contrived many complicated theories in an attempt to explain this type of light variations, but none was really satisfactory. For instance, never in the case of the Cepheids does the spectrum show the existence of a faint companion as in the case for eclipsing variable stars. My father showed that Cepheid variables cannot be eclipsing binaries, and he advanced the theoretically important hypothesis that they are pulsating stars. In other words, these Cepheid variables are single stars, whose light output and size both change. As the star expands, it becomes brighter, but in expanding, it cools slightly and thus appears to shrink and grow dimmer. As the star shrinks the gas compresses and begins to heat up, which makes it expand and grow bright again. And so it pulsates in some sort of regular rhythm peculiar to its own nature. As is to be expected, the spectra of these stars show periodic wavelength shifts to red and to blue, indicating that the gases on the surface of the star are oscillating back and forth as the star shrinks and expands. There is something odd about stars that cannot attain their equilibrium but vibrate in endless pulsation between too large and too small, too cold and too hot. Yet the pulsation explanation was soon accepted by the astronomical world, especially after Sir Arthur Eddington[1] in 1918 developed a theory of pulsating stars that was based upon his researches on the construction of the stars in general.

My father spent several more years studying the nature of open clusters (also called galactic clusters) and especially the nature of globular clusters. The open cluster is a loosely assembled group of stars with no heavy concentration in the center. They appear for the most part near us in our Milky Way. Globular clusters, on the other hand, are beautifully symmetrical and compact. They are found preferentially in the southern Milky Way, and they are very remote. The studies of these clusters resulted in the publishing of many papers. A very important series of 19 papers was published under the general title *Colors and Magnitudes in Stellar Clusters*, mostly in the *Astrophysical Journal*, between the years of 1917 and 1921. Some of the subjects treated were linear dimensions of various clusters and their luminosities, masses, spectra, and stellar densities; their internal motions; and the Cepheid variables found in them. He found that the globular clusters as a class appear to be rapidly moving in our galactic system. He also noted that for the stars at large, the fainter ones are usually reddest but that the contrary was true for stars in the globular clusters – the brightest are reddest. The reason for this is that in this type of cluster we are dealing mainly with giant stars; the dwarfs are too faint to photograph easily. The majority of stars in our own neighborhood in the Milky Way Galaxy are dwarfish. The discovery of the globular cluster type of stellar population is considered one of Shapley's most important contributions.

The real importance of the Cepheid variables became evident when my father found that they could be used as a yardstick for determining the size of the universe. I once asked him how it all began, this plunge into space that led finally to his important discovery. He explained as follows:

> "One of the physical factors, that the theories let us deduce from the eclipsing star light curves, was the hypothetical distance to the binaries. Those distances were for some stars exceedingly large. In the big table of the ninety orbits are many faint stars that appeared to be farther off than we had, up to then, considered were the bounds of the universe. To be sure, no one had very seriously estimated the size of the stellar universe – but it was surmised by some to be about 7000 light years in diameter. [A light year is a measure of distance used by astronomers, equal to the distance traveled by light in one year and equivalent to 5,880,000,000,000 miles. Seven thousand light years is 41,160,000,000,000,000 miles but as you can see, writing miles uses up too much space, so after this we too will talk in light years.] This estimate was terribly big compared with the distances measured trigonometrically of neighboring bright stars like Alpha Centauri, Sirius, Procyon, and others. Russell had marveled at these large distances but did not make much fuss about it because our distances were, after all, hypothetical. But I was much bemused by this indication that the universe is measurable and that some great revelations were ahead."

When my father arrived at Mt. Wilson and became the technical assistant of his Missouri University professor of astronomy, Frederick Seares, he was given some freedom from the routine Selected Areas photometry job with the large Mt. Wilson telescope, the 60-inch reflector. Dr. Bailey[2] at Harvard was at the time discovering variable stars in the globular clusters. He suggested to Shapley that he might examine these variables, for it seemed likely that they were distant – perhaps more distant than the eclipsing binaries. My father pitched in, found more of the variables, assiduously read the literature, including Miss Leavitt's[3] *Harvard Circular* about the variables in the Magellanic Clouds and Hertzsprung's deduction from the spectroscopic evidence that the Cepheids (like Polaris) were giant stars. He thought to himself, "If those faint Cepheids in the Milky Way and those in the Magellanic Clouds are cats of the same breed, then the clusters with the seemingly faint Cepheids, and the Magellanic Clouds, must be *very* remote." Thus, quietly the stellar system grew up to be a big, but measurable size. The eclipsing star monograph had led the way to a new and powerful method of estimating distances.

The beginning of this Cepheid research was in 1908 when my father was still a college freshman taking Astronomy I and Miss Henrietta Leavitt was studying Cepheid variables in the Magellanic Clouds at the Harvard Observatory. She noticed that when the variables were listed in order of increasing brightness, their periods of light variation were also arranged in order of increasing length. As all the stars in the Cloud can be considered to be at approximately the same distance from the Earth, the stars that appear brighter really are brighter and those that seem fainter are really fainter. Therefore, we can draw a curve that illustrates what astronomers call the Period-Luminosity Relation; it shows that the longer the periods of light variation, the brighter the Cepheids are. Observations of a great number of Cepheids showed that those of brightness, A, for example, all have periods of less than one day. Cepheids of brightness, B have periods of 5 days. And Cepheids of brightness, C have periods of 15 days. We can only observe how bright a star appears not how bright it actually is. If we could know how far away it is we could tell its true luminosity; or putting it the other way – if we could know the actual brightness, and how bright it appears, we could find the star's distance.

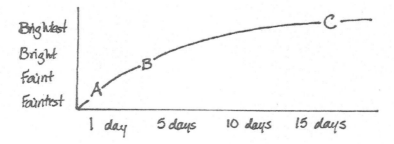

When my brother Willis was a tree climber many years ago in Cambridge, I used to send signals (Morse code fashion) to him perched in a treetop, using a 100-watt light bulb in my room. Of our messages I remember, only one because I was exasperated not to be able to finish it. I signaled, "For dinner we are having chocolate pudding" but by the time I got chocolate spelled out and was beginning with pudding, he was down out of the tree and in the kitchen to see if it was true, because anything chocolate was especially fine with him. Another time he came in to check my light to see if I was really using a 100-watt bulb, because to him up there in the tree it seemed no brighter than the feeble light of his flashlight that he was signaling with. If we had been as interested in science and mathematics as we were in chocolate pudding, we could have computed the distance from the tree top to my room because we knew the real brightness and the apparent brightness of my light bulb. Elementary textbooks tell us that the apparent brightness falls off inversely as the square of the distance. Of course, if it was a foggy night we would have to make allowances. Similarly, in the universe we now know there is interstellar dust that dims the starlight and must be taken into account. But this is something we shall deal with later.

My father set upon the difficult task of establishing the true or intrinsic brightness of the Cepheids. This he did by setting up a scale based on eleven variable stars that were close enough to the Earth that their distance could be measured by statistical parallax. Once he had established the real brightness for the Cepheids of each specific period and had observed the average apparent brightness, the actual distances could be determined. And so, with this measuring rod, wherever a Cepheid may be found, the period will indicate the true brightness; the observed apparent brightness then measures the distance of the Cepheid and also of the cluster of which this Cepheid is a member. Thus, he began exploring the sky and sorting out the clusters and nebulae that belonged to our Milky Way system and those that were far beyond our own galaxy. The universe began to take on a new size and structure.

Let us go back in history a little to see what eminent men of science thought the universe looked like a few decades ago. Just before the turn of the 20th century, a famous Dutch astronomer, J.C. Kapteyn,[4] began an investigation that resulted in a new theory of the structure of our Milky Way system. It took many years to complete the task he had set himself. Only a few years before his death in 1922, he summarized his findings in a sketch that supported his idea of the galaxy. It showed a flattened watch-shaped disk with the sun close to the center. Kapteyn also introduced a scale of distances indicating the approximate size of our Milky Way galaxy. He and his students measured and recorded nearly half a million stars, although at one time he did have the help of a few inmates loaned to him from a Dutch prison.

The Kapteyn Universe was the prevailing idea when Shapley, armed with his new measuring rod, began investigating the Cepheids in globular clusters. Eventually he plotted the distances of these clusters on two-dimensional diagrams in three different planes in order to get a three-dimensional idea of the location of the globular clusters in space. The amazing thing these diagrams showed was that the globular clusters were half on one side of the Milky Way circle and half on the other, and that there were more of these clusters in one particular direction of the Milky Way (galactic longitude 270° to 360°). What was the meaning of this concentration in the southern hemisphere – in the constellations of Sagittarius, Ophiuchus, Scorpio, and Centaurus? The first and most obvious deduction was that this was where the organization of these clusters was centered. And it is interesting to note that the presently accepted center is less than two degrees from his pioneering determination.

It was as early as 1917 that Shapley took what he calls the leap of faith. To continue in his own words: "that point in Sagittarius, I reasoned, is not only the center of the higher system of globular clusters, but also the center of the whole Milky Way galaxy. The Earth, the Sun, the naked-eye stars are far off center; they are near the rim, not the center."

I remember once some student came up after one of his lectures asking, "Is it true, Dr. Shapley, that you measured the size of the Milky Way with a 12-inch slide rule?" where upon he replied, "No, that is not true at all. It was a ten-inch."

I asked him once to describe to me what it felt like to come upon such a startling discovery, for as Dr. Bart Bok, a great expert on the Milky Way, has said, "With this revolutionary work, published in 1918, Shapley did for the Milky Way system what Copernicus had done for the solar system. Just as Copernicus had shown that the Earth was not the center of the solar system, Shapley showed that our Sun was not the center of our galaxy."

My father remarked, "Of course it was something to marvel at, but I had added more to the unknown than to the known so it was an incentive not to stop and cheer but to go humbly on." In his chapter in *Moments of Personal Discovery* [ed. by R. M. MacIver, Harper and Brothers, 1952] is an account of this dramatic moment in his career.

At first among his fellow astronomers there was much opposition to my father's radical findings, but gradually he gained some support for his theory, and in 1920 the National Academy of Sciences staged a debate[5] between Shapley of Mt. Wilson and Dr. Heber Curtis, then of Lick Observatory. Curtis defended the conventional theory. His opponent of course defended the Shapley theory. Even at the conclusion of the debate the new ideas did not find immediate general acceptance. Kapteyn, one of the doubters, placed the Sun at the center of the galaxy in his final diagram, published four years after the announcement of the Shapley discovery. As Dr. Bok says, "At the time there were good reasons to doubt Shapley's conclusions. Kapteyn and others had shown by straightforward analysis of available star-counts that the number of stars per unit volume of the sky dropped off in all directions away from the Sun, which seemed to prove that the Sun was at the center."

The two disputed theories may be outlined side by side as follows:

CURRENT (1920) THEORY	SHAPLEY'S NEW THEORY
Our galaxy is probably not more than 30,000 light years in diameter, and perhaps 5000 light years in thickness.	The galaxy is approximately 300,000 light years in diameter, and 30,000, or more, light years in thickness.
The clusters, and all the other types of types of celestial objects except the spirals, are component parts of our own galactic system.	The globular clusters are remote objects, a part of their own galaxy. The most distant cluster is placed about 220,000 light years away.
The spirals are a class apart, and not intra-galactic objects. As island universes, of the same order of size as our galaxy, they are distant from us 500,000 to 10,000,000, or more light years.	The spirals are probably of nebulous constitution, and possibly not members of our own galaxy, driven away in some manner from the region of greatest star density.

This debate was scheduled for a special evening session of the normal three days of National Academy of Sciences meetings.* On the afternoon of the big day occurred my father's first introduction to the famous Dr. Albert Einstein who was making his first visit to America. My father arrived just as the meeting was getting under way. The first speaker on the program, Dr. Charles E. St. John, was presenting his paper on the red shifts in the spectrum of the Sun. My father sat inconspicuously at the back, but one of the members spotted him and came over whispering, "How's your German?" He rather mystified, replied that it was O.K. "Fine, we want you to sit down front in the seat next to Dr. Einstein and translate what Dr. St. John is saying." The paper was particularly interesting to Dr. Einstein because St. John was an ardent

---

*   This account of the NAS meeting is not entirely accurate. See Notes, Chapter Four, Note 5. – Eds.

believer that the Theory of Relativity was nonsense and he thought that his spectrograms of the sun proved his position.

As he walked up to where Dr. Einstein was sitting, my father was thinking how completely inadequate his talking German was. There were the briefest whispered introductions. Shapley fidgeted with embarrassment and Einstein nodded with a grunt. My father proceeded to translate as best he could from pigeon-English to pigeon-German this interesting talk. At the end Dr. Einstein made the comment, "If Dr. St. John is correct then we must abandon the Relativity Theory and start over again." My father was much impressed with this remark. It showed that here was a man who wants to test his theory – not just defend it. When he shook hands with Dr. Einstein at the end of the meeting Einstein said, "The next time that I come to America I shall know English better," meaning perhaps that as a translator, Shapley left something to be desired.

In the evening came the much-publicized debate. The audience consisted of some 200 of the top scientists in America with the president of the National Academy presiding.

Dr. Curtis got up first and presented his views. He spoke well and with conviction. Supporting the Kapteyn concept, he argued that Shapley's figures were exaggerated ten-fold and he listed various other astronomers' reliable estimates of the galactic dimensions as follows:

Wolf	About 14,000 light years in diameter
Eddington	About 15,000 light years
Newcomb	Not less than 7000 light years; a later estimate – perhaps 30,000 light years in diameter and 5,000 light years in thickness
Kapteyn	About 60,000 light years in diameter

He compared a so-called average star in the neighborhood of our Sun about which we have definite information as to its true brightness, with an average star in a distant globular cluster. He assumed that these two average stars are comparable and pointed out that, if we are to accept Shapley's distances for the globular clusters, this average star would either have to be enormously brighter than the average of star brightness in our neighborhood or it would mean that star clusters at excessively large distances have an exaggerated concentration of luminous giant stars; this is not the case for nearby clusters. If, however, the globular clusters are not as remote as Shapley claims, these difficulties do not arise.

Curtis admitted, "While it is not impossible that the clusters are exceptional regions and that there exists a unique concentration of giant stars, the hypothesis that cluster stars are, on the whole, like those of known distances seems inherently the more probable. Shapley's deductions as to the much greater dimensions for our galaxy depend almost entirely upon the sizes and the internal relationships of the proper motions [velocities perpendicular to the line of sight] of eleven variables." Curtis here refers to the eleven variables of known distance that were used to determine the intrinsic brightness of distant Cepheids, as described earlier in this chapter. In Curtis's opinion, "so small an amount of presumably uncertain data is insufficient to determine the scale of the galaxy."

Curtis was a strong advocate of the theory that spiral nebulae were island universes, galaxies similar in size and content to our own Milky Way galaxy. He reasoned that if the spirals are island universes, it would seem reasonable and almost probable to assign to them dimensions of the same order as our galaxy. If, however, their dimensions are as great as Shapley's 300,000 light years, these island universes must be placed at such enormous distances that it would be necessary to assign what seems impossibly great true brightnesses to the exploding new stars or novae, as they are called, which are seen to appear from time to time in these spiral nebulae. If Shapley's dimensions for the galaxy were right, it would seem necessary to include spiral nebulae in our galactic system. For this reason, the inflated size of our galaxy did not appeal to Curtis. There were difficulties in assuming that they were a part of our system. First, they were not evenly distributed in the sky as were the galactic nebulae. Second, their velocities were found all to be very much greater, in no way comparable to the speeds of other nebulous objects definitely within the bounds of our galaxy. Curtis concludes his views as follows:

"There are many points of difficulty in either theory of galactic dimensions and it is doubtless true that many will prefer to suspend judgment until much additional evidence is forthcoming. Until more definite evidence to the contrary is available, however, I feel that the evidence for the smaller and commonly accepted galactic dimensions is still the stronger; and that the postulated diameter of 300,000 light years must quite certainly be divided by five, and perhaps ten. I hold, therefore, to the belief that the galaxy is probably not more than 30,000 light years in diameter; that the spirals are not intragalactic objects but island universes, like our galaxy, and that the spirals as external galaxies, indicate to us a greater universe into which we may penetrate to distances of ten million to a hundred million light years."

There was applause. Curtis sat down and Shapley got up to present his views. He was prepared and his arguments were well organized but he had difficulty feeling at ease in front of this distinguished audience of senior scientists. He was an upstart – 30 years younger than Curtis. This was his first important public show and he was visibly nervous. But this, he now remembers, was the last time he experienced nervousness in public speaking.

He began his arguments by pointing out that as a consequence of the exceptional growth and activity of the great observatories, with their powerful methods of analyzing stars and of sounding space, we have reached an epoch when our conception of the galactic system must be enlarged to keep in proper relationship the objects our telescopes are finding, and that the solar system can no longer maintain a central position. "Recent studies of clusters and related subjects," he said, "seem to leave no alternative to the belief that the galactic system is at least ten times greater in diameter, and at least a thousand times greater in volume, than recently supposed." While Dr. Curtis supports the view held a decade or so ago by Newcomb, Eddington, Kapteyn and other leaders in stellar astronomy, Shapley pointed out that nearly all of the astronomers that Curtis lists now subscribe to a larger universe, in the light of new discoveries. When Newcomb, for one, was writing on the subject some twenty years ago, it should be noted that knowledge of those special factors that bear directly on the size of the universe was extremely fragmentary compared with our information today. If he were writing now, with the knowledge of those relevant developments, it is more than likely that Newcomb would not maintain his former view on the probable dimensions of the galactic system.

Shapley continued to analyze the differences in opinions between Curtis and himself, answering one by one Curtis's objections, and paved the way to show that his estimate of at least 300,000 light years was sound. This value was, of course, antecedent to the discovery of the absorption of starlight by interstellar dust which cut galactic dimensions in two. His speech continued as follows:

"Curtis accepts the results of recent studies on the following significant points:

A. The globular clusters form a part of our galaxy; therefore, the size of the galactic system proper is most probably not less than the size of the subordinate system of the globular clusters.
B. The distance derived at Mt. Wilson for globular clusters relative to one another are essentially correct.
C. Stars in clusters and in distant parts of the Milky Way are not peculiar; that is, uniformity of conditions and of stellar phenomena naturally prevail throughout the galactic system.

"We also share the same opinion, I believe, on the following points:

a. The galactic system is an extremely flattened stellar organization, and the appearance of the Milky Way is partly due to the existence of a distinct cloud of stars and is partly due to the result of depth along the galactic plane.

b. The spiral nebulae are mostly very distant objects, probably not physical members of our galactic system.

"Through approximate agreement on the above points, the way is cleared so that the outstanding differences may clearly be stated: Curtis does not believe that the numerical value of the distance I derive for any globular cluster is of the right order of magnitude. The present problem may be narrowly restricted, therefore, and may be formulated as follows: Show that any globular cluster is approximately as distant as derived at Mt. Wilson; then the distance of other clusters will be approximately right (see point B), and the system of clusters and the galactic system will have dimensions of the order assigned.

"In other words, to maintain my position it will suffice to show that any one of the brightest globular clusters has roughly the distance I have claimed for it, rather than a distance one tenth of this value or less, which would be in line with Curtis's estimate. Similarly, it should suffice to show that the bright objects in clusters are giants, rather than stars of solar luminosity.

"An argument much insisted upon by Curtis is that the average absolute magnitude (the so-called true brightness) of stars around the Sun is equal to or fainter than solar brightness, hence, that average star we see in clusters are also dwarfs.

"Curtis apparently ignores the fact that in treating a distant external system we naturally first observe its giant (most luminous) stars. If the range in brightness is not mutually extensive in the solar domain and in the remote cluster (and it certainly is not for all stars of all types), then the comparison of average means practically nothing because of the obvious and vital selection of the brighter stars in the cluster. The comparison should be of nearby cluster with distant cluster, or of the luminosities of the same kinds of stars in the two places.

"Suppose that an observer, confined to a small area in a valley, attempts to measure the distances of surrounding mountain peaks. Because of the short base-line allowed him, his trigonometric parallaxes are valueless except for the nearby hills. On the remote peaks, however, his telescope shows green foliage. First, he assumes approximate botanical uniformity through all visible territory. Then he finds that the average height of all the plants immediately around him (conifers, palms, asters, clover, etc.) is one foot. Correlating this average with the measured angular height of plants visible against the skyline on the distant peaks, he obtains false values of the distances. If, however, he had compared the foliage on the nearby, trigonometrically measured hills with that on the remote peaks, or had used some method of distinguishing various floral types, he would not have mistaken pines for asters and thereby obtained erroneous results for the distances of the remote peaks. All the principles involved in the botanical parallax of a mountain peak have their analogues in the photometric parallax of a globular cluster."

After attacking Curtis's use of an average star, Shapley goes on to defend his use of Cepheid variables as a yardstick for measuring the galaxy:

"Curtis bases his strongest objection to the larger galaxy on the use I have made of the Cepheid variables, questioning the sufficiency of the data and the accuracy of the method involved. But I believe that in the present issue there is little point in laboring over the details for Cepheids, for we are, if we choose, qualitatively quite independent of them in determining the scale of the galactic system, and it is only qualitative results that are now at issue. We could discard the Cepheids altogether, use instead either the red giant stars and spectroscopic methods, or the hundreds of B-type stars upon which the most capable stellar astronomers have worked for years, and derived much the same distance for the Hercules cluster, and for other clusters, and obtain consequently similar dimensions for the galactic system. In fact, the substantiating results from these other sources strongly fortify our belief in the assumptions and methods involved in the use of the Cepheid variables.

"When we accept the view that the distance of the Hercules cluster is such that its stellar phenomena are harmonious with local stellar phenomena – its brightest stars typical giants, its Cepheids comparable with our own – then it follows that fainter, smaller, globular clusters are still more distant than the 36,000 light years found for the Hercules cluster. One-third of those now known are more distant than 100,000 light years; the most distant is more than 200,000 light years away, and the diameter of the whole system of globular clusters is about 300,000 light years."

One consequence of the conclusion that the galactic system is of the order of 300,000 light years in greatest diameter, is the previously mentioned difficulty it gives to the comparable-galaxy theory of spiral nebulae. The Shapley dimensions did not comply with Curtis's island universe hypothesis, nor did van Maanen's recent measurements of rotation in various spirals. For these spirals to exhibit an observable rotation they could not possibly be at the excessive distances required by the island universe theory. Shapley concluded his argument with these words:

"But even if the spirals fail as galactic systems, there may be elsewhere in space stellar systems equal to or greater than ours – as yet unrecognized and possibly quite beyond the power of existing optical devices and present measuring scales. The modern telescope, however, with such accessories as high-power spectroscopes and photographic intensifiers, is destined to extend the inquiries relative to the size of the universe much deeper into space and contribute further to the problem of other galaxies."

So this, then, was the famous debate; the two men had presented their opposing views. There was no discussion from the floor, just routine applause and they applauded the young man the most. Perhaps it was because he was Director Hale's prodigy or maybe because his evidence looked good. Unlike political debates, the participants were best of friends at all times, having one common goal – the discovery of the truth. Years later Dr. Curtis was the director of the University of Michigan Observatory when I was attending that university. I had concrete evidence over and over again of his and my father's mutual friendship and respect. Curtis was a conservative, and more intent on establishing that spirals were extra-galactic than that the revised scale of the universe was right or wrong. But he finally agreed with the new scale, or at least with putting the Sun and planets on the edge of the galaxy, as the globular clusters insisted.

The National Academy of Sciences concluded these meetings with a banquet to which my father was invited. Dr. Einstein sat at the head table. The after-dinner speeches my father remembers, by weary old men, were soporific, deadly. He amused himself by gazing at the guests at the head table who were also trying to stay awake. He noticed Dr. Einstein leaning over and whispering something to a Belgian delegate who immediately bit his lip in order to keep from laughing. "What was so funny," I asked the Belgian afterwards. Dr. Einstein, who had listened to garrulity for nearly two hours, had whispered – "I've got an entirely new concept of eternity."

During that ordeal, rewards for hookworm control were tediously bestowed by one elder statesman, then by another. Dr. Osterhout of Harvard at my father's table moaned profanely "Jesus H. Christ!" and Raymond Pearl of Johns Hopkins groaned, "Yes, and the H. stands for hookworm!"

It will be interesting now to look, from that evening in April of 1920, to see what turned out to be right and wrong about each of the two men's views. At that time most astronomers believed that the evidence was against the existence of any obscuring haze of interstellar material in space. But, in Dr. Bok's words,

"Two major discoveries in the late 1920s and early 1930s settled the question. First Bertil Lindblad of Sweden and Jan H. Oort of Holland showed that our galactic system, as a whole, is in rapid rotation, and that the center of rotation was located at a distance of 25,000 to 30,000 light years in the direction of Shapley's center for the globular cluster system. Then Robert J. Trumpler of the University of California and Carl Schalen of Sweden found that astronomers had been wrong in supposing that there was no general interstellar haze. They demonstrated that the light of an average star in the Milky Way and at a distance of 5000 light years from us was dimmed through interstellar absorption by at least one full magnitude. The revised computations, made necessary by this discovery, confirmed Shapley's conclusions regarding the direction of the center of the galaxy, though they reduced its estimated distance from 50,000 to 30,000 light years."

So the new methods were sound and the direction of the center was correctly located, but because no allowance had been made for the then unsuspected cosmic dust, the diameter proposed by Shapley was too large.

Distances of these orders of magnitude cannot be known exactly, but present-day estimates for the dimensions of our galaxy stand at 100,000 light years in diameter, about one-fifth that in greatest thickness, with the center about 27,000 light years distant from our solar system. Larger and more powerful telescopes and improved methods of probing the spiral nebulae have since shown that Curtis was right about the spirals; they are outside our Milky Way system, island universes; galaxies in their own right. Van Maanen's measures of supposed large rotational velocities proved erroneous, hence removing the biggest obstacle to accepting the island universe theory.

We should point out that the title of the Debate was *The Scale of the Universe*, and not *What Are the Spirals*. Shapley clearly won the scale argument, but Curtis set up another subject and he won the spiral argument. One of my father's worst scientific mistakes, he says, resulted from his trusting the work of his personal friend van Maanen. He hesitated to think that van

Maanen's measures of rotation in the spirals were illusory, and therefore he was skeptical of Curtis's favoring the position of the spirals as exterior to our galaxy. Curtis, on the other hand, distrusted van Maanen and held to his Island Universe theory. But as soon as my father saw his error, he acquiesced and became one of the leading students of spirals as outside systems comparable to our own galaxy.

To conclude, we note that my father's discovery of the peripheral location of the solar system, even before it was accepted by his colleagues, stirred up much public interest. Such streamers appeared in the newspapers as SHAPLEY PIN-POINTS UNIVERSE HUB. There would be a picture of him and, next to it a picture of Sagittarius with an arrow pointing to the center. The caption under the pictures would read STARGAZER SHAPLEY and SHAPLEY'S CENTER. Shapley's center would be described as "that jolly place a mere 175,000,000,000,000,000-odd miles away." Concerning the publicity my father commented, "We make all this funny flurry about things as old as the stars. Sometimes I suspect I know what they're twinkling at."

CHAPTER FIVE
The Young Director

W e haven't finished talking about astronomy – it will come up several times more, for one cannot very well isolate astronomers from astronomy; but let's move on now, as my father did, to the Harvard Observatory. The residence that had been the Pickerings' for so long was now the Shapleys' new home. The director's office in C-34 with the famous round table was my father's new headquarters and he quickly made himself at home there. The great circular desk became crowded with his many new projects. Once, in the presence of some visitor he remarked, "It's about as well organized as a city dump."

In 1921, when my father arrived, the Harvard College Observatory was purely a research institution. It had professors but no students. Its instruments were not as large or spectacular as the telescopes on Mt. Wilson, but even a 24-inch telescope, for example, taking a several-hour exposure, is a powerful instrument for photography of faint stars. However, the Harvard Observatory had another type of gold mine. My father's predecessor, Professor E.C. Pickering, with unexcelled foresight, had established over the years a photographic plate collection of vast proportions, covering the sky from pole to pole. There were few problems in astronomy to which this photographic library could not provide stimulus for further work. The expansion of research projects and facilities was therefore rapid.

On the Harvard Observatory staff at this time was Professor Solon I. Bailey. We have mentioned him earlier as the man who was discovering variable stars in globular clusters. Another leader was Professor Edward S. King working on photometric observations determining the magnitudes of the planets and the Moon; he had developed an ingenious method for obtaining the brightness of different portions of the Moon's surface. There was Mr. Leon Campbell whose specialty was long-period variables. He guided the amateur organization A.A.V.S.O. (American Association of Variable Star Observers). These 70 or so amateur astronomers (later several hundred), located throughout the United States, observed systematically the light variation of some 300 to 400 variable stars, with Mr. Campbell in charge of the analysis of their observations. And, of course, there was Miss Cannon, already familiar to us, working on her *Henry Draper Catalogue* of stellar spectra. Also on the staff were Henrietta S. Leavitt and Antonia C. Maury, as well as Miss Ida E. Woods and Miss Arville D. Walker, junior research workers, and there was Mrs. Shapley.

My mother's scientific contributions were sizable and significant. Her measurements of magnitudes of variable stars and of clusters greatly aided my father and others in getting answers and in writing papers. During my father's stay in Pasadena she did much computing, and there are a number of papers in the scientific journals to show for it – hers alone, and hers in collaboration with others. In Cambridge she continued her scientific work although little by little she became too busy with her growing family and her duties as hostess to the large Observatory family to do as much as she would have liked. Uniquely she was glad for her ten-day hospital vacations after the births of Lloyd and Carl. Then she was able to work on her orbital computations with virtually no interruptions.

In 1921, my father was younger than all members of his staff. It might have been an awkward situation, but the Harvard people treated him well. Professor Bailey, the acting director for the two intervening years between Pickering and Shapley, and who might have been made director, was helpful in easing my father in. He made one of his many trips to Harvard's Boyden Station[1] in Arequipa, Peru, to take over the observing of southern objects not visible in the Cambridge skies; the station was rather run down and confused at that time. Later when he came back, at my father's suggestion, he wrote the *History of the Harvard Observatory*, not an exciting but, on the other hand, an accurate volume. Dr. King, the next in line, was always friendly, saying he liked having a young director, as did Miss Cannon, Mr. Campbell, and the others. Mr. Gerrish, the business manager of the Observatory, did worry him a little about budgets and tried to hold him down from too ambitious undertakings.

This was my father's observatory staff and he instinctively began to explore all their possibilities – giving encouragement to all the Harvard investigations as well as attention to his own work. New photographs of the sky were taken wherever needed. He delved into the rich store of plates taken over the past 70 years verifying and augmenting his past work. Progress was made. Results were published. He was unorthodox and highly imaginative in his research approach, and his rate of production of important ideas was prodigious. As an administrator he set a new high in the quality and quantity of research work of his observatory. He continued the policy of his predecessor in concentrating upon the great projects like the classification of two hundred thousand stellar spectra (Miss Cannon's work) and the cataloguing of vast numbers of exterior galaxies (the *Shapley-Ames Catalogue*); but he also encouraged specific investigations and brought to Harvard some of the most brilliant research workers in astrophysics and stellar astronomy. Way back in Pasadena he had complained in a joking manner that as soon as a man becomes a good research scientist they make him into a bookkeeper – but we have seen that he sought and accepted gladly the directorship, and his bookkeeping didn't seriously interfere with his scientific work.

He was never satisfied with good enough. For instance, the weather in Peru was excellent for observing except during the two full months of their rainy season. He soon began a search for a better site and in 1927 the South American station was moved to Bloemfontein, South Africa. At the same time, he acquired a new 60-inch telescope for this new southern station and engaged Dr. Paraskevopoulos (known as Dr. Paras, to save space) as superintendent.

He worried about the safety of the irreplaceable photograph plate collection that was at that time housed in a non-fireproof building. As a result of my father's talent for making friends for the Observatory and for raising money for its expansion and improvement, as Pickering had done before him, Building D came into being. The observatory acquired a fireproof structure for the valuable plates and library as well as a much-needed auditorium and more offices.

One of his outstanding early moves was the inauguration at the Observatory of formal graduate studies in astronomy. No graduate courses in astronomy had been given and no degrees in this field awarded. But now the Observatory became rich in student activity and thereby richer in research ideas. The first Ph. D. in astronomy was awarded to Cecilia Payne[2] (later Mrs. Payne-Gaposhkin[3]) in 1925; the second to Frank Hogg in 1929. In all, 50 doctorates were awarded during the 30 years of my father's directorship. In this period Harvard rose from a non-existent graduate department in astronomy to one of the foremost in the country. Of the 50 men and women who earned the degree, all but seven remained active in astronomy; eight have become directors of observatories.

Encouragement of the amateur astronomers was another of my father's sidelines. In the Fall of 1922, he inaugurated Open Nights at the Observatory. These Open Nights were held for the public who applied for the free tickets, a system made necessary because space in the lecture hall was limited. The visitors could listen to an illustrated lecture, ask questions of the various hosts stationed around to receive them, and look through the 15-inch telescope that was housed under the green dome (a conspicuous Cambridge landmark). My brothers Willis and Alan, when they were of high school age, were often asked to assist at the Open Nights. I can see them now in their dark serge suits, guiding the visitors up the creaky circular stairs that led to the green dome or standing before the illuminated transparencies in the meeting room after the lecture. The visitors would be examining these self-explanatory photographs. My brothers would be ready with answers to: Why do the stars twinkle? Do the canals on Mars contain water? What causes the red spot on Jupiter? These were questions not too difficult for the sons of the director, especially since it was allowable to say, "Astronomers don't know the answer to that question yet." If the sky was cloudy the public that came anyway received rain checks for another night to have their look through the telescope. I have often wondered but never remembered to ask if the Observatory gave rain checks for rain checks for rain checks when it kept on being cloudy every scheduled time, and what was the longest struggle for a clear night. Cambridge weather could stay bad longer than the weather of practically any other observatory.

While most of the Open Nighters were probably only curious, some were inspired to make astronomy their hobby. In 1924, my father helped organize the Bond Astronomical Club (named for the first director of the Harvard Observatory) whose members were enthusiastic amateurs interested in keeping informed of the current advances in astronomy. They met once a month at the Observatory throughout the academic year. Later he also invited the Amateur Telescope Makers of Boston to hold their meetings and establish their workshop at the Observatory. These amateurs proved their worth during the war by building military optical equipment, and later helping Harvard build newer instruments. One of these amateur telescope makers was a professional pianist. When my mother heard of this, I, and later on Lloyd, took lessons from him. His touch on the piano and his interpretation of Chopin were superb, but his touch for the delicate grinding of lenses proved so exceptional and suddenly so remunerative during the war that he became a professional in the art of lens and mirror making, practicing more his hobby and less his piano.

As I have mentioned earlier, my parents maintained a pleasant social atmosphere at the Observatory with frequent teas and parties. My father was always looking for an excuse to have a party, and if there seemed to be none, he'd plan a party anyway and manufacture a reason for it later. "I'm a selfish person," I heard him once say, "I like to see people have a good time." For example, a distinguished visitor comes to town without much forewarning. Perhaps it was Professor Boris Gerasimovič of Kharkov, Russia, or maybe

Dr. Hagihara of Tokyo, Japan, or someone else from where you will – almost everyone, it seemed, visited Harvard. Up goes a notice on the bulletin board, FUN AND FROLIC IN THE HOUSE TONIGHT AT 8 TO MEET … DRESS UP OR FANCY. Miss Walker, his invaluable secretary, would have the job of spreading the word to those who might not happen to see the bulletin board that afternoon. My mother would have six-hours-notice to get the house ready and refreshments bought and prepared. "How many people do you think?" she'd ask.

My father would say, "Maybe 25, maybe 75," which was little help to her, but really one couldn't know until the party began. So, she had to buy X cakes and cookies and ice cream, make coffee and punch, and set out X cups and spoons and napkins. The party was always a success. There was always enough food; any leftovers were fed to the Shapley kids for the next few days.

Yes, everyone had a good time at my parents' parties – even the shyest new student or the most confused foreigner. The atmosphere was informal, even though the guests often came in formal attire or in fancy costume. There was always a variety of things to do at these parties of mixed ages and temperaments; rugs rolled up for dancing in one room; bridge tables in another; ping-pong set up on the extended dining room table. Perhaps at one time in the evening my father would divide the party into two or three groups for charades, whereupon each group would isolate itself to choose a word, plan their pantomime acts and gather props.

One time my group, I remember, chose the word "fortunate." We needed a golf club for the first syllable, a baton and some music stands for the second, a dish of something for the third, and a diamond bracelet for the whole word.

"Mildred, do you think you could find these items or facsimiles thereof?" and I'd run upstairs to look. Up there I'd meet Willis on the same mission for his group, and my mother hunting up props for group three. Before the action began my father made an announcement of warning: the penalty for calling out the answer, before the show was finished and the last egg laid, was that the offender must come to the front and do a word all by himself. I had found only a long-handled child's shovel, but our golf champion was so real-istic that there was no doubt that he was swinging his club with the rest of the cast tremendously interested and agitated by-standers. For the second act we were all seated in orchestra fashion going through the motions of playing as well as or better than Benny Goodman's big band, but our Benny Goodman was waving a baton frantically trying to stop his wild soundless musicians; with hand to his ear he obviously wanted a better A from us. I have forgotten how we acted out the last syllable except that ice cream was involved. The whole word was acted by my father alone. He put on an old moth-eaten coat, turned up the collar, donned an old battered hat, saved just for such an occa-sion, and with his hands in his pockets and a cigarette butt in the corner of his mouth, slouched over, he made an excellent bum. He ambled across the stage, spotted a diamond bracelet on the ground, looked to see that he was not being observed, picked up the heirloom (Woolworth's best), and ambled off stage again. Our word was easily guessed, but that wasn't the point. It was the fun for the doing, and the watching and laughing that counted. The funny side of everyone came out in these charades.

If you think it took much acting on my father's part to make a convinc-ing bum, you are mistaken. Once when returning alone from Europe he had just gone through customs with his one piece of luggage and walking fast but slightly hunched over with fatigue or concentration. He was stopped as he reached the taxi exit. "Just a minute, sir." An official was frisking him, suspi-cious of a slight bulge in his coat. "OK, you can go on." My father proceeded, reflecting, and musing to himself, "I must have looked like a jewel smuggler with diamonds sewed inside my coat lining."

A great many of our parties had at one time during the evening a Virginia Reel, a sober type of square dance in which all the guests could easily partic-ipate. It was a tradition begun by my father that Miss Annie Jump Cannon, with the guest of honor for her partner, should lead this dance; and she did it with the grace and dignity of a queen. Miss Cannon didn't jump or dance but when she led the Virginia Reel she was in her element.

We had get acquainted parties in the Fall for the new students and personnel; we had a party with a ship-board theme to celebrate the going away of people to the International Astronomical Union meetings in Europe; we had spring lawn parties or Tea and Turmoil when the snowball and spirea bushes were in full bloom. Outdoor tea parties usually ended in a quasi-baseball game on the south lawn. There was once even a touch football game. In our family scrapbook there's a wild picture of my mother and various senior staff members all running hell-bent to recover the ball.

Harlow Shapley hits a home run at the Bond Astronomical Club picnic (May 1955). The ball is visible near the top of the trees at the right.

Even the more formal winter teas were not altogether without a light touch. When, for instance, Professor Bailey was leaving for the Arequipa Station and was presented with a traveling bag, my father also presented him with a hand towel, saying it had been reported that the station was short on towels.

One of our fancy dress parties comes to my mind now. It seems that my father had just been to Mexico City, getting an honorary degree from the national university. The recipients were given gowns, capes, and academic hats, all of which were brought home. The garb was so exotic and colorful that my father felt he could not wear it in academic parades, but still he wanted to show it off. So, a masquerade party, with everybody instructed to let themselves go. They came – fifty or so dressed in the best styles, from ballerinas to queens. Dr. Bok was Oom Paul Kruger of the Boer country; the Gaposchkins were in Elizabethan clothes; somebody came as Red Riding Hood, another as Alice with mirrors, and so forth. My father, of course, wore his Mexican outfit and was mistaken for a Tibetan priest.

Another party was held in celebration of the discovery of Planet X. Pluto was its later name but in those post-discovery days we called it X or the Trans-Neptunian planet. So, we had a Trans-Neptunian party – strange clothes, strange language. Mrs. Payne-Gaposhkin and my father talked in a Trans-Neptunian dialect. Somebody composed a song and the music was in appropriate style. Everyone was there. Even the staid and proper Agassizs, generous patrons of the Observatory, came with pleasure and George Agassiz sang nobly in his whisky tenor.

One evening, I remember, my father came down the stairs from A-17 in his usual brisk manner as we were clustered by the dining room door waiting for his arrival. He had a special look of triumph on his face. "Bill," he said to Willis, "Go around and turn off 15 lights!" It was a big house and we were always forgetting to turn off lights all over the place, so my brother had an easy assignment. When he came back, we all went in to dinner and my father, throwing some papers on the table as he sat down, announced, "We've done it!" My mother seemed to guess but the rest of us were all eager with, "What? What do you mean? Done what?"

"We've achieved our goal of fund raising, thanks, among others, to the sustaining, friendly and financial interest of George Agassiz and Gerard Swope.[4] Building D is as good as built. It calls for a party – how about a Hard Times party this Friday?" We all agreed of course; there was always plenty of enthusiasm for parties. "Any conflict on the calendar for Friday, Gretchen?"

"No, only an Observatory Hard Times Party," my mother replied, one step ahead of him. "How many?"

This was always her first question and she never got a very satisfactory answer. "We'll invite everyone," he said.

The next morning my father got an Observatory artist to make up a poster for the bulletin board which informed everyone: POVERTY SELE-BRASHUN – HARD TIMES – COME IN RAGS OR OLD FASHIONED.

The Shapley parties became almost famous. Now whenever my parents travel in America or abroad, they meet people who like to recall and relive those celebrations. But perhaps I am placing the emphasis incorrectly, for of course it wasn't all fun and frolic at the Observatory. Continually the staff gathered together in serious manner. In these early days, colloquia were started. Various members aired their researches, discussing their progress and results. Visiting astronomers were invited to give talks on their work. Later these meetings were called Hollow Squares indicating a new arrangement in the lecture room. A more informal atmosphere was obtained by arranging a group of tables in a large square with participants and audience seated around the outside. However, plain listeners were discouraged from coming; everyone was expected to participate in discussion and questions.

To keep up with the times, we must from time to time introduce new members to the Harvard Observatory staff. Professor Harry Plaskett from the Dominion Astrophysical Observatory in Canada came to Harvard in 1927 to join the staff. He took a leading part in the direction of researches of advanced students and instruction in theoretical astrophysics. Bart J. Bok came from Holland in 1929 to study at the Harvard College Observatory on an Agassiz Research Fellowship. After receiving his degree, he joined the Observatory staff where he remained until 1957. He had great influence on the graduate students whom he guided. His strong personality, a mixture of joviality and seriousness, was felt by everyone. His specialty was the structure of the Milky Way and he quickly attained leadership in this field. Miss Cecilia Payne, who, as we have said, received her degree in 1925, has remained at Harvard to the present time, and as Mrs. Payne-Gaposchkin is known as an astrophysicist of world-wide fame. In this period Dr. Payne wrote an important monograph, on *The Stars of High Luminosity*.

The Observatory's photographic collection continued to attract scientific visitors from all over the world as well as to elicit many requests from American and European observatories for observational data. Among the foreign visitors of this period were Dr. P. ten Bruggencate of Germany, Professor B.P. Gerasimovič of Russia, Dr. L. Hufnagel of Poland, Professor E.A. Milne of Oxford, Professor S. Rosseland of Norway, Dr. A. Unsöld of Germany, Father Georges LeMaître of Belgium, Dr. K.F. Ogorodnikov of Russia, Dr. Ernst Öpik of Estonia, to name only a few. Some of these visitors stopped here only a few weeks – others stayed a few years.

One of my father's early experiments was a series of radio talks, 22 half-hour lectures on different phases of astronomy, by nine members of the Observatory staff. It was a pioneer adventure for those days. The next year these lectures were put into a book, *The Universe of Stars*, which proved to be a very successful volume.

The summation of one of my father's research projects was achieved in a Harvard Monograph entitled *Star Clusters* which was published in 1930. Not only all of Shapley's work in this field was included, but also a survey of the work of others, particularly the pioneer researches of Professor Bailey on the variables in star clusters. In the appendix is a virtually complete bibliography on the subject of star clusters – 812 entries covering the period from 1875 to 1930. Also, in 1930 my father completed a popular book *Flights from Chaos*, based on a lecture series he gave at New York University. In easy language he described and explained the Universe as scientists of that day saw and understood it, and he traced a continuous train of systems from the atom to the metagalaxy. At the bottom end of the series of material systems he left a blank space, which has since been filled in, pretty much as he expected it would be, by the identification of the sub-atomic particles called nucleons and mesons. He also left an unfilled line at the top of his table, of which he wrote that "a number of possible fillers come naturally to mind. We want to write in at once something that transcends the material universe. Some would offer 'The Absolute' as an appropriate class name. Others would suggest 'The Mind.'"

But this entry so far remains unfilled. I remember being curled in the easy chair in the upstairs study doing my homework while my mother was at the long desk working over her checkbook. My father walked in with the question, "Gretchen, what do you think of Flights from Chaos for a title?" They discussed it at such length that finally my Virgil and I got up to find a quieter place to study. He was afraid that the title might imply fleeing from chaos and hiding under the desk, rather than flying from chaos to order.

In collaboration with Miss Helen Howarth, my father brought out a third book, in 1929. Called *Source Book in Astronomy*, it contained excerpts from classical and fundamental treatises and monographs on all phases of astronomy, covering the years from 1500 to 1900. This book was one of a series, for there were also Source Books in physics, in mathematics, in biology, and other sciences. My father was one of the general editors.

As we can see my father was busy, as was everyone else at Harvard Observatory. Miss Cannon, after thirteen years' labor completed, in 1923, the cataloguing of stellar spectra – nine volumes, 225,300 stars. The printing took another decade. The value of this catalogue is beyond estimation – it is one of the staples of every observatory today. One afternoon, as the project neared completion, my father came to Annie J. Cannon's office for a chat on work and things in general. Between them they decided that the catalogue should have an extension – an extension to the fainter stars in the Milky Way. On the spot they mapped out a program for the *Henry Draper Extension* which added two volumes and 46,850 stars, and 13 years to the project. At this conference, I was no ear-witness but there was another that comes to my mind, that I stepped in on many years later when I was of the silk-stocking age. Of course, there were many such conferences. My father liked to seek out his colleagues in their offices. There he could sit and discuss a work with less interruption and with less tension perhaps, than in his director's office. To inquiries, at such times, Miss Walker would say "Dr. Shapley has misplaced himself somewhere," and that is what she told me that day when I finally hunted him down in Miss Cannon's office. The local telephone system was out of order and I had been sent to report that it was dinner time. He got the signal just by noticing me standing in the doorway, but the conference wasn't quite finished, so I lingered to listen to their talk. After a moment Miss Cannon turned to me.

"Do you know the first time I met your father – I must tell you!" And she interrupted herself with her infectious laugh. The laugh didn't mean that her story necessarily contained a joke – only that it was a happy recollection for her.

"It was in August 1913. The meeting of the International Solar Union at Bonn (Germany) had just closed and the Harvard delegation was traveling on a day train to Hamburg for the meeting of the Astronomische Gesellschaft. Having read an interesting article on *Die Deutsche Sprache* in the morning paper, I handed it to a boyish looking compatriot who had just joined us in the compartment – none other than Dr. Harlow Shapley, the most recent Ph. D. in astronomy of Princeton University. The next Fall when your father returned from his fellowship travels abroad, he said, 'Do you recall that editorial on *Die Deutsche Sprache*? While in Hamburg, I met the man who wrote it.' And ever since, your father has been meeting the man. No matter how busy he is, the human touch, the personal contact is there." Miss Cannon laughed, I giggled and my father looked a little embarrassed.

"I always get into trouble with Miss Cannon" he remarked, "But there's a better story. Did I ever tell you of the time I got all dressed up in Copenhagen and took the famous Annie to a swell dinner in a swell restaurant, and then found that I was without resources – I had changed my clothes. I borrowed the needed numerous kroner from my guest much to her delight and my embarrassment." I laughed, and so did he, and Miss Cannon laughed until there were tears in her eyes. Then we noticed that Willis had joined us to give a second call to dinner.

"Well, we'd better get over to the house before Gretchen sends the rest of the offspring after us," he remarked, as we all said goodbye to Miss Cannon. We started walking over the covered bridge that connects building C to building A. "Gosh, I planned to get in a haircut this afternoon," he said smoothing the thinning hair on top of his head.

"Hmm, going to get your ears lowered," was Willis's comment. "I was there two days ago – the Italian barber is in good shape."

"Pop, you don't need a haircut much," I said, looking him over critically.

"Maybe not, but by next week I'll need one too much."

"He goes just to talk grand opera with the barber," Willis explained.

Now we had arrived in A-17 and were racing down the stairs where the rest were waiting. "Pop and Miss Cannon were telling stories," I explained as we all went in to dinner.

"Bridge game tonight?" Alan asked hopefully.

"Maybe," was the answer.

Sometimes on his rare free evenings, if our homework was finished, we played bridge. It was in Jasper with our suffering parents and relatives that Willis, Alan, and I learned the game. Now we were better – good enough to fill in at Observatory bridge parties when a fourth was needed. But thinking back to our Jasper visit, in the beginning we weren't very successful. My mother was a good player and a fast one – she plays all card games well and fast. My father was a good player too – always trying to squeeze an extra trick out of the game. He would take what seemed a long time to plan his strategy while the other three waited. Then zim bam bam, he'd put one card after another down on the table with exaggerated force, finishing the game so fast that we could hardly get our cards down on the successive tricks in time. In spite of remarkable parental patience, our apprenticeship wasn't always peaceful. I remember my father once shouting to Willis, who was his partner, "You must lead out the trumps. Not leading out trumps is more dangerous than driving a taxicab in London!" The rest of us burst out laughing, but Willis, somewhat irritated, mumbled something to the effect that fathers are embarrassing and "if you were me and had you for a father, you would complain too."

"But I am my own father!" was his surprised remark. Our mouths fell open in disbelief. "Finish the game, Bill, and then I'll explain."

The game was over, and my father began the strange tale.[5] "My father and grandfather married sisters – Sarah and Kate Stowell – and both brought forth young, and thereby complicated the Shapley-Stowell genealogy. For now, my father, Willis Harlow Shapley, is the half-brother of my uncle who is also my first cousin. My mother is my father's aunt, and her father (because my mother's sister married my grandfather) is my great-grandfather as well as my grandfather, in this way making me my own father."

The words went in one ear and out the other – we just sat there dumb.

"Here," he said, and took the score pad, "I'll make a diagram. The Shapley-Stowell trees are a bit twisted and confused, you can see."

"It looks sort of indecent – like intestines," I remarked. We had all crowded around him to watch him draw, and as the sketch took shape we could see it proved his point. He was his own father, he was his grandfather, and he was his own son – any way you looked at it!

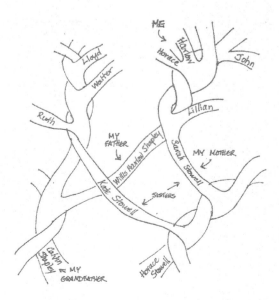

This evening of bridge wasn't interrupted with an explanation of the Shapley-Stowell tree or the more conventional Betz family tree, but it broke up just the same because at one point, Willis, Alan, and I could not agree as to who would watch for half an hour while the other two played with our parents.

"I'll settle it!" my father said. "No bridge!" He picked up the deck and zing, zing, zing, zing, zing – he put down five cards face up on the table.

"What's this game called?" Alan asked.

"Don't know – I'm inventing it on the spot. Let's call it Hells Bells," he said. "OK, we have a seven, an eight, a king, a five and a deuce. Make a hundred out of it, using each card only once."

"The king is equal to 13?" I asked, stalling for time.

"Yes."

"Got it!" shouted Willis.

"So have I," called Alan, right after him.

"Well, Bill?"

"You take the 7, add the 8, subtract the king. You've got two. Multiply this by the deuce. You've got four. Take the square root and you have two again. Multiply it by the 5. You've got ten. Square it. One hundred!"

"Good. Write it down on this piece of paper and see how it looks."

"I did it another way," Alan said. "Take the king and subtract the 8 and take the 2 from it and you've got three. Subtract this three from the 7 and you have four. Multiply this four by 5 squared; four times twenty-five is a hundred. Mine's more straightforward," Alan remarked, and he reached for the paper to add his formula to it.

$$\left\{5\sqrt{[(7+8-K)]2}\right\}\left\{5\sqrt{[(7+8-K)]2}\right\} = 100$$

$$(5\cdot5)[7-(K-2-8)] = 100$$

"You and your squares and square roots," I said (now just in time, I was ready). "I've got a still simpler way! Add the king, the 7 and the 5. You've got twenty-five. Multiply it by the 8 and you've got two hundred. Divide it by the deuce and there's your hundred."

$$\frac{(K + 7 + 5)8}{2} = 100$$

"All right," my father said, satisfied. "Here's another set of five cards." And after these, he gave us another – and so we learned to do fast arithmetic under the pressure of competition, and it was a wonderful way to utilize incomplete decks of cards. In our house we had a whole drawer full of such decks with one or more cards missing. We played Hells Bells a lot. It was with this game that we first learned the meaning and value of factorial 3 and logarithm of 10. As we became more proficient, we introduced the inverse factorial and antilogarithms, and chose as a goal-number some integer other than one hundred, or chose fractions as the goal-number.

Alan, when he was ten, was once explaining this game to Professor Russell who was visiting us as he frequently did. There were a few house rules such as no dividing by one, no use of logarithms, and always all five cards must be used but not as squares or cubes of another number.

"And does little Lloyd play with you?" Professor Russell wanted to know.

"Yes," and Russell was delighted with Alan's reply, and often told about this apparent precocity. "Yes, sometimes he does, and we let him use logarithms because he is only six." This inept six-year old who joined us in our various games was to become a distinguished mathematician and an authority on and inventor of sophisticated games.[6]

Bridge, Hells Bells, and other card games were good indoor sports, especially in winter time, but we as a family were not addicted to cards nor did we neglect the outdoors. Sunday mornings when my father could get away from his work, he would join a group of Harvard biology professors on walks in the country. These Sunday morning walks of the 1920s were organized and led by the famous Harvard zoology teacher – one of Harvard's greatest – George Howard Parker. For a time, the botanist W.J.V. Osterhout participated, and the two made the event unforgettable for the younger scientists. About a dozen on the average took part, and they usually went off into the Blue Hills, southeast of Boston, or to the outskirts of Lexington and Arlington – countryside then, crowded suburbs now.

Also we children would design walks for ourselves. We'd take a long slip of paper and write down L L R L R R L R L L R, a series of Ls and Rs in random order. L meant turn left, and R, turn right. We'd go down to the Observatory front gate on Garden Street, consult our paper and turn to the right or left as indicated, go a block, consult our paper again and turn accordingly, and so on through the city streets. The strangest thing about these walks was that almost invariably we landed near or in the Cambridge city dump. Why, we couldn't figure out – but so it was; no matter how we juggled our letters we never arrived at an attractive destination.

In later years, around Fresh Pond, the Cambridge reservoir, my father walked with the famous medical scientist Walter B. Cannon – familiarly known as W. Bodily-Changes Cannon, because of his work in metabolism. His doctor had scared him, and to save funeral expenses, Cannon got my father to walk with him. Cannon lived for twenty years after that and succumbed finally to the results of his pioneer work with X-rays. Sometimes we children joined them on these nature walks, an experience which taught us to keep our eyes wide open.

Every October, the A.A.V.S.O. had their banquet meeting. Sometimes my father was chosen toastmaster or, as they called him, Grill Master, at this banquet. At one meeting in 1924 when, I think, Mr. Campbell was president of the Association, the minutes of that after-dinner speech went something like this:

"After a few remarks Leon Campbell passed up further responsibility by choosing Dr. Shapley Grill Master. First Dr. Shapley, as Master, pronounced a long eulogy on the sooncoming first speaker of the evening; that he had all the virtues on the calendar; that he was a friend of the friendless, and enemy of the enemy-less. He then introduced Dr. Shapley, the director, as that paragon and Dr. Shapley, the Toastmaster sat down. Up rose Dr. Shapley, the director, and, in words that flashed and glittered, he told of the work astronomy had accomplished in the past year. Among the ten highlights he cited, perhaps one of the most important results was the return to the island universe theory in the study of the spiral nebulae, and he stated that some of the galaxies were over a million light years away, thus in just a few years, even within young memories, increasing the extent of the whole knowable stellar universe from 3300 light years as estimated by Newcomb, to Shapley's 2,000,000."

As we remember, before becoming an astronomer my father had been a newspaper reporter, and the technique and habits of that calling he instinctively applied wherever he went – shorthand, quick sizing up of personalities and situations, an eye and an ear for a scoop. Hence Harvard achievements frequently made news more promptly than could have been possible under a different type of leadership – an asset indeed to an administrator's ever-present need for money-raising. Spotting and recording highlights in astronomy was for him a natural undertaking; and once started, the highlights became the regularly expected attraction at the annual meeting of the A.A.V.S.O.

Harvard was the Western Hemisphere's distributing agent for news of discoveries of new comets, asteroids, novae, and other spot news in the astronomical field. Interesting episodes sometimes enlivened the routine. Even experienced people excitedly made false discoveries – often reporting, as comets, ghosts caused by reflections from a nearby bright star, in the multiple-lens telescope. But the real discoveries were more exciting. Much later my father told us this story.

"One day, Roger Lowell Putnam, former mayor of Springfield, Massachusetts, and the boss and trustee of the Lowell Observatory in Flagstaff, Arizona, which was founded by his uncle, Percival Lowell came into my Cambridge office in an excited state. He looked around carefully to see that we were safely alone, then in a hoarse whisper said, 'I think we've got it!' Influenza? Religion? Or just what? – This was about February 10th, 1930. 'No,' he said, 'I think we've got Planet X!' For some years at Percival Lowell's Flagstaff Observatory they had been looking for the hypothetical planet X. A special telescope had been made and mounted and manned by the farm-boy amateur astronomer, Clyde Tombaugh. He had made and examined hundreds of plates, searching for the photographic trail of the proper length to indicate a planet beyond Neptune – the ninth of the solar family. Now they had something, and in order not to lose credit for the discovery, Roger Putnam had me record the day, the hour, and the minute of his announcement to me. 'Don't tell anybody – not even the family.' But suppose I talk in my sleep? Why the delay in making this exciting announcement? They wanted confirmation with more plates, it was stated, and wanted to get an orbit computed – and some other excuses were made for a delay that I could not quite understand. Finally, the announcing telegram came, and then I knew what those sentimental astronomers were waiting for; it was the March 13th birthday of Percival Lowell. Although he had died some 15 years earlier, Percival Lowell was on the job – his inspiration had put it across."

The adopted symbol of the planet, ♇ , suggested by my father and possibly independently by others, is the combination of the letters P and L. The name Pluto was first suggested by a little girl in Oxford, England.[7] The god of the outer darkness she told astronomers is Pluto, and that word starts with P and L.

And so the first decade of my father's directorship came to a close. The number of scientific workers had trebled, and the fields covered by the investigations by the members of the staff had expanded and diversified. Each year between fifty and a hundred papers embodying the results of these investigations were published from the Observatory. The Observatory had a new endowment, and as a result some of my father's dreams were coming true. Building D was built. The Oak Ridge Station was established and most of the Cambridge telescopes moved out of town to a site where the skies were darker. There was a new 60-inch telescope for the South African Station and another, a 61-inch, for the Oak Ridge Station. It was the beginning of a golden era of astronomy for the Harvard College Observatory. The round table was now moved to D-35; the surface always covered with a variety of enterprises – administrative, research problems of his and others, and various other personal projects. The inner separately rotating bookcase and curio container, as the years went by, collected objects without restraint, for here my father was his own housekeeper – snapshots of friends, biological specimens, books unusual and books currently useful, cigars, fossils, souvenirs from travels including bottles of ants preserved in alcohol. He always carried a few ant bottles in his coat pocket for emergencies. He had ants from Bikini, the Mexican Garden of the Gods, the Taj Mahal, the Egyptian Pyramids, the Cedars of Lebanon, and other remote places that now I don't remember; and he had an ant from Stalin's banquet table in the Kremlin. This ant, which he found in the floral arrangement, was an ordinary insect but it had the distinction of being preserved not in American wood alcohol but in Russian vodka.

CHAPTER SIX

The Golden Era of the Harvard College Observatory

O ne morning in 1932 the Universe came to our breakfast table. I remember my father unrolling a scroll one yard long and two feet wide as we moved aside the food and dishes and wanted to know, "What is it?" The four corners were held down with water glasses.

"There's your universe as of right now," he said. "We put the finishing touches on it last night." Here was a diagram of the *Shapley-Ames Catalogue* of 1249 external galaxies. "Each symbol represents a galaxy like our own Milky Way system."

We began asking questions. "What are the circles?"

"The open circles are the bright galaxies, brighter than magnitude 12 – the dots represent the galaxies between 12th and 13th magnitude. The bigger the magnitude number, the fainter they are."

"And this curvy line?"

"It indicates the central line of the Milky Way. You can't discover many external galaxies there because we are inside our watch-shaped galaxy looking toward the edges and our view is pretty well obscured by Milky Way dust. If we look up or down from our inside position, we have a better chance of seeing through and beyond. Notice these groupings?"

"Clusters of galaxies?"

"Yes, this spottiness is interesting, isn't it?" My father began rolling up the Universe again so that the maid could serve the coffee.

"And now what do you do?" I wanted to know.

"Breakfast," he replied.

"No, I mean about the Universe."

"Go deeper – begin looking for and cataloguing the fainter than 13th magnitude galaxies. I'd like to carry it to the 17th magnitude in favorable regions; and we must have a better look in the regions of sky where we have so far found only a few galaxies. Also, we must study these groupings. It appears that galaxies gravitate and move in groups."

"If we have clusters of galaxies," I said, "perhaps we can have clusters of clusters of galaxies and clusters of clusters of clusters of galaxies." The thought was overwhelming. "I think I'll eat breakfast. It's easier."

Now, some 11,000 breakfasts later, I am prepared to appreciate this map of the sky, this catalogue of external galaxies. The first part of the project alone took two years of laborious work even though practically all the necessary photographic plates were already in existence. The position of every object had to be checked and the photographic magnitude (brightness) measured on three plates. When extended as my father had planned, this project made an important contribution to the Harvard Annals series, a sequel to the *Henry Draper Catalogue* of stellar spectra also contained in these volumes. Miss Adelaide Ames, who had through this work with my father attained an international reputation in the field of external galaxies, devoted seven years to research at the Harvard Observatory.

As you can imagine some really important things came to our breakfast and dinner table. We children became slightly blasé, not always appreciating the real significance of things. I, for one, remember more my father's enthusiasm and excitement than that which had caused it. It was nothing unusual at the breakfast table to talk science. The night's progress was discussed as one would discuss the day's progress at the evening meal.

My father's day at the office began at nine and often didn't end until midnight or later. He issued a standing invitation – "I'm free to see any student between midnight and three." By his bedside was a Dictaphone and a memo pad as well as stacks of papers, and probably a detective story to "help put me to sleep." If he didn't sleep well or if ideas came to him in the night, he could switch on his bed light and record them into the Dictaphone or shorthand them on his job list. For the past fifty years, at least, he has always written down work schedules – generally a list of BIGS and SMALLS, and in addition he keeps from month to month a list of DREADS. Sometimes a DREAD is answering some disagreeable or otherwise difficult letter, or finishing up a manuscript, or attending to some administrative red-tape. Eventually as the DREAD list grows, he will set aside a few days and make a drive to finish these conscience-dictated tasks.

Two rings on the door bell was a routine signal at breakfast time. One of us would run down with a mouthful of toast to the reception hall to gather up the mail from a box container built into the front door. My father would look over his mail as he sipped his coffee or ate his rye-crisp (nobody else liked it) or reached for a banana. You can see it was easy to fool him when he was absorbed. He'd jot down a few notes in the margin or at the bottom of some of the letters; to others, he'd say "wastebasket" and hand the advertising junk to one of us to dispose of as we liked. Some of it he would give to my mother saying, "your department," – bills to be paid. Then he would gather up what he couldn't dispose of, and along with a finished cylinder from the bedside Dictaphone, he'd head for the other side, as he called the Observatory. On the way over, he was likely to be stopped by one or more persons, and an on-the-spot conference would take up a few minutes. By the time he reached his office and laid down his load, Miss Walker and her assistant would have a full morning of work set out for them. Miss Walker, in turn, would have various messages to relay, a few questions to ask, and a few letters and papers needing his signature.

On March 23, 1932, Building D was dedicated in the presence of representatives of several eastern observatories. The dedication ceremony was made the occasion for a conference on astrophysical problems. Among those taking active part were President Lowell of Harvard University, Professor Arthur Holmes of the University of Durham, England, Professor Lane of Tufts College, and Professors Brown and Schlesinger of Yale. The 300,000 photographic plates now were safe in their fireproof stacks, the valuable library was in its new fireproof home on the mezzanine of the auditorium. By strange coincidence, almost at once during a heated conference in Dr. Donald Menzel's[1] office, some students had set a small fire in a wastebasket; but nothing worse than this was possible in Building D. Dr. Menzel had joined the Observatory staff and had taken over the duties of Professor Plaskett who had been called to Oxford University. We shall presently speak further of Dr. Menzel who was affectionately known among the children of the Observatory family as Donald Duck.

Cambridge inevitably grew bigger and brighter, and, therefore, worse and worse for telescope work. As early as 1930 my father began to search the countryside within a 30-mile radius for an out-of-town site for the major telescopes. On various Sundays some of the family would go out with him, and perhaps some of the staff members, to explore available sites. Finally, a hill site, actually the highest hill in northeastern Massachusetts, was chosen. Mr. Fuller, in the township of Harvard, Massachusetts had a piece of land not good for farming, 40 acres covered with small trees and underbrush which he offered *gratis* to the Harvard Observatory. The Oak Ridge Station (later known as the Agassiz Station) of the Harvard Observatory came into being. A new 61-inch Clark reflector, the 16-inch Metcalf doublet, the 8-inch Draper, and a battery of patrol cameras were all moved out to Oak Ridge, where the sky was darker, and they could be more effective. A residence was built for the superintendent and a one-story office and dormitory building was constructed. An attractive guest cottage, a gift of the Agassizs, was built for weekend and vacation visits of Harvard astronomer families. My father had much enthusiasm for these woods and so did others at the Observatory. On Columbus Day, a holiday, all the Observatory people, old and young, went out to Oak Ridge, incidentally for a picnic and particularly for building the Summer Palace, a prefabricated five room house that the directions said could be put up by four people in one day. So, with 40 people, it also took only one day. It was a jolly occasion that I missed because I was away in Michigan at college. However, the next summer we Shapleys lived in it for two weeks and if not as elegant as its name suggested, it was nevertheless a good solid palace for summer living.

My father blazed trails in these woods. A tree was pruned and made safe for children's climbing. Dr. Bok put up a swing. During this operation, while he was still up in the tree arranging the ropes, Johnny Bok and Carl Shapley down below had a violent quarrel with much screaming radiating out through the quiet woods. My father told us afterwards that he came crashing through the underbrush taking a shortcut from the trail to see which boy had broken a leg. He found the two boys simply quarreling over who was to be first on the swing, while Dr. Bok sat calmly up in the tree like God on High watching the fight.

The woods were lively. There was fun. There was also mishap. Willis and Alan continually had unpleasant experiences with poison ivy. Lloyd was almost immune, and Carl didn't explore. I somehow avoided being troubled by it and became so nonchalant with the idea of my immunity or good fortune that I didn't trouble to learn to recognize the plant. Once I was sitting by the road in the shade waiting for my father and my brothers who were detained talking with some visitors. We were all going to Hell's Pond nearby to swim. I was in my swimsuit waiting patiently in this leafy spot. The car sputtered up beside me. Instead of saying, "get in; let's go" in his usual cheery way, my father looked at me in a very strange way and so did my brothers. "Go and wash right away with a very strong laundry soap. Maybe it will save you!" But it didn't save me. After that, I knew how to recognize poison ivy.

Then, there was the time various students, a group of young ladies, and Dr. Theodore Sterne, a member of the staff, were spending the weekend at Agassiz Cottage. Dr. Sterne had an encounter with a pursuing swarm of hornets, and he came helter-skelter through the woods. Not knowing how to rid himself of his attackers, he charged into the cottage among the defenseless ladies, thinking that perhaps he could drown his trouble in the shower bath.

But, in general the days spent at Oak Ridge were extremely pleasant and peaceful. There were various places to go swimming. Hell's Pond was the favorite. It belonged to the Fort Devens Officers Club; perhaps the pond had a different name before the army got hold of it. Astronomers' families were considered harmless and so we were allowed to use this swimming hole which was better than some other holes nearby because it had a pier, a diving board, a handsome life guard and never great quantities of people. Dr. Menzel one summer decided that, even if he didn't complete some of his scientific projects according to his schedule, he would succeed in teaching his daughters and Lloyd and Carl Shapley, and various others to swim. And true to his nickname, Donald Duck, he succeeded in making many ducks out of timid landlubbers among the Observatory children.

"Pop, the phone is for you – long distance, I think." I had answered the telephone as we were about to go into dinner.

He took up the receiver, said "yes," listened a moment and then – "Jesus Christ, *No!*" He slammed down the receiver and just sat there by the phone.

I had started to go but the conversation was so short that I was still beside him. Finally, he got up. "Adelaide Ames drowned this afternoon." He said no more – gave no particulars – he hadn't waited to learn them. An hour later he and Colonel Ames, the stricken father, were on the long sad ride to Squam Lake in New Hampshire.

A few weeks later, in August of 1932 the International Astronomical Union (I.A.U.) met in Cambridge. It was a grand occasion but saddened a little, of course, for many of the Observatory family. Miss Ames had been active in administration as well as in galactic research and she was in charge of arrangements for the entertainment of the I.A.U. at its forthcoming meeting in Cambridge.

For all of us there was much activity and excitement during the two weeks that the I.A.U. guests were in town. The entertainment was preceded by a total solar eclipse conveniently located which, we claimed, we provided. It seemed that practically all the astronomers of the world were present. The Observatory personnel and all the Shapleys were drafted for work on reception committees, at the information table, as guides or hostesses for the 350 international guests. There were general meetings covering the various branches of astronomy. There were visits to places of historical interest, visits to Massachusetts Institute of Technology (M.I.T.), Harvard University, and Wellesley College, and an excursion to Oak Ridge where the Astronomer Royal, Sir Frank Dyson, laid the corner stone of the new 61-inch telescope building. Sir Arthur Eddington gave a formal evening lecture at M.I.T. There were three big luncheons in the residence, and at the end of the I.A.U. meetings a big party. It was on this occasion that the catholic priests Abbé LeMaître[2] and Father O'Connell startled us by playing bridge with great skill. My father tells the story this way:

> "LeMaître offered to take my bridge hand, pairing up with Father O'Connell, when I was called out of the game by a late guest or something. Oh no, I said to LeMaître, don't bother, for while watching our game, he had pointed to the five of diamonds and asked, 'what do you call him.' I told him, and later he pointed in the same inquiring manner to another card and asked, 'what do you call him.' Why Father, we call a spade a spade – it is the seven of spades. 'Ah so,' he said. Therefore, I was reluctant to impose on the other three by giving LeMaître my hand. I should not have worried for I soon noticed from a distance that the opponents, Mrs. Carol Rieke and Arthur Sayer, Harvard graduate students, seemed to be having a hard time of it playing against the two reversed-collar men. Later I looked more closely and saw a sweet look of triumph on LeMaître's face. He had just bid and made a small slam, with queen high! It takes an expert to bid such a hand and successfully play it. He dropped ace and king on the first and only trump lead. Naturally, I was amazed at the performance – this skill by the What you call him? kibitzer. Father O'Connell saw my dismay and puzzlement. He came up to me and said, 'Perhaps I should explain that LeMaître is a

much-experienced bridge player, and his inquiry about those cards was simply his seeking names in English which he knew only in French."

My father was headed for his offices after playing a game of volleyball with some energetic graduate students and other volunteers. In the basement of Building D there was a spare – for the moment – room in which a net had been erected. He encountered Miss Dorrit Hoffleit[3] in the hallway. "I want to see you in about ten minutes if it's convenient," he said to her, and went to find Dr. Bok who was one of his most valuable advisers in student matters. Miss Hoffleit was a diligent scientific worker who had received her master's degree but believed that was as far as she could go, scholastically.

When Dorrit Hoffleit came into my father's office he was sitting at his big round table. Dr. Bok was sitting nearby, looking stiffly formal.

"We were just wondering why you don't go on working for your Ph. D.," my father began.

"But I don't think I could ever pass the examinations," she answered, astonished.

"Go back to your office and think it over for a while," he replied.

Miss Hoffleit had scarcely got back down stairs when Dr. Bok stamped into her little office, firmly shut the door and sat down. Pounding her desk with his fist, he exclaimed, "Dorrit! When God suggests that you do something, it is your DUTY to do it."

Dorrit recalls: "The next morning I registered for classes, and this little incident and big encouragement made me happier than anything else that happened to me at Harvard."

My father had just come back from a business trip to New York where along with other jobs he – to use his words – "picked up a gold medal." Miss Walker greeted him with, "President Lowell and President Lowell's secretary have been trying to reach you on the telephone. Something urgent about an overcoat."

"So, *he* is the owner of this greenish garb." My father looked down at the overcoat he was wearing. "On this trip, I was, for the first time, mistaken for a panhandler," he jested. Harvard professors at the Faculty Club were always having trouble in picking up the right hats, rubbers, raincoats – or at least my father was – and sometimes the tangles took weeks to straighten out. This time, detained after a dinner meeting, he came out late to the coat rack in the hall to find only two overcoats left, neither of them his. So, he chose the best fitting of the two and went home. That same night he had to catch the night train to New York. It was winter; there was nothing to do but go off in the leftover overcoat. And in that coat, he was "successful in raising a substantial fund for the Harvard College Observatory" as he afterwards told President Lowell, who was a man of substantial wealth.

My father picked up several medals from time to time. He once told us he felt like the general who received one medal by mistake and everyone else decorated him because he'd received the first one. "I was awarded the Rumford Gold Medal when the American Association for the Advancement of Science came to Boston – not, I think, for my work but because they could count on me for a good lecture. So much publicity in advance was given about this famous Rumford Medal that on the night of the bestowal some gangsters – one woman and two men – attempted to steal it out of my hands on the pretense of photographing me and it with a fake camera. The Academy president and I fought them off in the hotel corridor and got into the ballroom slightly nervous! After the address, a policeman escorted me to the Cambridge subway and home, and I still have the gold, but I won't tell you where."

Beside the Rumford medal, there was the Bruce Gold Medal, the New York Academy of Sciences gold medal, the Royal Astronomical Society Gold Medal, and the Draper Gold Medal. He has said of them, "I really should melt them down and have a party!"

In the 1930s there were seven honorary degrees awarded him: Oglethorpe, Pittsburgh, Pennsylvania, Princeton, Harvard, Brown and Toronto

Universities. The University of Toronto, like British universities provided a beautiful scarlet gown, and a diploma was handed to him by Prime Minister Mackenzie King. As my father tells it:

"When this gay scarlet cape was draped over my bulging form, I thought Ha! This will please Gretchen, when I strut in color. But, alas! I was deluded, for as I paraded off the stage into the wings a pair of hands reached out and stripped me of my gown. Those thrifty Scots!"

It was generally known that Shapley was a popular lecturer. In Miss Cannon's words, "His unusual appeal as a speaker, on almost any subject to almost any audience, may be explained readily by a remarkable sense of humor, combined with a comprehension of human nature and a breadth and versatility of thought." Few scientists have possessed the ability that comes quite natural to him for lucid and inspiring presentation of scientific discoveries. In December of 1929 he gave a short talk before the American Philosophical Society, entitled *Ten Unsolved Mysteries of the Stellar Universe*:

> *"I am asked the question 'Why the 200-inch Telescope?' But first I should like to ask you a question – why not have some two hundred-inch intellects such as those of Aristotle and Benjamin Franklin? Are we not about to see farther than we have vision? To reach farther than we can grasp? As yet, that is not the case, I think, and in telling you of some of the unsolved mysteries of the stellar universe I hope to show that we have already visualized the great mysteries, that we have competent detectives on the job, and in one or two of the simpler cases we are nearly ready to ask for an indictment.*

> *The ten major mysteries that I have listed here will be unraveled not alone by the giant telescopes. Possibly one-third of the unraveling will be done by the interpreter and by mathematical theory, and another third by the moderate sized telescope that costs hundreds or thousands, instead of millions; but probably a third of the celestial mysteries that perplex us now will yield only to the powerful and penetrating giant telescopes, the greatest of which will be the proposed 200-inch reflector in California.*

In this outlining of unsolved mysteries, we shall begin near at home and travel to the bounds of the universe.

First Mystery. What are the perplexing wobbles of the whirling planet on which we live? The Earth does not rotate uniformly, and its axis of rotation does not stay put. The poles of the Earth wiggle over the Arctic and Antarctic maps. Recently Commander Byrd triumphantly dropped the American flag at the South Pole. Did he hit the exact spot? Perhaps, but the pole will soon wander away and give another explorer a chance. If Commander Byrd missed, the wandering pole may itself find the flag some time.

To be sure, these irregular motions of the pole are only a hundred feet or so in a year's time. The astronomers can map them accurately by observing the stars that pass directly overhead. We call the wiggles latitude variations. The mystery has been partially solved by astronomical detectives; two villains are involved – the weight of the yearly fall of snow is one, and the other is a slight deformity of our planet. It is not wholly homogeneous.

Second Mystery. Where is the original home of the comets? There are probably tens of thousands of these objects – of these swarms of meteoric dust and stones wandering in our solar system. But they die off so rapidly under the wear and tear of the Sun's intensive radiation and planetary perturbation that in a million years few of those now known will be left. Those that exist now must have come into existence more than a billion years after the planets were born. Did we pick up the present crop of comets from the wastes of space within the last million years?

The big telescopes should assist in getting the answer – they will follow the faint receding comets to the bounds of the solar system and help to analyze their light and motions. Big mathematics will also help.

Third Mystery. Why does the Sun rotate so slowly? And the moons of Mars, why so little and so speedy? If, and when, a giant passing star, some billions of years ago, wrecked our Sun's atmosphere and thus incited the birth of the Earth and other planets, was that event an actual graz-

ing collision rather than merely a close approach? That is what we now suspect, and the great solar telescopes may check up on this suspicion through the analyses of the atmosphere of the Sun, which might still show some effects of an ancient disaster. I have in mind a special telescope for solar research – an instrument of large caliber and long focus that will look into the private life of the Sun and help to resolve these puzzles.

The Fourth Mystery involves the source of energy that lights the stars. We on the Earth live on the bounty of the Sun, and all of our energy, in the last analysis, comes from that star – but how do the Sun and other stars get their stores of energy that have been pouring into space for thousands of millions of years? It must come not from the burning of their materials, not from the heat of shrinkage, not from electrical or mechanical or chemical sources – such energy stores are all too little. We have a clue to this mystery; the clue is that stars are transforming matter itself into energy – only a clue as yet, but the little and the big telescopes, exploring space and analyzing stars and nebulae, may eventually solve this great mystery – the source of energy – the fundamental problem of the existence of stars and life.

Fifth Mystery. Is this universe running down? Are we progressing to the heat-death of the Universe? It seems so. The stars appear to exhaust their own material. They tend to grow little, old, and cold in the course of thousands of millions of years. Matter transforms into radiation and disperses throughout the Universe. Will radiation sometime or somewhere change back into matter? This is the mystery of mysteries – it is indeed the question of the death of the world. We have only vague clues. Big telescopes and powerful minds may tell us more someday. Now we search, think, and wonder.

Sixth Mystery. Every hour millions of dust-like meteors crash into the Earth's atmosphere. Whence do they come? What is their past? What are the obscure secrets they hide concerning the evolution of the planets and the stars, and the evolution of the Universe in general? We know how to tackle those meteoric mysteries – just give us research room, and time, and powerful telescopic equipment and we shall contribute a bit to knowledge of the age and development of world-stuff. We compute the ages of stars as something like twenty thousand million years, but what came before the stars? Just give us room and we shall see what we can do.

Seventh Mystery. What are these baffling dwarf stars that are found in the neighborhood of the Sun? They are the size of planets but as massive as stars. They have us stumped for the present. Probably there are millions of them, but they are so tiny that we can see only the nearest ones. They appear to be gaseous, like all stars, but unbelievably dense – two or three thousand times as dense as lead. Their further discovery and analysis are problems for big telescopes.

Eighth Mystery. Our Galaxy is a great organization containing thousands of millions of stars, our Sun being one of this vast number. The nucleus of our Galaxy is hopelessly hidden behind dark clouds of matter far out in space, in the direction of Sagittarius. Light cannot get through. We cannot see that remote and mysterious center around which the Sun and its neighboring stars revolve with a speed of two hundred miles a second in a period of two hundred million years. The 200-inch telescope, outfitted with powerful accessories, can help in this problem, for gravitational forces operate right through the dark intervening dust clouds. Can these forces be best discerned by measuring the motions of stars which are too faint for existing telescopes? Will we be able to feel the gravitational pull of this great galactic nucleus, though we cannot see the stars that are pulling?

Ninth Mystery. Why do the other galaxies of stars, that lie far outside our own, run away from us with terrific speeds? The great spiral nebulae, now known to be island universes, composed of billions of stars, all appear to shun us – to fly in all directions. Is this real motion? Or is it a relativity effect? Or some deeply significant but as yet undiscovered prop-

erty of space and time? Only the large telescopes can contribute facts for the solution of this remarkable situation.

And finally, the Tenth and perhaps most hopeless Mystery: Is there a limit to the explorable universe, a limit to creation? Or do the galaxies extend on and on into impenetrable depths of space? Already the astronomers are measuring galaxies that lie a billion trillion miles away, so far away indeed that light takes more than a million centuries to reach the earth. The great telescope now under construction – the 200-inch reflector – should go further and tell us either that we now approach comprehension of the whole galaxy of galaxies, or that we must have still greater telescopes and deeper thoughts before we can hope to grasp and understand the total of material creation."

As a current footnote to the above speech, my father says, "Of the foregoing, numbers 1, 2, 3, 6, and 7 are partially solved by 1962; and numbers 4 and 8 almost completely answered; but numbers 5, 9, and 10 are still deep mysteries."

This period from 1920 to 1940 could be called the golden age of astronomy at Harvard, but as my father has pointed out "although during these twenty years our knowledge of the sidereal world doubled, the list of things we wanted to know has trebled or quadrupled, leaving us more ignorant than before, but also making us keener than ever to attain the spiritual satisfaction that only the struggle to comprehend can give."

In these years, as we have seen, with the aid of large numbers of photographs of the sky, made both at Harvard and at Harvard's southern station, my father was studying the structure of the Milky Way and of the nearby galaxies, especially the Magellanic Clouds, and the distribution of galaxies in space. He was one of the first to demonstrate that galaxies tend to occur in clusters and that the Milky Way galaxy is a member of a local cluster. The *Shapley-Ames Catalogue* showed the clustering.

Along with the glamorous life went a lot of ordinary family living. "Look Pop – I'm now officially an operator of motor vehicles; it says so here in fine print!"

My father was engrossed in some papers, and replied, "So?"

"Now, can I have the car for the afternoon? Alice[4] and I want to take a drive into the country. Look," I said, and I dropped my brand-new license on top of the pages he was reading.

"Good," he replied, "it looks genuine," and pulled out his to compare.

"We'll be back at five," I added, getting up to go.

"Have I said yes to something?" he asked. "Goshalmighty! My license has expired!" Looking at his watch, "I'd better go right now while I think of it and get it renewed. Want to come along?"

"All right, but I hope it doesn't take too long. Alice and I had planned to go out while the afternoon is still nice."

So, my father and I drove down to the Cambridge City Hall to the motor vehicle department. I demonstrated my good driving talents and he didn't seem overly nervous.

When I got past Harvard Square, and this square is more complicated to drive through than the name implies, with no hits or errors my father let out his breath and said "Fine – except you nearly took the pants off that policeman on that turn!"

City Hall was no marble edifice – just an old-smelling, old-looking, old creaking building. But the vehicle department was efficient, swinging into high gear as soon as we came up to the counter. Name? Professor Harlow Shapley. Address? Harvard College Observatory, Cambridge. Eyes blue, hair brown, height? Five foot seven. Weight?

One fifty-five. Witness signature – your signature – over here for eye test. Color test was OK; eye test, too.

"Read this." My father was handed a card to read on which was the preamble to the Constitution of the United States. He read it to himself while I stood beside him affecting a superior air. "Well?" said the man.

"Very interesting," was my father's comment.

"Read it *out loud*, Professor!"

He did, and so it went on record that my father, the Harvard professor, actually could read. And also, he could write, although at one of these driver's examinations, was it in New Hampshire or in Massachusetts, he was caught spelling the word traffic with one letter f.

My father's absent-mindedness led to slightly erratic, though never reckless driving habits. I remember when we were young and trusting, my mother would take special pains to gather us together, like a mother hen with baby chicks, way over to one side of the driveway. She was never sure when my father started the engine whether the car would move forward or backward. There was an incident once with a NO U TURN sign in Central Square. When the policeman came up to my father charging that he was breaking the law, my father explained that he understood that the sign meant "No, *you* turn." He was lucky that the officer only gulped, mumbled something, and motioned him on.

Years later, my mother tells me, there was one dramatic incident on the New Hampshire highways that, I can imagine, went something like this:

My father, to himself: "Do I hear a siren – yes, and I think I make out a motorcycle cop in my rear-view mirror. Probably late on his way home to dinner. – (long pause) – Do you suppose he is following me? – Let's see, 40 miles per hour; that's reasonable. I'm on the right side of the road. – He can't have anything on me. – (long pause) – He's still following. – What could be wrong? –Maybe my rear license plate has dropped off. – Well, got to stop since it is evident he wants to look me over. Heavens to Betsy! – Where's my driver's license? I've succeeded in coming away without it. – Now I'm in a fix unless this State Trooper understands professors."

State Trooper: "Are you Professor Shapley?"

"Yes," my father mumbles, obviously startled to be so readily recognizable by the police.

"Your wife telephoned us to stop you and hold you. She is following behind in her jeep. You have evidently left home without pajamas and the lantern slides for your lecture."

My father said, "OK" and "thanks" and he didn't bother to tell the State Trooper that he had also left home without his driver's license.

Perhaps that afternoon Alice and I didn't have time for our drive but there were plenty of other times and we shared many adventures together. Alice Hodson was a Radcliffe student who lived with us during the school season. Later she married a Harvard astronomer and became Mrs. Fletcher Watson. Her assignment was to care for my brother Carl and do some dusting in the downstairs rooms each afternoon. This gave my mother some free time and it gave me a sister, for Alice became an integral part of our family for three or more years. Although she was four years older than I, we became good pals and had lots of fun being crazy together. She was clever, had a bright personality and a fine sense of humor. Once we went into Boston to a deluxe vaudeville and movie theater. It turned out to be more deluxe than we had calculated. Combining our limited funds (we were both on allowances and usually broke) we had enough for the tickets of admission but lacked ten cents for the subway fare back home. It was a dismal thought to come this close to a pleasant evening's entertainment and turn around and go home without, so we went bravely in and enjoyed the show. Afterwards Alice went boldly up to the theater manager, successfully playing the girl in distress and asked him for a dime for the subway.

We also went through a phase when we were fresh-air fiends. Even in freezing weather we would drag our mattresses and blankets out of the fourth-floor bathroom window onto the roof garden, and there we'd sleep, bundled up like papooses with our faces to the stars. More than once in the middle of the night we would have to drag everything back in, the rain finally awakening us. In the quiet of the night with only the sound of the telescopes moving and an occasional streetcar roaring up or down the hill, our outdoor chatter and giggling must have surprised some of the astronomers working through the night.

Alice and I did homework together – I, my high-school Latin, she, her college Latin and Greek. We listened to the radio together, dieted on jello and milk together, or ate homemade bread, a whole loaf at a time, together. Along with our fresh air craze went the exercise craze. On Sunday morning in spring we would rise at four or five in the morning. There'd be only a suggestion of dawn in the sky and we'd be off with a little sustenance in our pockets for a hike from Cambridge to Reading, from my house to her house. We estimated the distance to be between 12 and 14 miles allowing a little for getting lost along the way. We'd arrive in time to have a fine Sunday breakfast with her family and then go back by train or maybe Alice's brother could be inveigled to drive us back in his car to Cambridge or once, but only once, we walked back again after an hour visit. That time found us in a bad shape the next day; we hobbled about like a couple of suffering old ladies.

Alice had much artistic talent, especially with flowers, and she was in her element, making our house beautiful for parties. Together we planned the details for many of the Observatory parties that my parents gave. The Ship Party was our design. We tilted the wall light fixtures, found some real life-preservers to place around the walls, stuck up a mast in the middle of the drawing room to dance around, and wrapped sheets and a strip of red paper around the partition where the drawing room, library and hallway entrances joined, trying to imitate a funnel. We made a ramp with railings over the last flight of stairs from the reception hall, using one of the outside boardwalk sections for a gang plank. On the bulletin board went a notice to the effect that the S.S. Sea-Sick will give a gala party Saturday night and warned people not to come ordinary. So, we got sailors and pirates, captains and admirals, tramps, and tourists with no, or with excessive, baggage. Some came in native costume of foreign lands. My mother dressed as a gypsy with dangling beads and hair down in two long braids. More than one person came up to her in mock seriousness wanting to know if she had gypsy blood in her. My father was a whaling captain and went around most of the evening with one stiff (as if wooden) leg. His dancing in this manner was amusing. People were issued, at the door, strange looking tickets covered with ominous warnings. My brothers were at the ship entrances to examine and punch the tickets and they looked over the arrivals with suspicion. There was dancing and eating and bingo and ship horse racing. Much home-made paper money was issued for the gambling. Everybody was rich and happy.

In June of 1935, Albert Einstein was to receive an honorary Doctor of Science degree from Harvard University. For this occasion, my father invited him to make the Observatory residence his headquarters while he was in Cambridge; "and please bring your violin," he added. Assuredly Einstein would have preferred a small insignificant hotel room to being a house guest. He craved privacy, disliked and found receptions tiring, and disliked talking science at large gatherings. Perhaps it was my father's guarantee that he would be allowed the privacy and rest that his frail health demanded and perhaps the bring your violin also encouraged Einstein to accept our invitation. It is true, my father hustled Einstein into a taxi from his train, and he waved his hand to shoo away newspaper photographers and reporters who begged for poses and a short statement from the celebrated long-haired man. The very shoo was visible in the newspaper picture that appeared the next day of Einstein and my father sitting in the taxi. The Shapley children were advised to be natural and friendly but for the most part out of the way. To my embarrassment Carl found the opportunity to ask Einstein why he didn't get a haircut. Einstein answered, "because barbers talk too much." Perhaps he thought that a seven-year-old boy also talked too much, perhaps not. He seemed to me a man with generous thoughts, even for children.

There was no typical Observatory party planned for him. Instead, a few competent musicians were gathered, and a few guests were invited to relax and enjoy the informal music making. Among the Observatory family and friends were found the makings of several string quartets, but with the serious lack, at that time, of an experienced cellist. One of my father's assistants, Jenka Mohr, herself a good violinist and violist, was given the task of finding one.

Emboldened by the idea of building this chamber music around Einstein, she called up the Boston Symphony Orchestra's first cellist. She mentioned Einstein's name and asked him if he would be free to join this famous scientist and others in playing some chamber music. Evidently the symphony player was unimpressed by the name of Albert Einstein or ignorant of it. He asked, "And my fee?" So, Miss Mohr thought again and this time she remembered a Boston Symphony bassoonist[5] who played the cello as a second instrument. This man was more receptive to the idea of joining our group of scientists for an evening of music. He mentioned he had a prized autograph collection.

"Do you suppose Dr. Einstein would be willing to give me his autograph?" Miss Mohr assured him that Dr. Einstein would, and so this professional came into our amateur midst. He blended well. On his own hunch, he brought along his bassoon and demonstrated it to the string players. And he received his fee, Dr. Einstein's autograph.

Einstein enjoyed the chamber music – he accepted the invitation to stay on for a second session – later recalling those two evenings with much pleasure whenever he met my father. He played an excellent first violin, especially in the quartets of Brahms and Haydn. He and Miss Mohr did a Bach partita for two violins. And he happily listened to other players trying their interpretations. Professor Louis Silverman, who had taught my father calculus 25 years earlier at the University of Missouri, came down from Dartmouth College to play with Einstein – a high moment in his musical life, he claimed. My father later arranged for Einstein to play privately with a famous quartet, one member of which was Professor Silverman's son, Raphael.

I sat next to Dr. Einstein during one of his self-imposed intermissions. We watched a Harvard professor and a Boston banker, Professor Pratt and Mr. Jones pound out some Bach for four hands on our piano. They did some high-speed sight reading each smoking his pipe furiously as they went along. Occasionally, one or the other would get lost; they'd stop and make a fresh start, all with such a jolly yet serious attitude, obviously enjoying themselves and completely oblivious of the audience. At one point, Dr. Einstein turned to me observing, "I notice in your father such an enthusiasm for life and for people. You on the other hand have a quiet nature. But you are young; when you become older – ." It was true, I was full of emotion and joy for this evening of beautiful music and congenial company, but I could share it with no one. I could give Einstein only a smile and a nod.

It was eleven o'clock – time to close this memorable evening of music making. The musicians were packing away their instruments. All the guests had said good night to Dr. Einstein but still lingered, reluctant to see this evening end. Einstein whispered to my father, "Why don't they go home?" My father assured him that they were on the verge of leaving. Einstein whispered again, "You know, they remind me of TIME – always going but never gone."

Dr. Einstein's wife, Elsa, had not been able to accompany him for the weekend in Cambridge – or perhaps Dr. Einstein had arranged for her not to come. In any case, she sent up many instructions for her husband's care, two of which I remember well. He must under no conditions have cigars and he must drink only Sanka coffee. My mother was conscientious about the Sanka coffee instruction, and she was careful to have all cigars out of sight. On the second day, however, Einstein noted that the others had cigars. He reached for one. "But Dr. Einstein," my father began, "Your wife!"

"*Ach mein Weib*, never mind her," and he got his cigar.

The morning after the musicale, my father, after joining Einstein for a leisurely breakfast, went over to his office to do two hours' work on things that couldn't wait. After the first half hour he was aware of a headache and a nervousness that he couldn't control. He came back to the house, stormed into the kitchen and spoke to the maid. "Mary, for heaven's sake, make me a cup of real coffee as fast as you can. I can't survive on this Sanka that is so good for Dr. Einstein."

"But Dr. Shapley," she replied, "you have had the real coffee! Mrs. Shapley instructed me that only Dr. Einstein should be served the Sanka."

There were other Shapley contacts with Albert Einstein. My father and I drove up to his summer home on Saranac Lake the following year to deliver to him personally an invitation to attend the Harvard Tercentenary celebration. My father had been hard at work on various phases of this celebration; he was on one of the committees that selected for the Harvard Corporation the sixty scientists and scholars who were to receive honorary degrees at the special commencement ceremony. Much later, my brother, Lloyd, working for his doctor's degree in mathematics at Princeton University, spent a month as assistant to Albert Einstein, but withdrew so as to have a wider mathematical experience. Another time Lloyd and my father made a call on Einstein at which time my father asked him if he would not consider the possibility that the so-called constants of nature are not all constant in value: the gravitational constant, the velocity of light, Planck's quantum constant, the charge and mass of the electron and the proton. "No," said Einstein, "only over my dead body," or words to that effect. "I sounded silly to him," my father recalls, "but I still think I may be right – especially about the variability of the gravitational constant when the Universe was young, say, in the Primeval Atom days, according to the LeMaître and Gamow theories of the origin of the Universe – but maybe not."

On the way to Stockholm in 1938. Lloyd, Martha, Alan, and Harlow Shapley with Annie Jump Cannon

Willis and I had gone with our parents to the 1935 Paris meeting of the International Astronomical Union. The glittering reception to meet the French officials of state, the formal ball, the sightseeing in grand manner – all this entertainment was an unforgettable experience for us who were under age for the astronomical sessions, the real purpose of the gala gathering. Three years later the I.AU. held their meeting in Stockholm and then it was Alan and Lloyd's turn to go.

They weren't prolific in sending news back home or describing it afterwards, so I can only assume it was as brilliant as the one I had attended in Paris. After this Stockholm meeting the Shapleys divided; my mother and the boys traveled for a while in Europe and then went home; my father took a flying trip down to South Africa to inspect Harvard's southern observatory. In 1938, flying to South Africa was more adventurous than it is normally today, as we learned from a series of postcards that came back to us.

The first postcard told us that he boarded an aqua-plane in Southampton. They headed for Rome, which was clouded over, and so landed in the harbor of Brindisi. The weather forced them to spend the night in a hotel there instead of going on to Athens for the night. In this way he missed a banquet that had been planned for him in Athens by the Greek Minister of Education.

The next postcard said that his plane stopped only twenty minutes in a Grecian harbor where the astronomer, Dr. Plakidis, greeted him with an armful of flowers from the previous night's banquet. The flowers were for Mrs. Shapley whom they assumed was accompanying him. My father presented them to the first lady he came to in the cabin of the plane, much to that lady's astonishment.

From Cairo we got a postcard saying it was hot. The next card reported that the plane was flying up the Nile to Khartoum, where the Blue and White Nile rivers come together with great volume and force, and there they would have their next overnight stop. A second card coming from Khartoum said that he had been to a movie, Deanna Durbin in *100 Men and a Girl*, and also a film of a lion hunt which pleased the cheering black boys in the audience.

The next postcard came from Kusumu. His plane had continued up the river to Lake Victoria and at Kusumu he had expected to see stars from the north pole to the south pole since he would be at latitude 0°; his usual luck, however, held out just as it had for the 1925 solar eclipse – it was cloudy! But, he collected some Lake Victoria ants and, having misplaced his vials, put them in his tobacco pouch. They were promptly asphyxiated by the burley tobacco. After this came a postcard from Dar es Salaam in Tanganyika. He told of seeing with regret black soldiers being trained to fight white men's wars. They were marching to fifes playing *Ole Black Joe* and the waltz *Let Me Call You Sweetheart*.

Then came two cards, describing his flight over Mozambique forests. The pilot flew so low to avoid a thunderstorm that he all but clipped the treetops. It was more comfortable to lean back lazily and watch two tsetse flies buzzing on the ceiling than to look out of the window. He told of a bridge game he played with three British army officers. It seems his partner was always leaning over to look out of the window, hoping to see a herd of elephants, thereby displaying his hand to the opponents. My father who was losing became so annoyed that in order not to show his anger, he loaded his pipe, and "demmed if I didn't smoke up my zero-degree latitude ants!" The moral to this story could be: don't hunt elephants while playing bridge.

From Harvard Kopje (hillock) in Bloemfontein, South Africa, we had only his verification that the Harvard Southern Station existed. He was too busy then to send us postcard reports.

It was a memorable occasion when I had a chance to travel with my father. Daughters are more awkward to take around than wives; but my mother didn't habitually travel with my father on his many trips and out-of-town engagements. She felt it was too difficult to leave her responsibilities at home. However, in June of 1932, my father invited me to accompany him to Providence, Rhode Island, where at Brown University he was to receive an honorary degree, and then to proceed to the University of Pennsylvania for another. I remember little about the pomp and circumstance of either commencement beyond the academic processions and the usual speeches and awarding of diplomas. Benjamin Cardozo, Associate Justice of the United States Supreme Court, had also received a degree at Brown and was slated for one at Pennsylvania. On the train to Philadelphia we met and spoke at length with him, and he invited us to luncheon in the diner. My father, being slightly travel sick, declined but pushed me to accept, saying it was a feed with, and at the expense of, the most famous man I had ever met. So, Justice Cardozo and I had lunch together, a good lunch no doubt but it tasted like glue because I was enormously shy when I was on my own and I was conscious of using all my resources to hide from the Justice that I knew nothing about anything political, governmental, or historical. At the University of Pennsylvania my father gave the commencement address. It was entitled *On Running in Trails* and Cardozo was much impressed. He borrowed and used it – so he told my father – in his address to the University of Pennsylvania Law School that same afternoon, claiming it was much needed by beginning lawyers. Even in those early days, my father was thinking and speaking in fields outside of pure astronomy.

> *"Seeing so many of you before me who are similarly garbed, similarly equipped, similarly habited, I am reminded that there exist in many parts of the world various species of a subfamily of ants, the Dolichoderinae, whose individuals run in trails, in well-established paths, maintaining the same highways through generations. I personally know of several colonies of these trail-runner ants that have maintained for fifteen years practically the same path, extending thirty yards or so from the hollow trunk of the home tree across ledges, under leaves and grass, and over logs to some other tree or to bushes where their aphids are pastured or other food supplies are found. These species of ants are essentially blind; they run by scent; the nest odor is maintained along the trails through the constant passing to and fro of the hundreds or thousands of members of the colony. Indeed, the job of many of these organic automata appears to be the spreading of the smell, the maintaining of the path, the following*

literally in the footsteps of the former generations. In their semi-blindness they rarely try the new. The inherited social habits suffice year after year, generation after generation.

When a new brood of ants is hatched and passes through its preparatory larval stages, it is impregnated automatically with the colony odor. The education proceeds through the callow stage; the young callows are exposed to radiation, their body surfaces darken and become hard; the young ants become adults, and then dressed up with caps and gowns or analogous vestments of the formicine world, they start the endless patrolling to and fro, saluting each other with twiddling antennae, maintaining the status quo, keeping alive the social smell that has been established by their forerunners. Some bring back honey-dew or other foods to nourish the next generation of larvae and callows so that they too may go through their training to adulthood, and, with diplomas under their arms, start out along the well-established path, saluting each fellow in passing, checking up that he too is conforming to the colony's customs and is in good odor.

Occasionally, by accident or by some psychic aberration, a trail runner gets off the beaten path and ventures out alone. Usually he becomes wholly lost, or after random wanderings stumbles back on to the good old trail. Occasionally one or two of these vagrants is followed by a fellow or two, but the new divergent trail with its slight and uncertain odors has relatively little appeal; devoid of vision these timid adventurers hurriedly smell their way back to the well-scented customs and go on running to and fro, twiddling antennae with those who do likewise, happy apparently to keep clear of those realms that have not the proper social fragrance.

If a natural calamity disturbs the aromatic trail of the Dolichoderinae, consternation and helplessness ensue. If a strange insect appears, blind fighting results – then back to patrolling out and in; a sudden obstruction on the path, brief excitement follows, and the trail is re-established with as little diversion as possible from the former path, and on they go as before; a sudden depression, and there results wholly thoughtless and random movements, the goal apparently being to get out of the depression and on to the travelled way, back to the old order, back to the beaten path, no matter how circuitous or absurd it may be, back to the saluting, the twiddling, and the maintenance of the old social aroma.

I believe it to be right and natural that the social insects remain static and blind in an illuminated and non-static Universe; but not so for us the social primates. The world of insects is terrestrial; they are adjusted through long geological experience to the animate and inanimate environment. The world of the primate, on the other hand, is cosmic, and though his geological experience is recent, he is in touch with the world of stars, of atoms, of consciousness, of beauty. His is an expanding environment, made so by himself. He expands with it, in outlook and comprehension only by getting off the scented trails.

I have no advice, Mr. President, to give your Bachelors, Masters and Doctors. In spite of our highly specialized information they know more, much more than we do. For three reasons they are wiser: they have acquired their fragments in a later stage of expansion; the hard economic times have probably inspired them to take their medicine more seriously; and they have not yet had time to forget.

It is clear that I, who am many years behind you graduates, am in no condition to advise you; I shall confine my advisory remarks to those of my own station. Are we who help to administer university education, and who try to advance learning along special lines – are we contributing to the high ideal of the expansion of universal knowledge? I think we are doing something – slowly in some directions, unknowingly in others, but on the whole methodically. I point to a few places where we are venturing off the old trails or straightening out their bends.

Administrators and faculties are beginning to realize that in about fifty per cent of the fields, included in college and university training, the body of knowledge has more than doubled and the methods have completely changed in the past generation. We are assured that equally great changes will occur during the next generation. In these fields – and practically all branches of science are included – the original college training of the older instructors may be seriously detrimental. Imagine any attempt at teaching physics or physiology now from a textbook of 1900, or with the college training of 1900.

In this expanding universe of knowledge, fairness to the modern student demands that the instructor be rejuvenated continually, or retired early. The rejuvenation is simple and should be joyous. It merely involves further study by the instructor, preferably, of course, creative, progressive research.

I hope we shall in the near future see the inauguration of the plan of the Free Student, in the colleges and universities, and perhaps also in preparatory schools. This plan looks toward the salvation of talent and genius – it is for those who cannot properly be bound by credits and academic rules. The Free Student is the young poet, inventor, experimenter, artist, dreamer, who is congenitally or temperamentally dumb or impotent outside his own passion; or one who would clearly lose his flair in the process of routine education. Most of us need and desire the discipline of classes and credits. But every year there are some who might justify freedom; who would grow by association with libraries and laboratories; and to whom in due time, for practical purposes, the academic insignia could be given. Abnormality, I insist, must be encouraged, for the world advances only through the deeds of abnormal men.

A further indication that we are making progress in adjusting college and university curricula in the expanding intellectual environment is our recognition of the possibility of creative work in science and the arts for undergraduates as well as graduates, if under proper inspiration and guidance. When a subject is properly approached, study and research will be the same word.

There is no need of my airing again my prejudice (or my view, if you are kind enough to let me use the softer word) that the only worthwhile goal for a university is the advancement of learning. To the school and the college, we can delegate the conservation of accumulated facts and attitudes; but the university should conserve nothing, except the ambition to advance. It should be in continual intellectual turmoil, it should doubt and test and explore. It should be no place for a static mind or for the methodical exploitation of sports and social graces.

But I am going too far and too fast – we cannot as yet unscramble the democracy of college and the selectivism of an institution of progressive scholarship. We are, however, tending towards this separation, or should be, by attracting to our universities' faculties those who cannot fail to inspire students with the spirit of inquiry.

In conclusion, I see the probability that the future goal of university education will not be the training for the proper and pleasant patrolling which we call good citizenship – that worthy standardization shall be retained for the school and junior college. But university men and women of the future will venture boldly off the established trails, they will make everywhere deliberate attempts to seek out the unknowns, not the known, they will think and dream for themselves and not merely go on with the thinking of the thoughts of past thinkers, and the dreaming of dead men's dreams."

Education and means for improving it were close to my father's heart. After building the Harvard Observatory into a world-renowned graduate school of astronomy, he began thinking about all the young people who would someday reach this and other graduate schools. He was concerned with the sizable quantity of human material that might be lost along the way because of financial obstacles or poor educational handling. His instincts for news-getting led to his close connection with Science Service, of which he was president for many years. One of his personal friends of thirty years standing is Dr. Watson Davis, the life-long director of Science Service. Through this association he played a major role, along with Watson Davis, in the establishment of the Westinghouse Science Talent Search, a bold venture, and a successful one, for selecting high school students with special aptitudes in science. Participation in the selection of the Talent Search winners was obviously one of my father's greatest sources of pride and pleasure. He points out that the plan has succeeded not so much in discovering high school seniors of high ability, but in encouraging about 20,000 high school students each year to take the qualifying examinations and undertake research projects. More than 300 receive honorable mention, forty win a trip to Washington, five receive large scholarships. For many years, my father was on the examining board, selecting those who were to get the top scholarships. The Westinghouse Educational Foundation pays the bill for the travel, examinations, the five-day visit to Washington where the students, about one-fourth of which are girls, meet the President of the United States, the Supreme Court, their congressmen, and visit the scientific institutions in the neighborhood. Many of the runner-up contestants who do not win the Westinghouse prizes receive generous scholarships from other foundations, colleges, or universities.

There was talent besides this to salvage. My father worked ardently to alleviate the sad lot of refugees both before and after America became involved in the Second World War. Dr. Bok has said, "Shapley's greatest human contribution came – as I see it – during the late 1930s, when he worked heroically to save German Jewish families from extinction by the Nazi regime, and when, by doing so, he strengthened the American cultural community." The problems of about 300 people went over his round table. Some very famous scholars were among those rescued. He helped to pension the old ones, and to get others away from Hitler's madness. Perhaps Dr. Bok does not exaggerate too badly; in a recent speech Bok said that hundreds of Jewish refugees every night thank God for Harlow Shapley. But my father looks on it differently; "it was our duty towards humanity, and it was our gain." As we mentioned earlier, my father made a point of entertaining and using visitors, especially foreign ones. Their presence frequently enriched the regular scientific colloquia held at the Harvard Observatory and through them, both staff and students were able to learn first-hand about research at other institutions here and abroad.

Ralph and Mildred Matthews on their wedding day, September 25, 1937

In this period there was also a family affair – my wedding; it was all a girl could wish for. I was married to Ralph Matthews, then a graduate student in music at Harvard, in the beautiful chapel in Harvard Yard, and a reception was held at the Observatory residence. It seems to me that people used this occasion to say thank you to the Shapleys, for particular reasons of their own, by giving the daughter handsome wedding gifts. I was overwhelmed by this undeserved manifestation, and all I could do in return, I felt, was to write individual thank you letters to one and all expressing my pleasure. I think it was with this self-imposed exercise that I became conscious of the importance of writing well.

In the following fall of 1938 came a hurricane, the worst Cambridge had ever seen. The historic Washington Elm went down, as well as many other beautiful giant trees. One of the chimneys of the residence blew over and toppled through the roof, piling up bricks and rubble on the floor of a third-floor bedroom. Oak Ridge suffered sad and severe tree damage. But the winds eventually stopped, and the cleanup began. Souvenir hunters came out and collected bark from the Washington Elm.

Before we bring this chapter to a close, there is one social event that must not be overlooked. Important enough to rate space and pictures in *Popular Astronomy* and the *Journal of the Royal Astronomical Society of Canada*, my father's one venture into show business was a smash hit. If this show didn't make Broadway, it could have been because after the Christmas holiday hullabaloo the astronomers had to go back to serious business, and if there were also other reasons, the cast was not disheartened, for the newspaper critics gave exceptionally good notices to the *Harvard Observatory Pinafore*.

During the search for a form of entertainment that would be suitable for a large number of guests of the American Astronomical Society scheduled to crowd the residence on New Year's Eve of 1929, my father remembered the discovery of an interesting manuscript some years earlier in the Observatory library. With a little searching Miss Walker found it again, and the more he examined this astronomical operetta, the more interesting it became. At a sudden preliminary meeting he had little difficulty in choosing most of the cast. With the exception of Professor Ransom of Tufts College, all the twenty or so artists belonged to the Harvard Observatory family.

The parody had been composed in 1879 by Winslow Upton, an assistant on the Harvard Observatory staff, soon after Professor E.C. Pickering became director. At this time, Pickering was designing and constructing one photometer after another and naming them with the letters of the alphabet. An astrophotometer is an instrument that measures the brightness of a star. Photometer P was pictured as a special refractory instrument, to which Mr. Upton was assigned on account of his physical prowess. The following song explained how it was:

"Two years ago I came to be
An assistant at the Observatree
I spent my time from day to day
In making computations for the Coast Survey.
My patent computations did so well for me
That now I am observing with Photometer P.

In the cool night air with S and P
I weary my eyes on photometree
Bright stars with H, faint stars with I
Blue doubles reserved for a cloudy sky.
So many close doubles were measured by me
That now I am observing with Photometer P.

I pulled the string or turned the screw,
Or drove the match as I was told to do.
I cranked the circle near and far
While S strained his eyes to catch the prism star.
I became so cranky they promoted me
To be an observer with Photometer P.

I turned the dome with so great a shock,
That I broke two windows and the Elliot clock;
I burst the gas pipe rolling the chair,
And created a blaze for the winter's scare.
For my worthy zeal they requested me
To try my strength on Photometer P.

Now Waldo, Wendell, Metcalf, Mann
Copy my example as far as you can.
Compute, observe, and – mark my word –
Your labor will gain its due reward,
If you are asked, "What reward shall it be?"
Say, "Let me observe with Photometer P."

Gilbert and Sullivan had written their popular operetta, *H.M.S. Pinafore*, and produced it with great success the year before. Mr. Upton used their music and wrote an astronomical libretto depicting the activities of the Harvard Observatory staff in the year of 1879. It may be that the innocent impertinence of satirizing his superiors from E.C. Pickering, the director, on down, was the reason why Upton's *The Harvard Observatory Pinafore* had not been presented at the time. Another reason why it was laid aside was probably because one of the staff members died soon after Upton's composition was completed.

Now, fifty years later, the manuscript was brought out, and my father with his usual energy and enthusiasm rehearsed his troupe and produced the show in less than a month's time. Frances Wright, whom we have already met as the present leader of the Observatory Philharmonic Orchestra, was the tireless accompanist keeping us in good rhythm while Jenka Mohr kept us on pitch with her violin. There were special chorus rehearsals. I remember we drilled the opening chorus to the operetta so relentlessly that I, for one, was finally singing myself to sleep with:

> "We work from morn till night,
> Computing is our duty;
> We're faithful and polite,
> And our record book's a beauty."

The six chorus girls comprised Miss Adelaide Ames, the nebular expert whom we have introduced earlier in this chapter; Miss Helen Sawyer, who later became Dr. Helen Hogg and is Canada's most prominent woman astronomer; Miss Henrietta Swope,[6] who leads a life dedicated to astronomy, at present at Mt. Wilson and Palomar Observatories; Miss Silvia Mussells, one of my father's valued assistants in his galaxy bureau who later became the wife of the Harvard-educated Irish astronomer, Eric Lindsay; Miss Irma Caldwell, Harvard Observatory computer at that time; and Miss Mildred Shapley, who is writing this story and, as my father puts it, has not been caught yet. We of the chorus rehearsed as if the reputation of the Harvard College Observatory rested solely upon us. But the principals worked, it must be admitted, as if the Observatory's fame was in their hands. Dr. Cecilia Payne, displaying her beautiful soprano voice as Josephine, the meridian circle reader, was easily the star of the show. Peter Millman, a Harvard Observatory graduate student, made the handsome hero, as Professor William Rogers, he was in charge of the meridian circle. Professor Ransom of Tufts College made a very convincing Professor Pickering, the director:

E.C.P.:	I am the captain of this little crew
All:	And a right good captain too.
E.C.P:	You are very very good, and be it understood
	I command a right good crew
All:	We are very very good, and be it understood
	He commands a right good crew.
E.C.P.:	Though moving by my right in society polite
	And among many men of note
	I am never known to wear,
	Though the ladies vainly stare,
	A tall hat or a swallow-tail coat.
All:	What never?
E.C.P.:	No never!
All:	What never?
E.C.P.:	Well, hardly ever.
All:	Hardly ever wears a swallow-tail coat.
	Then give three cheers and three times three
	For the gallant captain of the Observatree.

George Wheelwright played Mr. Upton, assistant observer on Photometer P, and it is he who proves to be the tattle-tale villain of the show. Leon Campbell played Professor Searle in charge of photometry. To the tune of *Little Buttercup*, Mr. Campbell sang:

> "I'm called an astronomer, skillful astronomer,
> Though I could never tell why;
> But yet an astronomer, happy astronomer,
> Modest astronomer, I.
>
> I read the thermometers, break the photometers,
> Mend them with paper and wax;
> I often lament that so seldom is spent
> A fair evening on star parallax.
>
> I write many letters, give aid to my betters,
> And often sit up late o'nights,
> To catch a few glimpses of the many eclipses,
> Of Jupiter's bright satellites."

Dr. Bok made a very impressive figure in the role of the pompous Dr. Leonard Waldo, L.L.D., director of the observatory at Providence, Rhode Island. Dr. Waldo was escorted by three influential men of Providence – Mr. Andrews, Mr. Sayer, graduate students, and Mr. Bowie, night observer of the Harvard Observatory – three men of ill-assorted sizes dressed in derby hats, frock coats and wing collars – typical citizens of Providence.

> L.W.: I reside in places three,
> Cambridge, Brookline and Little Rhodee;
> But the last of these I say is perfectly immense,
> Head Citizen: And so, say the influential men of Providence.

Citizens:	And so, say the influential men of Providence.
L.W.:	I am very full of knowledge rare, And could fill a professor's chair;
Head Citizen:	And so, say the influential men of Providence.
Citizens:	And so, say the influential men of Providence.
L.W.:	I am, at last an L.L.D. I'm very proud of my degree, For it shows that I'm a man of extraordinary sense,
Head Citizen:	And so, say the influential men of Providence.
Citizens:	And so, say the influential men of Providence, Professors, lawyers, ministers, The wise and wealthy men of Providence.

As the story unfolds discord and devious plotting are bred in the right good crew of the Observatree by the attempt of Dr. Waldo whose lightest word was corroborated by the influential men of Providence, to induce Josephine, the fairest flower ever blossomed on scientific timber to leave her position as assistant to Professor Rogers. The thought of losing Josephine was so devastating to Rogers that he plans with her to foil the scheme, since Josephine herself finds she cannot tear herself away from the meridian circle that is to her an object of passionate love. They decide that they can win over the director by having the faulty prisms of his new photometer corrected. So, secretly, they remove the prisms and attempt to take them to Alvan Clark's[7] to be reground, hoping in this way to win favor from the director. However, the director has been forewarned by the villain, Upton.

Computers:	Carefully, on tip toe stealing

	Breathing gently as we may,
	Every step with caution feeling
	We will softly steal away.
Josephine:	Goodness me! My catechism!
	Sam Magee! I've dropped a prism!
All:	She's dropped, she's dropped a prism!
E.C.P.:	Oh! My precious prism! *[hidden]*
Computers:	Haste along, with footsteps steady
	We shall soon be out the dark,
	And a horse car waits all ready
	To carry us to Alvan Clark.
Josephine:	Goodness me! My catechism!
	Sam Magee! The other prism!
All:	She's dropped the other prism!
E.C.P.:	Oh dear! My precious prism! *[emerging]*
	Hold! False assistant of mine,
	I insist knowing where you may be going,
	With these prisms so fine
	For indeed I suspect,
	The parts of my new instrument
	You scarcely are competent
	To tear and dissect.
All:	Indeed, we suspect
	The parts of his instrument
	She is scarcely competent
	To tear and dissect.
Rogers:	Dear sir, pray judge her not too hastily,
	For I can make the matter clear quite speedily;
	I saw the prism faces were not true,
	And so, I thought I'd have them fixed for you.

"Oh Polaris!" swears Pickering, but unmoved he sends Josephine to the observatory dungeons. Only a timely confession from Searle, the Professor of Photometry, saves her and Rogers from disgrace. He admits, "I taught them all I could and not a creature knew it." They are now capable of building a new photometer, he boasts. "A new photometer!" exclaims Pickering.

> Computers: For he himself has said it,
> And it's greatly to his credit
> That it is a photometer.
> For it may have been a telescope,
> Or a double-barreled microscope,
> Or perhaps a barometer.
> But in spite of all inducements,
> To belong to other instruments
> It remains a photometer.

Proficiency in photometry, in the eyes of the director, makes Josephine indispensable to the Harvard Observatory. In fact, it impresses the director so favorably and Leonard Waldo so unfavorably that the heroine is left to Harvard. Dr. Waldo seems completely assuaged by the unexpected offer of one of the fair computers to go with him and hover about him in his years of declination. And so, the opera ends with a burst of Pinaforean absurdity.

The cast of the Observatory *Pinafore* (December 31, 1929). Front row, L to R: Willis Shapley, Mildred Shapley, Adelaide Ames, Cecilia Payne (as Josephine, holding two prisms), Henrietta Swope, Sylvia Mussells, Helen Sawyer, Alan Shapley. Back row (L to R): Bart Bok, Frances Wright, Eric Lindsay, Prof. Ransom, Jenka Mohr, Harlow Shapley, Mr. Bowie, Arville Walker, Peter Millman, Mr. Sayer, Leon Campbell

The audience received the performance with unbounded enthusiasm. That evening was a high point of Observatory gaiety. George Agassiz said it was the best spoofing he ever saw. Frank Schlesinger, Yale astronomer, said only Harvard could do such a show. The applause was hard to quell but time was moving on. It was near midnight. As the ticking of the Observatory clock, connected with a sounder in the room, warned the company of the approaching end of the Old Year, all stood at attention, my brother Willis played taps on his flute, at the exact moment Professor King sounded the midnight bell, and everyone wished everyone a Happy New Year.

Now – back to work. Back to serious business. But the lines that describe so deftly their customary attitude kept astronomers laughing at themselves long after the show was over.

> "He must open the dome and turn the wheel,
> And watch the stars with untiring zeal.
> He must toil at night though cold it be,
> And he never should expect a decent salaree.
>
> His knee should bend and his neck should curl,
> His back should twist and his face should scowl,
> One eye should squint and the other protrude,
> And this should be his customary attitude."

CHAPTER SEVEN

Internationalist and Humanitarian

From the beginning of his scientific career my father has been world conscious. Astronomy, perhaps more than any other science, requires for its progress frequent exchanges of information among the observatories of different nations. The Harvard Observatory has always had on its staff a number of research associates from foreign countries – so much so, in fact, that someone at the Rockefeller Foundation said, "Oh yes, we call it the Broken English Observatory." Also, as we have mentioned earlier, Harvard has been a distribution center sending out, in this hemisphere, astronomical spot news and reports of discoveries received from all parts of the world. Not even wars curtailed this service, which demonstrates the ability of science to transcend national boundaries and the political differences between nations.

The international contingent of astronomers at the Observatory in 1939. Front row (L to R): Bart Bok (Dutch), Jaakko Tuominen (Finnish), Masaaki Huruhara (Japanese), Luis Erro (Mexican); Second row: Shirley Patterson (Canadian), Marie Paris Pishmish (Armenian-Turkish), Odon Godard (Belgian); Third row: Donald MacRae (Canadian), Zdenek Kopal (Czech), Richard Prager (German); Sergei Gaposhkin (Russian); Top row: George Dimitroff (Bulgarian), Cecilia Payne-Gaposhkin (English), Luigi Jacchia (Italian).

During the Second World War, astronomers of enemy nations continued to use Harvard Observatory as a clearing house in communicating new findings to each other. At the height of hostilities, a Russian astronomer on the Turkish frontier radioed his discovery of a new comet across enemy lines to Moscow and thence to America. One message from Romania was transmitted via Denmark and Switzerland and brought my father into conflict with a United States Navy censor. He finally was able to convince this censor that the words Popovici Strömgren at the end of the cable were not subversive code but the signatures of the royal astronomers of Romania and Denmark.

Cables had to be sent with discretion during the war. For instance, when an interesting nova flared up in the southern sky and the Harvard Observatory wanted a full record of this stellar explosion, one could not as before cable the station in South Africa: NOVA EXPLOSION PUPPIS

SHOOT NIGHTLY USING WHOLE BATTERY followed by the positional numbers and the word urgent. That would sound subversive. But the equivalent: MAKE SYSTEMATIC OBSERVATIONS OF BRIGHT NEW STAR IN CONSTELLATION PUPPIS NEAR STAR ZETA USING ALL TELESCOPES was satisfactory, and also expensive.

Peace must be kept for the progress of science and culture. My father believes all scientists should have a social responsibility to help keep the climate favorable for scientific advance. As cooperation across national boundaries helps to advance the sciences, it should aid human relations in general. He has been a tireless practitioner of the internationalism he preaches. He was the most active American scientist in planning of the United Nations Educational, Scientific and Cultural Organization (UNESCO) – a story that we shall tell later in some detail. He was one of the original organizers, and a member of the board of trustees, of the World-Wide Radio University Broadcasting Foundation. Its World Radio University goodwill programs, supervised by faculty members of Harvard, Yale, Princeton, Columbia, Brown, and M.I.T., were in the war years sent by short wave to foreign countries in 23 languages.

By way of illustrating his friendly interest in the people of the world, one can retell a few of his adventures in various countries that he has had occasion to visit and deal with. With no pretense to chronological order, I shall begin close to home with the Mexico story. This is the way my father has told it:

"In the early thirties I went on a health-vacation trip to Mexico – went by boat: New York, Havana, Vera Cruz, and then up to Mexico City. My host was Señor Joaquin Gallo, director of the observatory at Tacubaya, a suburb of Mexico City. Among other enterprises we went to the professional pelota game, I bet on it and lost. Gallo let me pay my gambling debt for 'that is a matter of honor,' he explained; but everything else was his fiscal responsibility. We went out to the pyramids and monuments in Teotihuacan and I climbed the Pyramid of the Sun. Near the top I found a nest of Harvester ants where their food of wild barley was very scarce. Incidentally, on two later trips I checked on them – their descendants are still in operation. Nothing notable happened on that excursion, but in 1942 the trip was different.

"The previous year I had been approached by Señor Luis Erro, a Washington diplomat and an amateur astronomer who had studied at the Harvard Observatory, asking me to help found a new observatory. Erro was a close friend of President Avila Comacho. He wanted us to lend telescopes and build a new one – a Schmidt type reflector. After some negotiating, we at the Harvard Observatory agreed to help in this noble enterprise of the awakened Mexico. George Dimitroff undertook the rush job on the new Schmidt; we boxed up and sent a couple of small cameras; and a plan was developed to take down to Mexico a score or so of American and Canadian astronomers – for this new observatory was to be a sort of international scientific enterprise. Then came December 7, 1941! Pearl Harbor! And a bloody war was begun. I thought that would end things astronomical in Mexico. But no! On the night train from Washington came Erro with specific instructions from President Comacho that the astronomy plan should proceed.

"So, we continued, and the following March off we went – about 30 astronomers to Mexico, Gretchen and I included, with books and telescopes. It was a grand occasion. Comacho and five or six ex-presidents of Mexico attended the dedicatory exercises on the hill near Tonanzintla, eight kilometers west of Puebla in the Cholula valley and east of the two great volcanoes, Popocatepetl and the Other One (Ixtaccihuatl) which we could neither spell nor pronounce. The ceremony was colorful – pomp and circumstance in abundance – and thousands of illiterate Indians looking on, much impressed. There were scientific meetings, and visits around the country. Henry Norris Russell and I got honorary degrees at a primitive ancient university in the west country – Michoacan. I was decorated with the Croix d'Honneur at Puebla by the Mayor. In some way I got into contact with the famous leftist labor leader – Vincente Toledano – and with the quiet acquiescence of President Camacho, I gave a spontaneous talk on galaxies to a quickly assembled hall full of electrical workers. After that Toledano was permitted by our government to come to the United States. The *New York Times* commented that astronomers could teach diplomats how to mend bad relations.

"We have been friends with Mexican astronomy ever since. Dr. Guillermo Haro, now the top astronomer of Latin America, studied at the Harvard Observatory. Felix Recillas came up to study with us. There he met another student of ours, Marie Paris Pishmish. A marriage eventuated – a union of a Catholic Mexican Indian and an Armenian Turk.

"In 1943 Gretchen and I took down a dozen or more physicists – motive: friendship and collaboration – and the next year, I selected and sent down four leading American mathematicians. That nearly finishes the Mexican story except to say that I was ceremoniously awarded the Aztec Eagle at the Mexican Embassy in Washington; and when Camacho finished his six-year term both Gretchen and I were invited to the inaugural ceremonies involving Camacho and his successor Miguel Aleman – again with all expenses paid. It was on that occasion that I was given an honorary degree by the National University of Mexico – another case of one undeserved honor generating others. Many distinguished foreigners lined up to say goodbye to President Camacho. When he came to me, he didn't shake hands, but enthusiastically gave me the *doble abrazo* – the top salute of friendship. I didn't know what to do; the best I could manage with President Camacho was to pat him reciprocally on the back. The other Americans present were much impressed."

Another of my father's south-of-the-border activities was the organizing of the Committee on Inter-American Scientific Publication, in collaboration with the State Department, Science Service, and Watson Davis. They arranged the publication in U.S. journals of the most important papers of Latin-American scientists, and, in turn, provided Latin American journals

– more than 1,000 of them – with authoritative surveys of developments in various fields of science. Some people in the State Department have said the project incited the best cultural relations we've had with any country.

The next is the Poland story. It started back in 1922 when my father and mother took an extensive Mediterranean cruise which ended for them in Rome where the International Astronomical Union was meeting for the first time. There, a very polite Polish astronomer, Professor Tadeusz Banachiewicz, introduced himself, kissed my mother's hand and asked for help – the loan of a telescope; the observatories of his country had been ruined by the war. My father said he would try; and when he got home, he recalled from Arizona a loaned 8-inch instrument that was in disuse. He had it fixed up and sent to Cracow in south Poland, where it has survived the Second World War. It was mounted in hilly country and has done much creditable work, such as discovering a comet and observing eclipsing variable stars. The Polish parliament voted thanks for the three-year loan; and when the period was extended, again Harvard was formally thanked. After that there were no more arrangements or thanks and the telescope, nearly 40 years later, is still busy in Poland! Later my father organized a committee known as Books for Poland and some of the Polish university libraries were rebuilt – mostly with books contributed by American university libraries.

After the Second World War, again came a request from Poland and again a telescope was sent. This time the 8-inch Draper camera, tube, mounting and all, was shipped for use at the new memorial observatory at Torun in north Poland, the birthplace of Copernicus. This 8-inch was the instrument that had been used by Miss Cannon in classifying the spectra of some 100,000 northern stars – a real treasure, historically – and appropriately it is now used in Poland by a woman astronomer, Dr. Wilhelmina Iwanowska, also working on stellar spectra.

As my father tells it,

> "I was, during the war years, an official in an American Polish society
> – the Kosciuszko Foundation. We worked on Polish relief in various

ways – food, books, letters, escapes. Professor Charles Smiley of Brown University was a valued collaborator. Money-raising concerts were held celebrating the music of Chopin and Paderewski and others. And then in 1943 came the big act – the 400th anniversary of the death of Copernicus and the publication of *De Revolutionibus Orbium Celestium*. We rented Carnegie Hall in New York and filled it. I had the hunch that in celebrating Copernicus and his revolution we could well honor contemporary revolutionaries – those who had also affected the direction and speed of social evolution. A committee of big shots helped in choosing these revolutionaries. First, of course was Einstein – then Henry Ford, the geneticist Thomas Hunt Morgan, Igor Sikorsky of the helicopter, and Walt Disney; but no politicians. Everybody came. The Polish ambassador was there and Wanda Landowska, the harpsichord wizardess, and delegates from various learned societies. President Roosevelt sent a message that I read to the assembly; Deems Taylor, representing Disney, who was on location, made a speech; Sir Henry Dale, President of the Royal Society of London spoke trans-Atlantically from London by radio – a grand stunt in 1943; he had to stay up till 3am! The music was appropriate – the citations pleasing. Einstein's brief speech in his pidgin-English was incomprehensible – so everybody loved it and him. The affair was a complete success – another good offering of internationalism."

At the Copernican Quadricentennial, Carnegie Hall, May 24, 1943. L to R: Dr. James Y.C. Yen, Jan Ciechanowski (Polish Ambassador), Harlow Shapley (National Chairman), Albert Einstein, Capt. J.F. Hellweg (Supt. U.S. Naval Observatory, Washington, DC), Dr. Henry Noble MacCracken (President of Vassar College and of the Kosciuszko Foundation)

Then, there is the Ireland story which had its beginning in 1946. Ireland is a split country – the northern six counties, including Armagh, where Eric Lindsay, a Harvard trained astronomer, is stationed, are a part of Great Britain – the other 20 or so counties are in Eire, where the Dunsink Observatory, long dormant, is now revived. Eire is Catholic; Northern Ireland is Protestant.

In 1946 my father was accompanying two prominent American astronomers, Joel Stebbins and Otto Struve, to Copenhagen where they were to take part in re-establishing the I.A.U. which had been suspended by the Second World War. At Copenhagen they set up many cooperating committees; it was mostly an occasion of hard committee work by representatives from Russia, U.S.A., United Kingdom, France, Spain, the Vatican, and Scandinavia. My father made the big address for the public of Copenhagen on galaxies, nicely illustrated and, he thought, eloquent. But his name was promptly dropped from the I.A.U. Galaxy Commission. "Was this dropping before or after the address," he asked.

"Oh! Oh! A dreadful mistake," said the membership compiler, as embarrassed as he could be – he, being André-Louis Danjon of Paris. Needless to say, my father is still on the Galaxy Commission!

Stebbins, Struve, and Shapley had various adventures on that trip, especially at the Shannon airport, but most of them trivial. For instance, on the return trip from Copenhagen, S., S., and S. got as far as Shannon where they were to change planes. But the weather was so bad that they were sent by bus to Tipperary and Limerick to a couple of strange hotels to spend the remainder of the night. War shortages were evident. One of the party found a bed but no sheets; another found sheets but no bed; perhaps the third one was lucky – the details are a bit vague now, and unimportant. But it was during the plane change at Shannon on the way over that the important Ireland story developed. While waiting for their flight to be called, they noticed in the crowd that was awaiting church dignitaries flying home to America from Rome, a gentleman whose face looked familiar. They inquired and learned that he was Eamon De Valera, Prime Minister of Eire, and one of the great men of those times and now. My father arranged for an introduction. In those few minutes of conversation an idea came to him and he proceeded to sell the Prime Minister this idea: A Baker-Schmidt type reflector which would be jointly owned by Armagh, Dunsink, and Harvard – and mounted on Harvard Kopje near Bloemfontein, South Africa. Both Irish countries joined with money and applause, and in a few years, this powerful new type of instrument was doing exceptionally well. The eventual written agreement that came out of this chance meeting was a document unique in history and symbolic of the willingness and desire to cooperate across religious and political boundaries, when something as remote and pure as the stars is concerned.

"To finish the story – much later, in 1958," as my father tells it, "I went to Armagh Observatory, in Armagh City which is in County Armagh, for three months of research on star clusters in the Large Magellanic Cloud in collaboration with Eric Lindsay. But Eric had a heart attack, and I had to work alone on the photographic plates in the observatory residence, situated in a lovely park. There was a party by the Prime Minister of the six northern counties, and by the Governor General (representing the Queen), and also by the vice Chancellor of Queen's University in Belfast. Down in Eire they also treated me too well. There was a special dinner with the faculty of Dublin's Institute of Advanced Studies. I saw quite a bit of De Valera. He had me met officially at the airport, with the red-carpet treatment."

De Valera has a substantial knowledge of mathematics and has maintained a persistent interest in science. He has sought Shapley's advice in a variety of scientific matters. In 1960 my father received a letter from De Valera asking him to recommend the best textbooks in algebra, calculus, and analytic geometry for a student friend whom De Valera wanted to advise. On official stationery headed in Gaelic: UACHTARÁN NA HÉIRANN (President of Ireland), BAILE ÁTHA CLIATH (Dublin). An excerpt of the letter reads:

> "I would like the books to be of such a kind that the proofs given on fundamental theory would be rigorous and not have to be replaced by other proofs later on. For instance, a proof of the differential coefficient of x^n which will hold for all real values of n, logarithmic and binomial functions, as well as for the fundamental theorems on series.

> "I would like to have your advice also on suitable textbooks for Mechanics and Theoretical Physics. Please pardon me for giving you this trouble, but I need advice and I am sure your judgment will be a sound one.

> "I hope you are keeping well. Should you find yourself on this side of the Atlantic do not forget to give me a call. I saw Dr. Lindsay a little while ago and was delighted to learn that his health is greatly improved."

From Sharon, New Hampshire, my father replied:

> "Dear Mr. President:

> "My inquiries in Harvard and M.I.T. yield these results:

"For the young student about to enter the university: (1) *A Survey of Modern Algebra*, by Garrett Birkhoff and Saunders MacLane, (2) *Differential and Integral Calculus*, by Richard Courant, two volumes, in English, (3) *Calculus and Analytic Geometry*, by George B. Thomas, Jr., of M.I.T. These are college texts used at Harvard, M.I.T. and elsewhere, and are considered to be the best.

"It is quite possible that I shall this year return to Armagh for a few days with star clusters and Eric Lindsay. At least I must get as far as London to attend an international conference on life in Space and the biology of Space travel.

"Life on this planet seems to progress erratically as usual, but possibly not too dangerously. I have too much to do – lecturing, consulting, travel, proof-reading of three books, and fussing about politics and spies and satellites. I hope you now have it easier. In presidential election years we waste a lot of time being democratic.

"The best of health to you."

My father continues the Ireland story: "So, when I was in London in 1960 with a British group conferring on life in Space, I received from De Valera, who was then President of Ireland, an invitation to an official luncheon in my honor in the President's mansion. Eric Lindsay and I drove down the 150 miles from Armagh – and what a luncheon! Maybe it was not *all* in my honor; De Valera was probably paying off social debts at the same time. Anyway, the whole cabinet was there, the top scholars and scientists, and some officials down from Belfast. I made a short talk and so did De Valera."

Out of these efforts there came, as with Mexico, an honorary degree, this one from the University of Ireland. The ceremony, steeped in tradition, was tri-lingual – Dr. Brown, president of Galway College, cited him in Latin; De Valera who was the chancellor of the University of Ireland, saluted him in Gaelic; and my father responded as best as he could in his native Missourian.

He considers the Armagh-Dunsink-Harvard project to be one of the finest things he ever managed, for in its way it brought some religious, political, and even economic peace to the cantankerous Irish. But, when later he met a certain prominent American cardinal at a banquet and proceeded to describe to him the A.D.H. telescope project, with some undisguised pride, for it gave, he thought, great credit to the Catholic De Valera, the cardinal brushed it off as of little consequence saying, "that man is always playing politics."

Let us proceed to the India story. Early in December of 1946 my father received a telegram signed simply Nehru, saying, "Will you please come to India to attend the Science Congress and inspect our scientific laboratories." His first reaction was that it might be a student prank, but, upon investigating, he was assured by Washington that the telegram was genuine. The Rockefeller Foundation was approached and quickly put up the necessary travel money. My father cancelled all January engagements, wired back OK, and on the last day of the year flew by way of Newfoundland, England, and Karachi to Delhi.

It happened that the day he left Boston he was unexpectedly elected President of the American Association for the Advancement of Science. Unexpectedly for two reasons, first because the retiring president was Harvard University's President Conant and two presidents of the society from Harvard in succession did not seem proper or possible, and second, at this time the red hunters were making headlines out of liberals, Shapley included. Nevertheless, the election happened, and he went to India full of honor. It also happened that Pandit Jahwaharlal Nehru was the President of the corresponding Indian scientific society, and this circumstance threw them together a few times – speaking on the same platform, dining together, and so forth.

But another incident merits mentioning here – a penalty for being conspicuous. The day before the trip to India, a newspaper reporter excerpted a whimsy from my father's talk to the astronomers and deliberately misquoted him. The occasion was a particularly dull meeting of the American Association for the Advancement of Science, and the reporter thought to enliven things by making his own sensation. At this meeting, my father had said "Science is going to advance, and we are going to have concurrently serious political problems; should we stop science; should we eliminate the geniuses among us? Of course not!" The newspaper version took another form.

"Shapley," said the reporter, "advocates extermination of the bright students!" As one can imagine, all hell broke loose! The other newsmen were shocked. Even the apology he got from the Associated Press had little effect, and for some years that reporter and the Harvard Observatory did not speak. That night my father flew to India, but this wild story got there first. The flare-up was not disastrous; it could, however, have cost him the A.A.A.S. presidency.

The Indian Scientific Congress was already in session when he arrived in Delhi; a large number of foreign scientists were attending. There were various honorary degrees conferred by the then Viceroy Lord Wavell. Only Russian recipients received more applause than the popular speaker on galaxies, and that was because Lord Wavell unexpectedly saluted the Russians in the Russian language to the amazement and joy of the Indian audience.

There was a side trip to Agra to see the Taj Mahal where on the marble steps he collected some ants. In spite of their exalted location, they were nothing special – the same species that he had found on the Kremlin banquet table and at home.

Shapley had been asked to give a principal address before the Scientific Congress; his subject was galaxies and also science and youth in America. He was president of the Science Clubs of America at this time. The University of Delhi had no auditorium large enough to handle the major sessions of the Congress, so a circus tent had been erected for the occasion. A special section was reserved for the faculty; the students overflowed into the aisles and peered from under the tent flaps, but my father recalls:

"To my surprise, one quarter of the tent, back of my platform, was blocked off. Funny business, I thought, with so many sitting on the ground. Before I went on, I asked the vice-chancellor, why the blockage? 'Oh, there are people there.' People? What people? '*Girls,*' he said. So that was it – girls and boys not together – segregated! It sort of annoyed me. I took a gamble that the Indian youths were not afraid of each other. This must simply be a surviving custom in an India that socially is not yet awake. Consequently, as I walked up on the stage toward the lectern, I detoured somewhat, stood on my tiptoes, looked over the barrier. Gosh, what a sight! Hundreds of beautiful girls in colorful saris, dangling earrings, and smiles. All screeching happy to see the Galaxy Man! And out in front, pandemonium – 3000 roaring males – delighted, angry, happy. I could not tell. But I carried on and began with 'I bring you greetings from our A.A.A.S., and from the Sigma Xi Research Society, and from the 200,000 students in the Science Clubs of America – greetings to your faculties, to you students out in front, and to those hundreds behind the screen.' More pandemonium broke out. And when at every possible opportunity I made a reference to women in science with a head toss to the barrier, the boys cheered and shouted. As I left the stage, I again looked over the barrier and waved at the applauding girls. The vice-chancellor came up to me, grasped my hand warmly and said, 'Dr. Shapley, you have done more for the liberation of women in education in India than anything that has happened before.' I replied with a nod and a grunt, but thought to myself, such is the reward of flirtation!"

Along with the formal, crowded sessions of the Congress, there were pleasant, quieter occasions. There was a supper with Nehru given for my father and two other scientists; they discussed world politics and some science. Nehru had an earned degree in science from Cambridge University. The conversation turned to my father's interest in ants; he recalls, "It seems that during his stay in British prisons Nehru wrote a series of letters to his talented daughter. These were later made into a book, and one chapter was on the insects found in a prison."

After the meetings in Delhi my father made a month-long trip to other colleges and universities. Always there were speeches and parties. In a government plane he flew all over India – Madras to Lahore, Bombay to Calcutta. The Astronomer Royal, Sir Harold Spencer Jones was with him for the visits to the two observatories – Kodaikanal, high on a mountain top, in southern India, and Hyderabad, in Deccan.

They took the over-night train from Madras down the peninsula to the Kodaikanal railway station from which they would go by taxi up a long picturesque road to the top of the high mountain. On the train they had a large compartment, but no bedding or pillows or anything else but the hard benches. Sleep was not easy so most of the night they told each other stories about their scientific lives. My father woke up first. When Spencer Jones came to, he felt a bit out of sorts; the morning tea, handed through the window, was good enough, but there was no hot water on the train to shave with. "I notice that you had no trouble," he said to my father.

"No" my father admitted, "no trouble. I shaved with my tea."

At the isolated Kodaikanal Observatory they were met by the director, Dr. Amil Kumar Das. Improvements for the observatory were discussed, and eventually the conversation turned to (we can guess) the question of high-altitude ants. "Oh, there are no ants whatsoever on this mountain," Dr. Das exclaimed; "It's too high!" My father was skeptical and upturned a few likely stones. Ants! Dr. Das was embarrassed, and probably thenceforth disliked Shapley who had exposed his un-omniscience to his staff and to the Astronomer Royal.

Another adventure my father told in a commencement address at M.I.T. "The longest bare-foot walk since early childhood I took along with Sir Harold Spencer Jones in January 1947. We were visiting the Temple of Madura in southern India. It is a very, very holy place. Our shoes were, of course, left at the court-yard gate of this extensive, but not very beautiful shrine. We gazed at the temple jewels, and at the statues of the lesser deities, under proper guidance; but when we got in sight of the statue of the Holy Mother of God, I was stopped. This far and no farther! Sir Harold could go a few hundred feet nearer and was permitted to bow and perhaps touch some relics. Why this discrimination, I asked? Is it because I have not been knighted? 'No,' was the answer, 'the English and the Indians are politically associated; so, the English have some privileges not accorded to Americans.' I could do nothing about it, except remember Lexington and Concord. A few months later, Sir Harold could not have outwalked me; the Indian independence was only one monsoon away."

"At the Bombay airport we were met by Spencer Jones's brother. He looked and acted so official that I asked Sir Harold what was his brother's business. With his customary solemnity Sir Harold asked me for a one rupee note and pointed to the signature thereon, without which the note was valueless. It was, of course, his brother's signature."

My father made addresses in Bombay, Lahore, Calcutta, and Allahabad. In Allahabad he recalls, "I was taken ten miles or so to the junction of the Ganges and Jumuna rivers on the most holy day of a great pilgrimage. There were a million worshippers – actually two million, but it is hard enough to get one million believed. They were from many sects; they came to touch the holy waters. Each river is sacred; their junction is doubly-so (actually four times), and the junction of the two with a mythical third river that comes straight up out of the bowels of the earth is nine times as holy. (Holiness evidently varies as the square.) We got a rowboat and went out to the visible junction of the two real rivers where thousands were getting holy treatments, and being cleansed of disease (they said), by washing in that surcharged water. Being skeptical, I tried it out: I dipped my left arm into the water, keeping the right out, as a control on the experiment. You know what? A few weeks later, I began to have neuritis in my right arm! It only goes to show you!"

Early in February he went home, making a report to Pandit Nehru on the enthusiasm but low estate of science everywhere in India. Some Indian students followed him home for further study in America. Astronomy in India is now beginning to look up. When Nehru visited America in 1955, his official tour brought him to the Cambridge-Boston area. Harvard University gave a luncheon in his honor. Oddly enough, my father was not invited, the reason being he was not a dean! But Nehru, when asked by President James B. Conant how he would like to spend the afternoon, said simply, "I want to see the astronomer, Shapley." Red tape was cut, and Nehru came to the Observatory escorted by officials and motorcycle police. He sat at my father's round table in D-35, and in the library, saw Menzel's moving pictures of explosions on the Sun. They have remained good friends and exchanged letters over the years. At one time my father wrote to Nehru of a brilliant but unemployed Hindu student, Vainu Bappu, who had studied at the Harvard Observatory. Nehru promptly got him a job. Now Vainu Bappu is the top astronomer of India and the new director of Kodaikanal. After Pandit Nehru's visit to America my father, worried by the prim and cool reception by New York bankers, sent a letter:

"My dear Pandit Nehru:

"Now that you are home in India, with the advantage that distance gives to retrospection, I venture to hope that you look kindly on the mélange that is America. We have here so many generations of high emphasis on materialistic goals, natural for aggressive immigrants in a rich virgin territory, that spiritual credits with us are scarcely more than varnish deep. The average goal has been success, not service; and success has been measured largely in dollars.

"The American people are far more generous, it seems to me, than are the big editors and the government.

"We were pleased and honored that you and your distinguished sister visited the headquarters of our Observatory. I have just heard from her office that I have been made an Honorary Member of the Indian Scientific Institution. That is also pleasant and appreciated."

Nehru replied:

"My dear Professor Shapley,

"Thank you for your letter of November 22nd.

"I found my visit to America not only interesting but rather exciting. America is of course a strange mélange. We all know of its worship of success and dollars. But I found something much more appealing to me and much more enduring there. This made me feel almost at home. In a sense America shows up the essential conflict that is present all over the world, a conflict of the spirit of men. I have come back therefore with a larger measure of confidence than I had when I went."

The Indians had invited my father to return, but he could not manage it in his heavy schedule until a sudden trip in 1960 got him as far as Moscow. For his second visit he flew over the Himalayas to Delhi. Again, he lectured to the Scientific Congress, and also in Calcutta, Roorkee, and Delhi University. He consulted on the new planetarium being built in Calcutta – the largest in the world. At Nehru's request, my father spent half an hour with him, talking about the population pressure problem and about scientific research. Nehru considers Shapley's *Of Stars and Men* a most interesting book, and it has now been translated into Hindi. It was on this trip that he was ceremoniously greeted at the airport by a delegation from the Ramakrishna Society, by the Delhi astronomers, and by the picturesque, white-bearded former mayor of Delhi who had built their fabulous American Embassy structure, designed by Edward Stone. The ex-mayor decorated the visitor with a garland of gold – gold thread, gold cloth, gold pincushion – all gold and dangling like the one later presented to Jacqueline Kennedy, only bigger than hers!

And finally let us sketch the Russia story. My father has made three trips to Russia: one in 1945, another in 1958 and still another in 1960. The first was to celebrate the 220th anniversary of the Russian Academy of Sciences, the second was for the I.A.U. meeting, and the third on business for the New York World's Fair to be held in 1964 – 65.

It was in June of 1945 that he headed a delegation of 16 American scientists to Russia. The Russians were preparing their first post war international gesture. They invited in hundreds of scientists to celebrate the anniversary. That 220 was no magic number of years, of course; it was just a pretext. A year or so later, when various people were accusing my father of being pro-Russian, he pointed out, "The Russians did not invite *me*. They liquidated some of their best astronomers, friends of mine. They had no reason to think that I was sympathetic with their system. It was President Conant who told me that the Harvard Corporation had asked that I represent Harvard. The first stage of the trip was arranged by Under-Secretary Joseph Grew and President Truman, and we were taken as far as Persia by the American Air Command."

To continue the tale in his words:

"There was some confusion among the 16 scientists that constituted the 1945 party. Somehow or other I became the boss – *der Führer* – and was that something! It meant that I hunted lost passports, mopped up the airplane after a rough weather calamity, made plans along the way and made the official speeches. Among the group were Detlev Bronk, now President of the Rockefeller Institute for Medical Research; Nobel Prize-man, Irving Langmuir; and others. It was just at the conclusion of the German war, and before the end of the Japanese phase. It was risky business but obviously a good cause. Flying out of Casablanca, south of the Atlas Mountains, something sprang a leak, forcing us to descend at the famous Biskra oasis in Algeria. In Cairo we were fêted by the Academy of Science in the fabulous Auto Club. The Academy President at that time was my friend, Dr. Mohammed Reda Madwar. We ate melon as one of the desserts at the banquet and all fifteen of us got sick, except the mathematician, James Alexander, who had stayed at the airport and so provided us with a control on the dining experiment.

"All along the way we were entertained as V.I.P.s. Changing in Persia to a Russian plane, we arrived in Moscow and found dignitaries assembled and nation-wide radio hook-up ready. I was asked to descend (*der Führer!*) and tell the Russians what we thought of them and the Universe. A few sentences were enough – then Dr. Ivan Bardin, the vice president of the U.S.S.R. Academy, stepped up to the mic and put in Russian what I had said, or perhaps he put in the mic what I *should* have said. We were put up comfortably at a good official hotel – just finished, and therefore with provisional plumbing. Presently, at this Moskva Hotel, I was looked up by Zdenka Kadla, a young astronomical student, who had heard the broadcast. Her English was near perfect, and she was assigned to the American delegation as a guide in the sightseeing. I got her invited to the American Ambassador's party for us, and she had her first experience with champagne.

"The Moscow Astronomical Society had a special meeting where I spoke on variable stars. Sir Harold Spencer Jones and the famous Indian astronomer Meghnad Saha, also addressed the society. Everyone was friendly, although after such a murderous war there was a general sadness evident; practically every family had lost at least one member on the battlefields.

"There was a side trip to Leningrad and to the site of the Poulkova Observatory. Sir Harold and I stood on the rims of great shell craters that marred the beauty of Poulkova Hill. The German armies, in their fierce and bloody drive toward Leningrad, had been stopped ten miles short of that city by the Russian resistance at Poulkova. In the bombing and cannonading the many observatory building had been destroyed, but some of the telescope lenses and the library with its famous Kepler and other manuscripts had been evacuated. The observatory was a ruin, as was the other important Russian observatory at Semeis on the Black Sea. There was no question but that Poulkova should be rebuilt. Spencer Jones and I remembered, as we stood among the ruins, that Poulkova throughout much of the 19th century was called the astronomical capital of the world. With the leading Soviet astronomers present, we planned for the future – planned as we walked among the huge dandelions, which may have owed their size to soil enriched by human blood.

"I met many Russian astronomers that formerly I had known by name only. Back in my student days at the University of Missouri, curiously enough, my first variable star astronomy was measuring a star that Dr. Sergey Blazhko, a Russian astronomer, had discovered to be variable. Naturally at that early time it pleased me to be tied up with a distant German-writing Russian in this professional way; to my amazement, I met Blazhko in Moscow in 1945, 35 years later!

"The government gave us three big banquets, and at the last one – the night before we flew toward home – the big shots were in attendance – Stalin, Vyacheslav Molotov, Nikita Khrushchev, Andrei Gromyko, etc. There were about 1100 at this feast which lasted four hours – plenty of caviar, vodka, fruit, orangeade, roast pheasants besides a regular full meal; we had stuffed ourselves so much with those hors d'oeuvres that we could do little with the roasts. About twenty toasts were proposed by Molotov, one of them being 'To the Visiting Scientists, especially to the Americans who have come so far.' Actually, he was slapping at the British who had not let their atomic scientists come to Russia. Later the officials handed me a great bouquet of flowers, but none to the British until I protested. To the Molotov toast I replied by elevating my vodka glass and shouting 'Thank you.' We were seated – the American delegation – about twenty yards from the government. Back of the government's long table was the famous Red Army Chorus, which sang patriotic songs, and the famous ballerina, Olga Lepeshinskaya. She jumped, twirled, flew, and since the stage was not quite wide enough, crashed against the wall, but without damage to stage or act. Later that night I met her – a petite comely piece! 'You are American, no? Then I can practice my English on you!' In her presence I was helpless – she could have practiced anything on me.

"It was at this banquet," my father goes on to tell, "that I did the much talked-of ant collecting. An ant of a familiar species had dropped off the flowers or bananas that decorated our table. At once, this *Lasius niger* started to crawl directly toward Stalin. 'Oh no!' I protested. My vial with Rexall's wood alcohol was quickly produced from my pocket, uncorked, and with a wet finger I gathered up the ant and put it to sleep, to the considerable interest of some of my table mates. The two nearest mates were a Cossack colonel and a fat surly Polish woman; he was interested; she was not. In fact, she was quite unfriendly when I made a social pass or two. Presently, another ant dropped off and started for Stalin. Oh no! And again, the vial, and from the Cossack, increased interest. But, said I, should those Kremlin ants when they awake in a Soviet heaven be soaked with Rexall's wood alcohol? No, it should be for them nectar and ambrosia! So, I drained off the alcohol onto a biscuit which I left where the unsympathetic Polish lady might get it; I filled the vial with vodka and inserted as ambrosia two fish eggs, that is, caviar.

"The vial was sealed later with paraffin, and for two or three years I showed it off to visitors. Then came a mystery – one of the ants had disappeared, along with the caviar which naturally could not remain cohesive in the strong vodka. What became of that ant?[1] The puzzle is not solved. Gretchen proposed the hypothesis that those who go to vodka parties cannot count very well; but that theory I resent. I prefer to think that some unknown enemy stole one of my Kremlin ants just to confuse me."

The second trip to Russia was to attend the meetings of the I.A.U. in 1958. Hundreds of astronomers went. The Russian government bore their expenses while they were within the country. The experience was pleasant. Moscow had changed much in 13 years. For one thing the skyscrapers had appeared. The astronomers lived in one – in the Ukraina Hotel; the great university was in another. The Shapleys spent one week in Moscow and another in southern Russia – in Yalta on the Black Sea. There, while strolling along the board walk, they saw Sputnik for the first time.

The third trip, in 1960, had as its purpose to present officially to the Russian government an invitation to take a big part in the 1964 – 1965 New

York World's Fair. Khrushchev had a cold and so the formal invitation was delivered formally to Gromyko. There were about a dozen Americans in this delegation. After the World's Fair assignment, my father went on to revisit India, as already reported, and then on to Australia.

Let us mention a bit more about Russian astronomers, and Russian sympathies here at home. At the close of the war, nine Russians came over to see our telescopes, and to buy some. They visited Harvard and other observatories. They brought a million dollars with them, hoping to order the making of really big telescopes, but we wouldn't or couldn't trade with them. The reason: the diplomats were starting the cold war.

Then, there was the ill-fated penicillin gesture, a story that my father tells as follows:

"One day in 1946 two or three Bostonians of high repute came unannounced to my D-35 office where I was doodling or perhaps working at my round table, and asked if I would go along with them on an international goodwill project. One of the men was of the famous Cabot medical family. Their plan was to set up in his honor an organization of which I was to be the national president. They proposed that we raise money – a lot of it – and give to the Russians a penicillin factory. It would be a tremendous show of good will, because there were in Russia five million wounded warriors, we were told, who would recover, at least many of them, if they could be treated with this newly developed wonder drug. The pharmaceutical houses in Russia were not yet up to it. The need was genuine, and we remembered that these Russians had sacrificed much to save themselves and the Western World from the curse of German Hitlerism. But, I asked, somewhat dazed by the invitation, why ask me, an astronomical professor? 'You are a natural organizer,' they said. 'You are a promoter of good causes,' and some other flattery. I told them, you should have national leadership. Why don't you ask Mrs. Eleanor Roosevelt to head the movement. She would be ideal. They were a bit confused by my suggestion; hesitated, hmmmmmed, looked at each other, and then came out with it. 'The fact is, Dr. Shapley, we did ask her, and she declined!' Mrs. Roosevelt did, however, endorse the project – and sat in on a planning meeting.

"So, I took over and worked out a beautiful plan of action. We would build a penicillin factory on a prominent street in Moscow, help train workers, and in a few months, have a pilot plant going – a gift from the Americans to our colleagues in the world's last war! It would do for the friendship of Russia and America what the Statue of Liberty does for the American French relationship. We would get the endorsement of prominent Americans, in government office and at large. We would raise two million dollars for this purpose, one million coming from one million American citizens, and, to demonstrate that we believe in the free enterprise system, as well as the social state as demonstrated by the million one-dollar gifts, we would get the second million from rich citizens, corporations, and philanthropic foundations.

"We set up a central committee in Boston – mostly of bankers, for they foresaw that trouble was ahead if we just drifted. The Secretary of State approved, the President, and, in fact, everyone whom we approached. I wrote letters, held a few press meetings, employed a professional money-raiser; and then, alas, clouds commenced to form on the horizon. The directors of an important bank were encouraged to withdraw from our project because some depositors protested. Other donors withdrew. Some money had come in before we could say *wait*.

"Well, those unhappy days need not be remembered and emphasized. The Cold War was getting started and probably would grow too fast for our dream to materialize. We waited a little, and then folded up – our Statue of Penicillin, which the Russians said they would be glad to accept, was stillborn. I believe the Russians had even suggested a site on Gorki Street, or a site next to the Tchaikovsky Music Hall.

"In retrospect I have a feeling that the Russians suspected from the first that we would not go through with this gift. Too bad that we could not have started much sooner and worked faster. I wonder if something else of the same sort will one day be erected to celebrate man's natural goodness."

The planning and birth of UNESCO (United Nations Educational Scientific and Cultural Organization) was another of my father's labors in the interest of internationalism. In 1944 he was president of the American Association for an International Office for Education. In the name of this association he wrote to the State Department officials calling on them to go beyond limited reconstruction needs in post war planning for international education. In the June issue of *Tomorrow* of that year he wrote under the title of *Education towards International Tolerance*:

"The world will not be brought nearer to heart's desire by the most skillful manipulation of boundary lines, the greatest ingenuity in economic reform, unless, simultaneously, the base for human happiness in social expressions is encouraged and sustained. In the last analysis, that means education. Moreover, in an integrated world, it means education on an international level. Knowledge begets social understanding, which in turn, generates the generosity of spirit that restrains blind primitivism."

The American Association for an International Office for Education had many prominent supporters. Mr. James Marshall of New York was the founder executive vice-president, and prime mover. Archibald MacLeish,[2] as an assistant Secretary of State, wanted to name the new agency UNECO. My father, however, objected, pointing out that the word culture could not easily include, for instance, chemical engineering. They argued over this point by phone from New York to San Francisco, where MacLeish was attending the U.N. formation congress. "If you leave the S for science out of the title of this agency, then the scientists will have to set up their own U.N. agency. Science won the war – why should it not openly take part in post-war management of affairs?" MacLeish yielded, and there was no difficulty in using the longer name – UNESCO. My father was commonly given the credit for putting the S in UNESCO.

In November of 1945 he was sent by the State Department to London to assist in the writing of the charter for UNESCO. He remained in the American UNESCO organization for two years and appeared before the 79th Congress to discuss UNESCO structure.

It appears now that UNESCO with its many member-nations is too big for efficient collaboration on many projects. In 1949 my father was sent for a week to Paris by UNESCO and the Economic and Social Council of the U.N. to work on a special international ten-member commission; its object was to study and recommend to the United Nations the setting up of international research operations. A report was issued two years later dealing with geo-medicine, mental health, calculators, arid zone research, weather, and the like – but nothing much came of this project, and the thick report now gathers dust in many libraries.

The International Geophysical Year (I.G.Y.), however, was an exception. More than 60 nations took part in this intensified program – the systematic study of the planet Earth and its cosmic environment. My brother Alan, who works in the field of ionospheric physics, was very active as the American vice-chairman of the 1957 – 1958 I.G.Y. He spent so much time traveling all over the globe in airplanes for the purpose of coordinating the I.G.Y. programs, that given a few days in one place, he began to feel ground sick.

My father appeared several times before committees of the 79th Congress on business other than scientific. One hearing was before the Labor Committee, in the interest of subsidies for unemployed artists, writers, and actors; another was before the Foreign Affairs Committee, to report on his 1945 trip to Russia; at another time he went before the Appropriations Committee to recover from the State Department broadcasting rights for short-wave cultural programs to Europe and Asia; and he also appeared before the joint House and Senate committee on atomic energy legislation.

His essay *A Design for Fighting* was in part included in the *Congressional Record*. He considers it the best paper he has written, from the standpoint of social usefulness. First published in *The American Scholar*, the essay was reprinted in *The American Scientist*, then in the *Atlantic Monthly*, and finally in several anthologies and foreign language publications. In it he reviews the tremendous rallying of American forces that World War II brought about and proposed that Americans make war with equal vigor on the enemies that assail the human qualities which we group loosely under the term civilization.

His preliminary list of those enemies include: (1) illiteracy; (2) premature senility including the chief disablers: arthritis, cancer, nephritis, disease of the circulatory and respiratory system and of the brain; (3) cultural uniformity, the deadening centralized manipulation of the minds and mores of the people; and (4) tyranny of the unknown, the unsolved problems in science and human relations.

Strangely enough, there is nothing in this essay to suggest that its author is an astronomer, apart from a few metaphors borrowed from his field. In one place, he lets star-bent apply to idealistic social planners. In another, he says: "I cannot escape the feeling that the human mind and human curiosity are really significant on this planet – even perhaps in the cosmos of geological time and intergalactic space."

Back in September of 1944, my father was already campaigning as an amateur politician for progress in social reforms. At Madison Square Garden in New York City he was master of ceremonies at a gathering of 20,000 sponsored by the Independent Voters' Committee of the Arts and Sciences for Roosevelt. He presented celebrities like Henry Wallace, Danny Kaye, Frederic March, Bette Davis, a senator or two, all in lively fashion, and himself made a seven-minute talk entitled *Revolt Against Stagnancy* which took eleven minutes to deliver because of the tumultuous applause all the way through.

From time to time he attacked American foreign policy, especially in relation to Russia and Greece, and argued for a closer Soviet-American cooperation. Because of his sympathies for all scientists of the world, no matter what their political convictions, because of his sponsorship of various committees working to help refugees, and because of his outspoken liberal and progressive ideas, many newspaper readers associated the name Harlow Shapley first with liberal politics and second, if at all, with galaxies and the dimensions of the universe. He repeatedly denounced the methods of the House UnAmerican Activities Committee (HUAC). "The most un-American activity I know of today," he said, "is the House Un-American Activities Committee."

In 1946 he was called before this committee to be questioned about his political activities as Massachusetts director of the Independent Citizens Committee of the Arts, Sciences, and Professions, and about other political connections he had. Previously a letter of his had been stolen from Martha Sharp's[3] files and handed over to the counsel of HUAC. She was a candidate for Congress, opposing the reelection of Congressman Joseph Martin, Jr.[4] The letter was harmless, ethically credible. At the hearing only the committee's chairman, Congressman John Rankin,[5] a friend of Martin, was present. He furiously sent out of the room first my father's lawyer, and then his stenographer who was present because he did not trust the committee's reporter. These expulsions did nothing to soothe my father's temper, and when he himself proceeded to short-hand the questions and answers, Rankin blew up again – snatched away the shorthand notes. With that, my father charged Rankin with using Gestapo methods and of acting generally in an un-American and discourteous fashion, and he walked out of the hearing room. Rankin followed and declaimed to the waiting newspaper reporters and photographers, "that man has held the House Un-American Activities Committee in higher contempt than anyone else has ever done." ("I considered that a very fine compliment," my father inserted.) "Shapley will be cited for contempt of Congress for refusal to answer questions and to produce documents in accordance with a subpoena," shouted Rankin. It was true that my father had refused to submit records of certain organizations because "I have no authority to do so, and I am not even a member of two of the groups under question." The contempt charges were dropped. Almost all of the newspaper publicity was pro-Shapley, deploring the behavior of the congressman, and my father's mail (it was very heavy) was 99 percent vigorously favorable. This episode was a signal victory for the liberals.

One newspaper said "The shadow of Galileo walked in Washington last week. When a despicable character like Rankin can haul before him one of the leading scientists of the nation and bawl him out because of political differences, this country has gone pretty low into the depths of political persecution." Another said, "The fact that Dr. Shapley is one of the country's most distinguished astronomers with an international reputation, draws extra attention to this situation, but it should not diminish the fact that any citizen appearing before a Congressional committee as a witness is entitled to dignified and courteous treatment, not only as his own right but because the setting itself should be one of dignity and courtesy, not brawling."

In the Jackson, Mississippi, *Daily News* appeared the following, under the title *Jittery John Again*:

> "Thursday happened to be a dull day for news in Washington and as per his custom, Congressman John Rankin seized the opportunity again to make a goggle-eyed chump of himself.
>
> "Jittery John's latest splash into the limelight was provoking an angry clash with Dr. Harlow Shapley, noted Harvard astronomer, whom he had summoned to appear before the so-called committee on un-American activities, whichever way you care to phrase it.
>
> "Jittery John, it seems, was downright angry at the moment. In fact, being angry seems to be John's normal frame of mind these days. He can foam at the mouth, figuratively speaking, every time anybody is mentioned who fails to measure up to his quaint standard of what constitutes Americanism.
>
> "Just why Dr. Shapley should have been chosen as a target for John's personal peevishness is not made quite clear in the press story from Washington. Dr. Shapley is a native of Missouri, has not participated in political pow-wowing of any sort, and is about as un-American as

the late Sitting Bull, but it seems that our John suspected the celebrated man of science, who has a string of degrees as long as your arm following his name, of being mixed up somehow with the PAC of the CIO in the recent election in Massachusetts wherein a Democratic candidate for Congress went down in defeat.

"Therefore, John summoned Dr. Shapley to appear before him in person in Washington – in person; mind you, not before the committee, for John was the only member present. That may be legal, as things are done in Washington nowadays, John contending that he was clothed with full power to act for the committee, but it was in itself a hellishly un-American procedure.

"Briefly, Dr. Shapley appeared before this star chamber session wherein our Congressman from the first Mississippi district sat solitary and alone, like God on His heavenly throne, and because he allegedly failed or refused to 'produce documents in accordance with the subpoena,' John attempted to snatch some papers from the astronomer's hands. Dr. Shapley resisted, and for this horrible offense he has been, or will be, cited for 'contempt of the committee' if Speaker Rayburn can be persuaded to give approval – and it is a 100 to 1 bet Rayburn won't.

"John Rankin may not realize it, but a lot of folks here in Mississippi, including his constituents, are getting damnably tired of seeing him making a blithering ass of himself in Washington. If he must have cheap publicity, and can't possibly get along without it, he might try swimming the Potomac river or jumping from the top of the Washington monument with only a balloon inflated with his own ego to ease him to the ground."

As a result of this dramatic row my father was commemorated by 1200 Harvard students upon his return from Washington. Overnight they had signed an endorsement of his position and at a public meeting in Emerson Hall they presented the manifesto and made speeches. My father remembers being terribly embarrassed, but the cause, he realized, demanded this painful opposition. And Harvard University, in addition to its students' action, has never failed to back up my father and others of its faculty in matters of public controversy, a fact which he attributes to the University's long tradition of sticking to its liberal thinkers.

My father continually spoke for abolition of the Un-American Activities Committee, the Loyalty Oath, and any other organization or activity that cramps liberties. In an article appearing in the publication *Fact*, he has said:

> "It is one of the misfortunes of scientific institutions, such as colleges and universities, that they live on the alms handed out by the rich and the self-assured, and therefore the anti-progressive. The second misfortune of colleges and universities is that they must have trustees, and the trustees must guard investments, and the investments mean conservatism, and conservatism almost always means reaction. It is a rare trustee of a college or university who believes that a scientist who is the least bit rampant as a citizen is a good investment. And here, to me, is the bitter consequence. The administrators choose safe deans and other officials, and deans and department heads can unconsciously cramp the career of a young upstart."

My father goes on to say

> "After I myself had returned from Washington from the abortive encounter with Congressman Rankin, I was promptly interviewed in Harvard by two famous refugees now on the faculty. Mussolini put a price on the head of one; the other was a pre-Hitler official in Germany. Both men asked for details of the proceedings. Both were amazed that I was pulled up by the American Gestapo on the basis of material obtained through a burglary. In part, Mr. Rankin's bitter annoyance at me was because I refused to identify stolen goods on the grounds of not wanting to be an accessory, and on the further grounds that I always decline to work with thieves and fences. Mr. Rankin really didn't like it. He said I was contemptuous, and he was right. Both of these famous

exiles from the fascism of Europe said that my experience was exactly the same as that of those who suffered with fascism in Italy and with Nazism in Germany. It's exactly the same pattern."

None of these experiences intimidated my father – in fact, it had the opposite effect. In March of 1947, he spoke to a gathering in Madison Square Garden – a so-called Crisis Meeting of the Progressive Citizens of America – on the same topic of un-American procedures in the government and the fight to establish civil liberties in the United States.

In these various aims he had often, as an ally, Albert Einstein; much correspondence on constructive plans for World Peace passed between them. On April 1st of 1948, Dr. Einstein wrote:

"Dear Dr. Shapley:

"I feel now sure that the people in power in Washington are pushing systematically toward preventive war. I have the impression that it is the duty of the leading intellectuals of this country to launch a strong appeal to the American public to vitalize strong opposition to this development before they have driven it so far that irrevocable steps have been taken and nobody can stop any more the course of events. In my opinion such an appeal can be effective only if it has the form of a strong counterattack. What is your opinion about it?"

In replying to Einstein, my father suggested the organizing of a conference to be held in late Spring in New York and proposed a detailed plan. He closed his letter with the following paragraph:

"It would be important if you would comment on the proposed conference on the Plan for Survival, or whatever we would call it. [Pattern for Survival was the final name chosen.] It is fortunate, whether or not it is decent, that the names, thoughts and ideals of scientists weigh pretty heavily in the public opinion of America."

Einstein replied:

> "I thank you very much for your letter of April 7th.

> "I am in agreement with everything you said and proposed in it. The new independent Council of Arts, Sciences and Professions should be the right frame for the conference you proposed. It is certainly very necessary to avoid connection with any Party if full concentration of all available forces towards the main goal: 'Action against Militarization of the Nation' shall be achieved."

And again, on May 7th he wrote to Shapley:

> "I am glad to give my consent to be a co-signer of the invitations for the sixty people to the sessions you mentioned in your letter and to the public meeting in Carnegie Hall. I am not able to participate in person but am gladly willing to give you a message from here by any means you think desirable."

Again in 1947, my father was active in establishing The Committee of 1000, to bring pressure to abolish HUAC, and became the active chairman. The 1000 succeeded in damping the wild ardor of HUAC; its chairman, J. Parnell Thomas,[6] was sent to Federal prison, but even as late as 1960, HUAC was still active, though subdued. The defense of the prominent scientist, Dr. Edward Condon at all costs was one of his aims.

The Progressive Party in 1948 nominated Shapley for Governor of Massachusetts. My father promptly declined this honor.

In 1949 my father was attacked by Senator Joseph McCarthy. In an interview in Reno Nevada, the senator told the world what a danger Shapley was. The Associated Press did not release his charges until they had got my father out of bed at the Harvard Club in New York and repeated what McCarthy had said. My father's reply in brief was that "the Junior Senator from Wisconsin has in his statement about me told six lies in four sentences – perhaps the indoor record for mendacity."

"That settled Joe," my father recalls, "and he didn't go on with his charges – all of which were false. He never pursued me much, nor did others, for I had full FBI clearance and had spoken out more than once against authoritarianism, whether in politics, church, or school."

My father is naturally proud of the fact that he and his scientific work have been officially recognized with honors by many countries including Austria, England, Sweden, France, Italy, and several other European countries, but *never* by Germany, Japan, Spain, or Russia – the totalitarian states. "I was not palatable to them," he claims; "or, could it be that they are really the better judges of my work?"

World affairs continued to absorb his attention. In collaboration with Hermann Herrey, an exceptional architect and reformer – an exile from Germany – he wrote a *Draft Proposal for World Security Through International Resources Development*. This treatise preceded Truman's Point Four of help to underdeveloped countries by a month or two, and was much discussed, though for various reasons the authors could not follow up on their plan.

Another effort was what turned out to be the unhappy Waldorf meeting of March 1949 – an affair that both lost and gained friends. From his paper *Flying Samovars*, published in the *Harvard Alumni Bulletin*, my father tells of this convention in New York: a conference on peace, for which there had been such high hopes – hopes for promoting understanding and goodwill.

> *"No matter how loudly Mr. Hearst and his kind shout that the New York conference was communist planned or communist operated, the statement is completely false. More than anyone else, I personally planned the conference beginning two years ago and presided at all the major meetings. By no feat of distortion can I be made out as communist, or fascist, or reactionary Republican. I am a member of no political party. No one could be more opposed than I to totalitarianism, whether it emanates*

from dictator, political bureau, or those who advocate minority-sup-pression legislation.

"The peace conference fell on unfortunate times. We did not foresee a year ago that the government would in March be selling the Atlantic Pact to a worried Europe and that a terrifically expensive armament program must be glamorized and justified. How to do it? How to get public and Congressional support? Frighten the people. Scare the togas off the Congressmen. Smear the anti-militarists.

"In transparent ways, built-up fears are sometimes employed. A Cabinet member publicly rumors a submarine off the coast – and Congress comes through with a big appropriation. Then no more of the submarine scare. Soon new billions must be voted. What will be our panic technique this time – flying samovars?

"Frankly, I am sorry that we had to witness the government's deliberate stacking of the conference with guests only from Eastern Europe and the pulling down of an American iron curtain against western Europe-ans, thus thwarting a major goal of UNESCO, and setting the stage for redbaiting. I am sorry the National Manufacturers Association could not carry out its truly intelligent plan of showing America to the visiting communists. I am sorry that we must repeatedly point out what should be obvious – that all of our work in science and the arts – of the past, of the present and the future – will mean nothing at all if the trend toward war is not stopped or diverted.

"In the opening address at the New York Conference for World Peace, I emphasized the fact that both Russia and America are so obsessed with each other's shortcomings that they overlook, or choose to ignore, their own shortcomings. I pointed out that racial discrimination in America is perhaps our most embarrassing social fault. The totalitarian curb on individual freedoms is, in the opinion of America, the prime curse of the Russian system. One country is said to export communistic social doctrines, the other economic imperialism. But why not practice toler-

ance, seek adjustments, and turn our fighting instincts and our human wealth to war on the real enemies of all mankind – to war on poverty, disease, ignorance, and baseless suspicion.

"The conference in New York, bravely sponsored by more than 500 leading American citizens, was impressive to those who took part. Serious, sincere, critical but friendly, all the meetings, from the initial dinner to the conclusion in Madison Square Garden, were oversubscribed, and hundreds sought to participate that could not be admitted. Much of the America public, however, obtained from the press and radio the impression that something evil and dangerous was happening."

The program carried a list of more than 550 sponsors from which an informed person could judge that the conference's backers ranged in their political orientation and social philosophy from a half-dozen outspoken communists to another handful of persons on the extreme right. The majority of the sponsors were not revolutionaries, but merely liberals or progressives who held the common belief that understanding and accommodation between capitalist and communist nations are preferable to tension, name-calling, and the risk of war. The pressure on the sponsors to withdraw their support was enormous. Amazingly enough, only a dozen or so out of the 550 succumbed to it. Several distinguished sponsors received anonymous death threats by telephone and letter. Others were butts for crude practical jokes, like 4am summonses to mythical meetings.

It took a great deal of fortitude even to go to a conference session. Nevertheless, in attendance were many big people: Dmitri Shostakovich, Alexander Fedeyev, Paul Eluard, Norman Mailer, and Aaron Copland, to name only a few. Outside the Waldorf, and Carnegie Hall, and Madison Square Garden were howling pickets, and curious or sneering crowds. Police protection was given to the participants going to and from the meetings. My father, who is so accustomed to liking people and being liked by people, experienced a strange sensation in being flanked by police and shouted at by an angry, misinformed mob. Nevertheless, as we have mentioned, thousands attended, and a thousand more were turned away for lack of space. But what happened constructively inside the conference rooms, the newspapers did not report, for, that, unfortunately, was not considered news.

Just after the close of the Second World War when the bombs had been dropped on Japan, my father joined a group of a dozen or so scientists and humanitarians to write essays under the general title of *One World or None*. My father, like most scientists, is a sensitive and humane man. He is always ready to help solve problems that various people put to him – personal, as well as scientific problems. He doesn't like to turn people down. There are some who regret that he has two lives and does not live alone for science, or, even better, for astronomy. Yet his interests have always been wide, his energies phenomenal. And as he has said so many times, all the arts we create and all the sciences we learn are not worth anything if the world goes to all-out war, and we fail to learn the art of living together in peace on this planet. While one half of him was worrying about people and trying to promote world-wide harmony, the other half was working with apparent full energy on galaxies and Observatory research problems. Let us now return again to the Harvard Observatory.

World War II, budget cuts, personnel away on war duty – nothing was easy. The years between 1940 and 1952, when he retired as the director, were turbulent and intensely busy for him. I was too far away to be an eyewitness to his activities. I had moved with Ralph and our children to Michigan and then to California. Only during summer holidays in New Hampshire, did I have the opportunity to know my father again, and even then, I was too much absorbed with three lively children to focus much attention on my parents, their current activities and interests. I remember once asking him, in 1944, I think it was, what he was doing these days, and he showed me the following list of current activities:

PART I Major Official Assignments

1. Astronomical research (variable stars, clusters, galaxies, metagalaxy)
2. Director of the Harvard Observatory (Oak Ridge, Cambridge, Climax, Bloemfontein)
3. Chairman of World-Wide Broadcasting Foundation Trustees
4. Chairman of Science Service Board of Trustees and President of Science Service, Inc.
5. President of the National Society of the Sigma Xi (national research society)
6. President of the Board of Trustees, Worcester Foundation for Experimental Biology
7. President of the American Astronomical Society
8. President of the Science Clubs of America
9. Member of the Research Committee of the American Philosophical Society
10. Member of the President's Advisory Committee on New Resources (Harvard University)
11. Life Member of the Corporation, Massachusetts Institute of Technology

PART II Middle-Sized Assignments

a. Guidance of Observatory astronomical research programs
b. Official investigator, Observatory War-time Optical Project, OSA
c. Member of the Editorial Board of the *American Scholar*, Phi Beta Kappa
d. Chairman, Corporation Library Committee (Massachusetts Institute of Technology)
e. President of the American Association for an International Office for Education (precursor of UNESCO)

f. Chairman, Department of Astronomy, Faculty of Arts and Sciences, Harvard College

g. Chairman, American Section of the International Astronomical Union

h. Vice President and Councilor of the American Philosophical Society (Philadelphia)

i. Vice Chairman, Foreign Policy Division of the National Research Council

j. Member, Rumford Committee of the American Academy of Arts and Sciences

k. Member, Steering Committee, Observatory Forum on International Problems

l. Chairman of Research Grants-in-Aid Committee of Sigma Xi

m. Member, Advisory Committee on Grants-in-Aid in American History, Library of Congress

n. Member of Class II Membership Committee of the American Philosophical Society

o. Chairman, National Science Fund Committee of the National Academy of Sciences

p. Member, Examining Committee, Boston Public Library

q. Chairman of A.A.V.S.O. Committee "On a new Astronomical Society"

r. Promoter, Institute of Planning, McGill University, Montreal

s. Chairman, Policy Committee of the American Academy of Arts and Sciences

t. Chairman, Committee on Inter-American Scientific Publications

u. Member of Harvard University Radio Board

v. Member, Advisory Board, Watamull Foundation (Honolulu)

w. Member, Conference on Science, Philosophy and Religion (N.Y.C.)

PART III Minor Assignments

1. Astronomical research projects for students

2. Trustee of the Damascus School for Girls

3. Trustee, Woods Hole Oceanographic Institution

4. Member, Policy Committee of the National Research Council (Washington)

5. Member of National Research Council

6. Vice President of "Friends of Norway"

7. Member of Executive Committee of Emergency Committee in Aid of Displaced Foreign Scholars

8. Member, Refugee-Work-Relief Associates

9. President of Examiner Club (Social and Scientific)

10. Member of Boston Joint Committee for International Cooperation

11. Trustee, Long Island Biological Society

12. Program Director of the Forman School (Litchfield, Connecticut)

13. Member of Visiting Committee, McCormick Observatory (University of Virginia)

14. Member of Joint Anti-Fascist Refugee Committee

15. Trustee of the Kosciuszko Foundation (New York)

16. Member, Princeton Graduate School Council

17. Associate Editor of the *Astrophysical Journal*

18. Member, Advisory Commission, NBC Inter-American University of the Air

19. Member of the National Radio Advisory Committee of "American Town Meeting of the Air"

20. Member, Visiting Committee on Meteorology (Massachusetts Institute of Technology)

He was busy and his work significant, I could see at a glance – Director of, President or Vice-President of, Chairman of, Trustee of, or simply member of – but what pleased me most then was that he found time for and enjoyment in a job not on the list, that of being Grandfather of! My father's summer home in Sharon, New Hampshire was a haven for friends and family, children and grandchildren. It was a place where one could get away from troubles and problems for a few days. His favorite way to relax was to play with his grandchildren or to go out into the woods, study the plant and insect life; and afterwards return more refreshed, to stars and people.

In spite of my not being there, I continue with confidence. I rely on my father, who tells a good story, and upon the abundant printed material. For instance, the *Annual Reports* of the Director of the Harvard College Observatory are revealing. Here are some notes taken from them:

One of the outstanding events of 1940 was the establishment by Donald Menzel and Walter Orr Roberts of the high-altitude station for solar research at Climax, Colorado. In 1941, the Observatory suffered a heavy loss in the death of Annie J. Cannon. 1942 saw the almost complete disappearance of graduate student assistants at the Observatory; war jobs had absorbed them. Shipping photographic supplies to the South Africa station became a problem. It was feared that the station would have to be closed for the duration of the war, but at the crucial moment a British shipping concern came to Harvard Observatory's assistance. In the 1943 report, my father stated that 32 members of the scientific staff were occupied full time in war work, leaving very few for work in research. Photographic plates and supplies continued to leave for the Boyden Station from the Cambridge headquarters at unrevealed times by unknown routes to unspecified South African ports. The 1944 report begins thus:

"To the President of the University:

"Sir, – I regret to report a disaster at sea – the loss of the S.S. Robin Goodfellow, with its crew and its cargo of important materials for war industries. Apparently, there had been engine trouble before the ship left port, and possibly a subsequent dropping-out of convoy. A relatively small item in the Robin Goodfellow's cargo, but large in the eyes of the Harvard Observatory, was a shipment of astronomical photographs on the way to Cambridge from the Observatory's station at Bloemfontein, South Africa. The loss was totally unexpected. The insurance rates on trans-Atlantic shipments had dropped to a very low figure, and our shipping advisors in South Africa and in America had assured us of the relatively high safety of shipments once or twice annually from America to South Africa – shipments of photographic plates and other materials necessary for operation of the station; we have had very high insurance costs but no losses whatsoever. For the past two years, we had attempted no return shipments from South Africa. Large quantities of photographic negatives are accumulating in our southern store house. Only twice have we had to ration our plate-hungry telescopes for a few weeks or months while waiting the replenishment of new raw materials from England or the United States. In number of photographic plates our loss by the sinking of the Robin Goodfellow is something less than 20 percent of a year's work."

In 1945 the graduate students were enrolling again and little by little, the staff returned to their research work. War had stimulated progress in technology in general and in certain phases of astronomy in particular, so various staff members returned with new skills applicable to pure research. It was inevitable that the Director was, in this period, obsessed with budget problems. Industries were offering scientists large salaries with which an institution with a fixed endowment and limited funds could not compete. Dissatisfaction with remuneration was bound to occur at the Harvard Observatory, at times even to the point of bitterness. Yet it is to the Director's credit that the very ones who complained most were the ones most unwilling to accept more remunerative positions proffered elsewhere. Somehow work for work's sake was as important as the more-worldly compensation. This, together with the prevailing feeling of good fellowship during his regime, held my father's staff together throughout many a trying economic year.

Yet his Galactic Bureau of computers was depopulated during these war years; for his own researches he retained only one part-time assistant. The same fate came to the Faint Variable Star Bureau, and to others.

Returning to the *Annual Reports*, we note that in 1946, foreign students began to appear again in the graduate school of astronomy; they came from Canada, Holland, Belgium, and Egypt. Foreign visitors also came to the Harvard Observatory from Argentina, Poland, China, Russia, Sweden, Mexico, and France. In this year, in order to facilitate the administration work and responsibilities in the Observatory, my father set up an Observatory Council which would be responsible for the scientific policies and programs of the Observatory and its out-of-town stations. Dr. Bok was made Associate Director, in charge of the Oak Ridge, later called Agassiz Station, in Harvard, Massachusetts; and Dr. Menzel was made Associate Director for solar work, with the Climax, Colorado Station his main responsibility.

New Mexico figured in two instances in the 1947 report. The Air Material Command of the United States Army asked the Harvard Observatory to investigate very seriously the possibility of establishing another well-equipped solar observatory near Alamogordo, New Mexico. The simultaneous operation of both the Climax Colorado and the Alamogordo New Mexico stations could be easily justified in light of substantial government support for solar work. Happily, both the new equipment and the new programs were almost exclusively devoted to what one could call pure research; there were no restrictions on the selection of problems and on the publication of results.

Also, with funds supplied by the Bureau of Ordnance of the United States Navy, Harvard made plans for building two meteor stations in New Mexico, twenty miles apart, to be equipped with special cameras for the study of meteor trails, learning in this way more about the Earth's upper atmosphere. Dr. Fred L. Whipple was the effective leader of this enterprise.

Thus, with the assistance of the government, two of the Observatory's five major programs were given new impetus; the departments of solar and meteor research were in prosperous condition. But the three other programs, variable stars, Milky Way structure, and the galaxies, were not yet completely rehabilitated.

1948 reported progress in all Observatory endeavors and mentioned Dr. Bok's and Dr. Shapley's efforts to reestablish the bureaus for the study of southern variable stars, galaxies, and the Milky Way structure. Forty thousand dollars a year for five years were estimated necessary to put in operation their large joint research on the hub of the Universe.

In 1949, my father gave a new summer lecture course – Introduction to Cosmography. Not too technical, this course carried only one pre-requisite – persistent curiosity. From the 1950 report we learn that Harvard began using two powerful new instruments – one a reflector, for working on galaxies 100 million light-years away, the other a coronagraph for studying the Sun only 8 light-minutes away. This year it was decided to limit advanced graduate students to 15. The Observatory Council found that the research of the staff members is aided with a few good students and delayed with too many. The total expenditures by the Harvard Observatory for the advance of astronomical science during this year came to approximately half a million dollars.

In the 1951 report we learn of Dr. Bok's visit to Bloemfontein, South Africa, of the death of the Boyden superintendent, Dr. Paraskevopoulos, and the retirement, after 50 years, of Mr. Campbell. The Harvard College Observatory has by now expanded, consisting of these seven stations: Alamogordo, New Mexico; Bloemfontein, South Africa; Boulder, Colorado; Cambridge, Massachusetts; Climax, Colorado; La Cruces, New Mexico; Oak Ridge, Massachusetts. In order that the widely scattered staff at the six out-stations and in Cambridge could keep in better touch with each other, a mimeographed House Organ was successfully tried out. In this H.C.O. Gossip Sheet my father had innocent fun exercising his talent as a breezy newspaper reporter, reminiscent of his Missouri and Kansas days.

The September 1950 H.C.O. Gossip Sheet indicated that there had been some vandalism at the meteor stations.

"SUCCESSFUL SUPPLICATION. A sign installed last winter at the meteor observing sites in New Mexico reads:

'HARVARD METEOR STATION NO.1 DONA ANA (or NO. 2 SOLEDAD)

'This station is operated by the Harvard College Observatory for the purpose of photographing meteors (shooting stars). The photographs are used to learn scientific facts about the upper atmosphere. This station and its companion at Soledad (or Dona Ana) are the only ones of their kind in the world. Please help us maintain these stations in the fine skies of New Mexico by refraining from molesting the equipment.

'Harlow Shapley

'Director, Harvard College Observatory'

"The supplication works. Now the hot-rod boys steal no more gas and oil; they vandalize no more the thyratrons and clocks. Presumably they now dash wildly toward the stations on their foaming broncos, with a yippee-i-yi, their six shooters a-blazing. They stop short, with a snort, rear hoofs a-grinding. They spell out the sign, and their jaws drop. They see the august signature, turn quietly, pick up their jaws, and jog off into the twilight – baffled, but better hombres.

"NEXT STEP. This success with sign advertising has suggested to an unholy one that we should follow up our triumph and do the next sign on a new angle. Instead of facing the lonesome trail, this sign would face heavenward and read:

'Dear God

'More meteors, please.

'(signed) Harlow Shapley'"

The 1952 report which is my father's last report to the university before his retirement as director of the Observatory contains a summary of his

32-year term. From ten telescopes to thirty; personnel also trebled; expenditures increased five-fold. Due to generous gifts to the Observatory, the budget showed a small surplus at the end of the year. A radio telescope is in the process of being installed at Agassiz Station, the only astronomical observatory in America equipped with such an instrument at this time. Speaking of his own work in this last report he says, "My scientific program currently includes researches on the extent of the Galaxy in the anti-center direction, the corona of stars surrounding our galactic discoid, the distribution of some 300,000 galaxies in the Inner Metagalaxy, and the structure and population of the Clouds of Magellan."

At this point let us return briefly to astronomy. In June of 1950, my father attended a symposium at the University of Michigan and presented a paper on his current research entitled *Comparison of the Magellanic Clouds with the Galactic System*. The Magellanic Clouds are two irregular galaxies, the nearest of the external galaxies to our Milky Way system. They appear virtually as two hazy, luminous star clouds not far from the south celestial pole, and therefore not visible to observers in the northern hemisphere. These clouds of stars were first clearly reported by the historian of Ferdinand Magellan's voyage around the Earth in 1518 – 1520, and they have become known as the Large Magellanic Cloud and the Small Magellanic Cloud.

At the beginning of the last chapter we were speaking of clusters of galaxies. It appears that these two neighbor galaxies are part of our local group, as are also the beautiful Andromeda Galaxy seen in the northern hemisphere and the two ellipsoidal dwarf galaxies in the constellations Sculptor and Fornax. To date, there are 17 known members of our local cluster of galaxies; but even as I write this, the number may have increased. At the time the Michigan symposium paper was given, 15 were known.

The Magellanic Clouds provide an excellent tool house for the astronomer, as my father points out in detail in his book, *Galaxies*. We have an all-over outside view of them, and they are near enough that moderate-size telescopes can explore their content. They help us in understanding our own

Galaxy; from our inside view, we have difficulty gaining a clear and complete picture. The Clouds also allow us to guess intelligently what the galaxies may be like that are too distant for our telescopes to resolve into stars, clusters, dust clouds, nebulae, novae, and variables.

Very early in the discovery and investigation of galaxies, or, as Heber D. Curtis called them, Island Universes, different galactic types were noted. There were spiral galaxies seen from various angles, front-on, edge-on, or tilted; some had tight arms, some were loose spirals; some were barred spirals with the arms starting from the ends of a central bar of stars. There were spheroidal or ellipsoidal galaxies of varying degree of elongation, and also galaxies of completely irregular form.

Our local group of 17 known members form an elongated cloud with our Galaxy and the Magellanic Clouds near one end and the Andromeda spiral with its elliptical companions and the open spiral Messier 33 near the other. It comprises three spirals, four irregulars, four ordinary elliptical systems, and six dwarf ellipticals.

An interesting structural series is revealed if we arrange the galactic types in order, beginning with spheroidal and going to slightly ellipsoidal, to very ellipsoidal, to tightarmed spiral, to loose-armed spiral, to vague spiral, to completely irregular. Some astronomers have ventured a hypothesis that this represents an evolutionary trend. The Magellanic Clouds fall in the irregular group or perhaps in a stage between irregular and spiral.

Also in my father's Michigan symposium paper, gravitational effects between galaxies are discussed, and apparent bridges connecting some of them. As early as 1940, he had discovered an asymmetrical extension of the Small Magellanic Cloud in the direction of the Large Cloud.

In these middle and later years my father made several experiments with a short-hand diary, but none of them were long-lived. He was simply too busy with the *doing* to take time to record any of it. In one of them, in 1942, he wrote, "yesterday I was horizontal – also a blood donor, but no connection."

We can see that shorthand notes even when translated are still cryptic. He was seldom seriously ill and more seldom admitted illness – horizontal was the most he would say. This entry brings to mind a story he told about one of his blood-giving dates with the Red Cross. He has always had abnormally low blood pressure so that any new doctor checking him will try twice before he believes what his instrument reports. When the pretty young nurse, so he tells it, prepared to take his blood pressure before the bloodletting, he said, "you've got a surprise coming." She looked at him strangely and went on with her work. When she registered no astonishment, my father's curiosity got the better of him. "Very low, wasn't it?" he remarked by way of conversation. "No," said this gorgeous blond, "perfectly normal."

Another two lines in the diary states "Got Annie and Dorothy out today, gave them the once over; and Mrs. Virginia Nail brought me an interesting wheat yield." Annie and Dorothy were star clusters that the galactic bureau worked on from time to time – they got these unofficial names because Helen Sawyer (Hogg) said "they are so cute!" A wheat yield, also known as a horse race, was more of the goofiness that came out of the hardworking bureau. These wheat yields were frequency diagrams in which the number of galaxies is plotted against brightness intervals.

Here is another diary line, one which needs no explanation. "Tonight I dine with Leopold Stokowski who has requested to meet me, which means only that he doesn't want to meet Harvard composers." Another entry: "Many short phone interruptions this morning: John Garfield called me to say hello, just because I like you; the *Boston Herald* wanted to know my definition of metagalaxy and universe." He told them: "Metagalaxy is the sum total of all galaxies, stars, planets, and cosmic rubbish. Universe is something more because it includes, as well, space, time, and intangibles in general."

Another item in the diary – "planned tomorrow night's Full Moonatic program." When I asked about this, he explained that he had assembled every month a dozen, plus or minus, graduate students – alert men and girls – for a gab session. "They would outline some of the difficult astrophysical puzzles and discuss possible solutions. These sessions were held on the night of the full moon when astrophotography would be futile; we called them the Full Moonatics. At the two-hour sessions some thought deeply, some thought wildly, some merely ogled the girls. A few bright ideas came from the brightest members of the group; on the whole everyone found these meetings profitable."

Still another entry: "then to bed, but had an uneasy night tossing with the budget – figured that the discovery and measure of galaxies is now costing us about $52 a hundred. Maybe with increased managerial skill it can be brought down, for the next hundred thousand objects, to $48 a hundred. Also estimated that the cost to Harvard University for our recent discovery of a basically important metagalactic density-gradient was 2.6 kilo-girl-hours, and an even dozen directorial headaches, counting the one I am going to sleep with right now."

Many of us, looking back on the post-war years, are unable to explain the hysteria that so many succumbed to. As we have mentioned, Rankin, Parnell Thomas, McCarthy, as well as others were calling my father red names. He washed it off. My mother, active during the war in secret work, was called to Washington on her own account to prove that she was a true-blue American. Her offense, it seems, was that she was married to my father. The whole thing was reminiscent of the Salem witch-hunts. She had her fight – and a complete victory.

During the war she worked on various aspects of ballistics, shock waves, jet engine heat flow, and later much computational work on meteors – accurate position measurements on Harvard plates made in New Mexico. This work performed at M.I.T. under a Navy contract lasted 13 years.

My mother's efforts in astronomy have produced a considerable bibliography and have made her for many years a member of the International Astronomical Union. Along with her ballistic and meteor work, she joined an ambitious project being carried out by Dr. Zdenék Kopal[7] – the *Catalogue of the Elements of Eclipsing Binary Systems*. In sending me copies of this large catalogue, Dr. Kopal wrote: "You should not allow the sterling but largely silent contribution of your mother to be lost in the glare of her scintillating husband."

Dr. Kopal, in the introduction to his catalogue, compares it with Harlow Shapley's Princeton thesis of 1915, *A Study of the Orbits of Eclipsing Binaries*, regarding that thesis as the direct predecessor to his work. Kopal's move from Cambridge, Massachusetts to Manchester, England, halfway through the work "deprived me," he wrote, "of the collaboration of the senior co-author whose name appears on the title page. May the junior writer," Kopal goes on to say, "use this opportunity to record publicly the debt of obligation which he, and all students of eclipsing systems, owe to the life-long efforts of Martha B. Shapley, whose expert help was already at the disposal of her husband, Harlow Shapley, in his work in the Princeton period of 1912 – 1914 and who, more than thirty years later, volunteered with the same selfless devotion, her assistance to the present undertaking. The measure of her contribution to it, by the part she personally took in reductions and supervision of computers engaged to assist us, is difficult to overestimate."

My mother considers Dr. Kopal's opinion of her contribution and abilities extravagant. Praise embarrasses her – she wants it neither on her own account nor as the wife of a well-known astronomer. Her pleasures come from her husband's successes in science, his general popularity, his big and little triumphs; this is indeed what makes her most happy.

Dr. Dorrit Hoffleit, now director of the Maria Mitchell Observatory on Nantucket Island, had another story to tell about the difficult years during and immediately after the war. Reminiscing with me, she recalled her happiest time at the Harvard Observatory, when she was encouraged to continue her studies to a doctoral degree; and her most unhappy moment, one she had never revealed before. In her words, "I was doing well at the Ballistic Research Laboratory in Aberdeen, Maryland, and my superiors were trying to make conditions sufficiently attractive for me to stay there. But I was homesick for Harvard and by 1948 I was ready to return to the Observatory at a decided monetary disadvantage, under 40 percent of my Aberdeen salary. Then, one of the security officers whom I saw frequently about routine laboratory matters took it upon himself to give me some friendly counsel. What he said cut deeply; 'If you go back to Harvard to work under Harlow Shapley you will, for security reasons, probably never be able to come back here.' Nevertheless, I took that chance; and within two months after my return to the Observatory, I was happily appointed a visiting consultant to continue some classified investigations for the Aberdeen Laboratory. Those were trying years for Dr. Shapley, and uneasy for some of his staff too."

But there were also more pleasant episodes. Mrs. Virginia McKibben Nail, my father's chief research assistant for several years, tells of one of the times she and her small daughter were spending a weekend with the Shapleys in Sharon. It seems that my father had just returned from a day at Woods Hole, attending a trustees' meeting at the Oceanographic Institute. The meeting had considered how a hungry and thirsty world might be fed by making use of seaweed and sea water. With this fresh on his mind he was full of talk about returning to the sea for food, and during the dinner conversation he mentioned "you can use the sea moss in cooking, you know." Nobody showed much enthusiasm. He brought up the idea several times without gaining any supporters. Nevertheless, he maintained his position, coming out finally with, "it makes a *delicious* dessert." My father, who likes every ordinary kind of food, with the exception of lemon meringue pie and canned pears, and likes almost any strange concoction, at least for sampling, would probably have liked a sea moss pudding, whatever it was. However, the matter was dropped.

Several months later Mrs. Nail was giving a small birthday party for my father. When dessert time came, she scored a complete triumph by serving a fancy gelatin pudding in a sort of wedding cake shape, garnished with fruits and whipped cream. It was beautiful to look at and delicious to eat. She had everyone guessing what it was and finally my father remembered – Sea Moss Pudding. So, the party fed on fruits from the sea but many landgrown fruits went into the sea moss masterpiece to help make it palatable.

When in 1952 the International Astronomical Union met in Rome, Pope Pius XII gave an address in French, on the subject of *An Astronomical Survey*, to the 600 astronomers assembled at his summer residence at Castel Gandolfo. He mentioned Shapley by name – the only living mentionee – perhaps because Harlow Shapley had been awarded the Pope Pius XI Prize for science and humanity several years before. Curiously, this prize of 50,000 lira took three or four years to arrive in America. In the meantime, the lira had dropped so steadily that my father feared it would go negative and he would have to pay the Vatican. Fortunately, however, the payment was made and at the original rate of exchange. After his address to the astronomers, the Pope stepped off his platform and came right to the Shapleys, who had protestingly been put in the front row of seats. As my father reports, "He scared us, or at least me. The Pope said he was glad to know that his 1951 Academy address, *A Survey of Modern Physics and the Age of the Earth*, had been made required reading in my Harvard Cosmography course. He spoke in good English while I was trying to muster a request in French – a request that he do for biology what he had so boldly done for physics and astronomy. I stuttered and said how honored I was, and he passed on, greeting the whole front row – in five languages!"

In C-21 at the Harvard Observatory hangs a Charles Hopkinson[8] portrait of my father and as is often the case, none of the family likes it! But some other artistic efforts we do like. It was the poet Robert Frost who suggested to his artist friend, Mrs. Enit Kaufman[9] that she include Shapley, President Conant and perhaps others at Harvard, in her caricatures of 100 Representative Americans, with novelist Dorothy Canfield Fisher[10] writing the accompanying text. My father claimed he was too busy and did not care to appear as a clown, with one strand of pink hair etc., but when the artist persisted, he did agree to hold still a few minutes. During these holding-still sessions he wasted no time. He took on a mental job – did some thinking about his current research problems. "When that thinking was finished, I had a crick in my neck," he remembers, "but she wasn't through with me yet, and so I had to think of something else. I thought of Frost, her host, and constructed a quatrain or two about the crick on

Robert Frost's farm and the crick in my neck. 'You are thinking of something wicked,' said the keen-eyed artist. No, only something mischievous, I replied. I quoted the poem and suggested that she get Frost to reply in verse. She tried, but he declined, saying that he had no ability in versified repartee."

The whole collection of sketches was exhibited in the National Portrait Gallery in Washington and it then traveled the country over. Among the hundred famous or notorious were Franklin Roosevelt, Justice Felix Frankfurter, Robert Frost, and Joe Louis.

Pencil sketch by Samuel J. Woolf

There was a pencil sketch by Samuel J. Woolf, printed in the *American Scientist*; and an Austin Briggs drawing that the family likes; and an oil painting done by a criminally insane artist doing time in the Iowa State Penitentiary; and a cut-out silhouette by a French countess. There were various photographs that we liked. One in particular of him sitting beside his round table "like a hop toad" to use his words, is a favorite in our collection of the more dignified poses. But of course, the more interesting pictures to us are safely pasted in the family album and are those exhibiting less dignity and more humor.

From the final H.C.O. Gossip Sheet comes the following notice, most likely from my father's pen:

"GALAXIES IN TROUBLE

"So long as the Director of the Harvard Observatory had to put in eight – or nine-tenths of his time on administrative details for the H.C.O. and for its extra-Cantabrigian operations, the galaxies were not much disturbed. He couldn't pry into them effectively, notwithstanding the over-time hours. But thanks to a proper and long-standing rule of the Harvard Corporation, he is officially relieved of said administrative details at the end of this year – thirty years is certainly by golly enough! Now there can be nearly full time with research and with a special course on cosmography in Harvard University. Somebody else must turn out the neglected lights, hunt down resisting contributors, make a dozen daily decisions, bad and good. The directing of such a grand institution as H.C.O. is fun; but assailing the galaxies, inquiring into the cosmic how and why, being a scholar of the stars, of protons, electrons, cosmons, space-ons, time-ons, is even funner. Yes, much funner.

"Already the worried galaxies are hastening away!"

Every year there was an Apple Blossom picnic at Oak Ridge which included everyone who had any connection with the Harvard Observatory – the attraction being apple blossoms, people, children, food, and baseball. The Apple Blossom Picnic of 1953 was an especially gala affair, since, besides celebrating apple blossoms, it celebrated that year the retirement of the Observatory's director. In addition to the large Observatory family, two amateur groups, the Bond Astronomical Club and the Amateur Telescope Makers of Boston were present, and seldom have amateur astronomers paid such a warm-hearted tribute to a professional as did this gathering at Oak Ridge.

The 61-inch reflector was gaily decorated for the occasion. The telescope was pointed to the zenith and from the top end were attached many-colored paper streamers which were draped down and fastened to the walls of the turret. A large paper spiral galaxy served as background to the platform where my mother and father sat receiving presents and praise. The decorators outdid themselves transforming this large and rather drab telescope room into a festive ballroom. Dr. Bok gave the main address; the newspapers afterwards were generous in their praise:

"Dr. Shapley's conception of his own job in the evolutionary scheme of things has kept him going at a pace that would wear out three or four men with smaller packs of energy than he has. Hard working, quick thinking, fast talking, Dr. Shapley has a heavy schedule that gives him a somewhat harried expression, but this look frequently gives away to a warm smile or a hearty laugh. He has made the Shapley Era of the Harvard Observatory a brilliant chapter in modern astronomy, through his own research and those of the outstanding scientists he has brought to Harvard, such as Fred Whipple, Zdenék Kopal, Donald Menzel, Bart Bok, Sergei Gaposhkin and and Cecilia Payne-Gaposhkin."

My father and mother sat on their throne, not knowing whether to be happy or sad. Various others in the group felt a twinge of sadness while they celebrated the ending of one regime and the beginning of another. But merriment was the order of the day. There were flowers and gifts: A handsome red leather chair was one; another was an album of color photographs of and in the director's residence. There was dancing, and a Virginia Reel led by the retiring Director. And at the climax of the festivities the turret roof motor was started, the turret began to revolve, and the colored streamers made a pretty sight as they twisted, stretched, and finally broke. In the hubbub, I overheard a comment of Charles Federer, editor of the popular magazine, *Sky and Telescope*. He said: "I've always been impressed by the

Shapleys' down-to-earth, friendly, unassuming attitude. I told Mrs. Shapley that once; she smiled and said, 'You mean our lack of dignity.'"

CHAPTER EIGHT

Assault on the Unknowns

"You should get out, way out, and keep clear of the successor" has been my father's advice for years to retiring officials. When his time came to use this advice, he made a firm point in having nothing further to do with the administration of the Harvard Observatory. "I never went back to my office and requested that the staff remember that I was out; from my offices as director in A-17 and D-34 and D-35." Following the long-established tenure rules at Harvard, administrative officers retire at 66 – that is, retire from administration; but, by special arrangement with the President's office, the retirement for teachers may be postponed to 68 or even 70. As planned, he took on a three-year teaching assignment, but never retired from personal research projects. He moved into C36-38 which had been Miss Cannon's suite of offices years before, and his famous round table was moved to Boulder, Colorado, where my brother Alan built a house around it.

Harlow Shapley, happily retired

My father and his research assistants continued their investigations on the external galaxies and the form and extent of the Milky Way. The work was centered on the photometric measures of star clusters in the Magellanic Clouds, and on novae, Cepheids and long-period variables. There were smaller investigations in related fields such as the finding of several hitherto unrecorded faint star clusters and planetary nebulae in the southern Milky Way; the cataloguing and spectrum analysis of nebulosities in the Small Magellanic Cloud. He supervised a collaboration with the Observatory of the University of Michigan in the survey of novae in the Magellanic Clouds, and studied the star population characteristics of the two Clouds, proving them to be similar in their content of supergiant stars and essentially equally distant from the earth.

Simultaneously with his research, my father devoted a great deal of his time to his lectures on cosmography in Harvard University. Cosmography, we should insert, is the field of study related to the cosmos as is geography to the Earth. More than a hundred signed up for this course each year. It was designed for the non-scientific student, primarily juniors and seniors concentrating in the humanities and social studies.

When my father retired from teaching, Harvard University could find nobody with the requisite taste for stars, atoms, biology, and philosophy to take over the popular course. "Not that I had these disciplines well in hand," my father says, "but every lecture was filled with by-play – poetry, biology, paleontology, mixed with galaxies and the spacetime complex." He reports that the essays handed in by the students at the end of the term were often marvelous, and those of the dozen or so Radcliffe students were among the best.

In 1953 my father edited a book titled *Climatic Change*, writing the introduction and the first chapter in which he explained, among other things, how to construct an Ice Age. He explained in the introduction to *Climatic Change* that:

> *"This volume is the crowning result of a conference held in May of 1952, when a score of students of the wide science of climatology, and three score of the especially curious, analyzed and debated the evidences of climatic change and the possible sources of such variation. We have included all the papers of this conference – long and short, simple and technical. This volume will indeed be something like the weather, soft and easy-going at times, occasionally cold, rugged and enigmatic, and at other times, whether tough or tender, possibly a bit monotonous."*

Further on he comments:

> *"Our climate is now reasonably comfortable over a wide latitude – neither too muggy nor too frigid. If solar radiation is the dominant influence in climatic behavior, one might futilely urge the Sun: Steady now, hold it! But do we really want an equable epoch? Climatic and continental changes usefully force us inhabitants of this Sun-controlled planet to evolve in adaptability. If the warm spell and vegetable lushness*

of the mid-Mesozoic era, which prevailed for a hundred million years, had persisted to the present, we almost certainly would not be here to write essays on climate. The flowers and bees and the other facets of life derived much inspiration and experience from the rising mountains and the climatic changes that together led terrestrial biology into the highly adaptable forms that successfully faced the oncoming Ice Ages and survived them."

After his teaching in Harvard my father was invited to be the William Allan Neilson Lecturer for three months at Smith College, but like *The Man Who Came to Dinner* he stayed two additional months. Once in referring to his lecturing to 2000 Smith girls he commented (but without conviction) "this astronomer's message at Northampton will soon be blown out of remembrance with gales of girlish laughter. 'I have looked at the universe,' the astronomer will say, 'and I see that man does not amount to much.' 'We knew that already,' they responded. It's hard to tell anything to these bright eye-some girls."

After Smith College came heavy work on *The Inner Metagalaxy*. This technical volume, which was published in 1957 by the Yale University Press, summarized three decades of trailblazing work on the problems of the galaxies. Beginning with what he and his associates had discovered concerning the Clouds of Magellan, he leads us through explorations of the north and south galactic polar zones, the canopy galaxies, and along the borders of the Milky Way. He discusses positional distributions of some 330,000 galaxies, the magnitudes of 170,000 and estimates the metagalactic population per cubic light year. He also deals in *The Inner Metagalaxy* with his discovery of the Earth's peripheral position in our own Galaxy. "We begin to suffer the consequences of the Earth's location in the dust-affected region near the galactic plane when we extend the galaxy survey from the polar zones towards the Milky Way," he says. "In regions of the Milky Way we are blocked by the smog in our own spiral." But here and there along the Milky Way are a few breaks in the dust clouds, so-called windows in the cosmic smog. Some of them are particularly interesting. One, for example, is found in the constellation Cygnus. It was here that radio telescopes first picked up signals which seemed to come out of the void. Later this radio source, called Cygnus A, was identified with a pair of dimly photographed, faint and very remote galaxies which are or were apparently in collision. Through this and other windows we can see beyond our own Galaxy and by studying these vistas here and there, we gain an idea of the distribution of remote systems.

My father's most popular book is *Of Stars and Men*, published in 1958. It has been translated into six foreign languages (Swedish, Italian, Spanish, Japanese, Russian and Hindi) and has gained him wide acclaim and many new friends.

In *Of Stars and Men*, he approaches the vastness of his universal subject with humility and wonder, while seeking to pin down the cosmic facts and bring order, shape and continuity to the elusive concepts of cosmography. There are tables, or alphabets, as my father calls them, of mass, space, time, and energy, to which the reader can turn when he wishes to get himself and things properly oriented. Many scientific fields are called upon to make this cosmic picture. For instance, now in various chemistry laboratories, primitive atmospheres have been constructed, containing such gases as ammonia, methane, and hydrogen. It is believed that such atmospheres must occur on other planets as they once appeared on the Earth. When the gas mixtures are bombarded with electrical discharges, simulating the effect of lightning strokes, amino acids are produced – the most important constituents of living organisms. Although there is much yet to learn, we have bridged, at least provisionally, the gap between life and lifeless.

Dr. Willem J. Luyten of the University of Minnesota has said that *Of Stars and Men* is Shapley's most important contribution. The American poet, Fred Winsor wrote to my father:

"I have just finished reading *Of Stars and Men*. If I may use a cliché that a thousand others must already have thought of, 'out of this world' comes first to mind. I am not competent to assay the gold therein, nor would you be interested much. Where I may, perhaps have better right to judge – the language, style, and art – I can only admire. It is a very, very fine piece of work. I hope it is widely read by the many of us who need it, priest, pedant, and politician, the old and the young, every person who hopes for a better future, or fears a worse one."

Of Stars and Men has been made into an animated motion picture which has won praise both here and abroad. In consultation with the author, movie-makers Faith and John Hubley[1] have interwoven color, design, animation, music, and narration in unfolding the tale that *Of Stars and Men* tells. I met the Hubleys in the summer of 1961 when they were presenting their film at the Venice International Film Festival. Mrs. Hubley confided to me, "You know, neither John nor I have had any science background. We are like the little animated man in the film, full of wonder and curiosity, and eager to learn."

The fact that my father had a heavy travel and lecture schedule did not discourage the Hubleys from frequent conferences. "We would ask him where he would be on a specific day and what would be his freest hour. We would meet at the predetermined point which might be anywhere in the eastern United States at the place and hour he chose (and some of the hours and places were strange) and, you know – neither he nor we ever missed an appointment!"

The Universe is explored in the first nine chapters of this book: Introduction – Nothing Merely Human; New Bottles for New Wines; On Being Incidental; An Inquiry Concerning Other Worlds; On the Hazards of Primitive Life; Rainbows and Cosmic Chemistry; The Fourth Adjustment; A Digression on Great Moments; Toward the Emergence of Organisms. The tenth chapter asks, "What Should Be the Human Response?"

In 1961 my father revised *Galaxies*, a semi-popular book that he wrote twenty years previously. It contains much recent information on a variety of subjects: Cepheid variables; the period-luminosity relation; globular clusters; heliocentric-to-galactocentric hypothesis; galactic surveys at Harvard;

Magellanic Clouds; types of galaxies. In the last chapter of *Galaxies* is treated briefly the problem of the expanding universe.

It is interesting to probe our universe, to the depths the present great telescopes allow, to see if we can observe any evidence of a center or any evidence of an edge. My father asks:

> *"Do our observations show any indication of a concentration, or a systematic thinning out, in the number of galaxies as we move in million-light years strides across metagalactic space? To save time, we go to the answer immediately, without bothering to present facts or arguments. The answer is, 'No bottom.' There is no indication of a boundary; nor is there good evidence that there might be one if we went out far enough. If our measuring rods were longer than a billion light years, or more sensitive to small density changes, we might find a falling off in some direction, or a clear trend toward some all-dominating nuclear cloud of galaxies; or we might glimpse clear evidence for a finite curved space; or, more likely, we might find as now no bottom and no excessive variation in the average frequency of galaxies."*

Further, it appears that all the galaxies, with the exception of a few nearby ones, are running away from us. We deduce this in the same manner as we did the motion to and fro of revolving double stars; from the faint spectra of galaxies we observe the Doppler shift of spectral lines toward the red end of the spectrum. There is a further dramatic point: The fainter the galaxy, the more pronounced is the red shift. In other words, the farther away these galaxies are, the faster they are receding.

Some alternative explanations of the red-shift – other than simple motion in the line of sight – can be suggested. Could it not be that the light quanta traveling over these super-great distances of perhaps six billion light years grow "tired" and undergo some change?

"Those quanta of radiation that ultimately make our spectrograms, have spent a million centuries or so traveling in space since they were emitted from the stars in the distant galaxies. The intervening space has some dust and gas in it, and everywhere it is being crisscrossed by the emitted radiation of millions of stars. In consequence, could not Earth-ward-bound quanta of radiation lose some of their energy and thereby increase in wavelength and [the spectral lines] move toward the red end of the spectrum?"

Or suppose that the fundamental constants of Nature such as the velocity of light, the mass of the electron, the gravitational constant are in fact not precisely constant over long intervals of space and time.

"If one persists in the conviction that galaxies, stars, planets, animals, and even matter evolve, why exclude categorically the primitive physical constants from the process of change, from evolving with time and space? It goes without saying that if the constants are not constant we need no longer strain ourselves to interpret the red shift as due to a velocity of recession; or, for that matter, strive to interpret anything else on the cosmic scale."

The time scale for the evolution of the Universe is another question:

"The age of the Earth's oldest rocks and the abundance of radio-active elements remaining in the Earth and Sun indicate the age of our planetary system, like the age of the expansion, as a few billion years. The nature and behavior of star clusters in the Milky Way, as Bok has shown, point to a similar age for our Galaxy. It is a thought-provoking circumstance that Earth, Galaxy, and the beginning of metagalactic expansion all appear to date from a rather recent epoch.

"However, it is hard to cram the whole past life of the stars into a short span of a few billion years. It does not seem sufficiently dignified that the majestic universe should measure its duration as scarcely greater than

the age of the oldest rocks on this small planet's surface, or little greater than the age of the life in the crannies of the rocks.

"It is puzzling to find many mixed double galaxies, with one an open spiral, the other a conservative spheroidal. They suggest a great difference in evolutionary stage, if not in age. Why the difference, if they have developed together?

"We may be driven, in our speculations, back to the long, long time scale, where there is duration enough to allow clusters and galaxies to evolve leisurely, while the stars grow old and die, or blow up as supernovae, and by way of reincarnation appear as second- or third-generation stars."

My father concludes *Galaxies* thus:

"Meanwhile it will be refreshing to test some of these hypotheses with well-placed observations. Dozens of unsolved galactic problems can be outlined. We are far from finished, or from being finished, in this combat with metagalactic mysteries. More measures, more correlations, more theoretical analyses – and then, if we like, a return to wistful speculation."

In 1957 my father lost a close friend in the death of Henry Norris Russell who was always more than a teacher and professional colleague. "In those early days at Princeton," my father recalls, "I, as an uncouth Missourian, was accepted by Russell with some reservation, but gradually I improved in standing, and at last became aware of my arrival when Russell very privately told me a deep secret – he told me just where in the woods four miles north of Princeton I could find the rare and precious fringed gentian. I had indeed made good!"

Henry Norris Russell, center, with Donald Menzel (L) and Harlow Shapley (R)

Russell was an extremely religious man. He was once asked to define the evasive concept of soul. He said, "by soul I mean the personality, the conscious individual who understands, feels, remembers, responds to us."

"Soul equals personality – I rather like that," my father continues his reminiscing. "But when Russell goes on to state, 'When the body dies the soul vanishes utterly,' I do not agree with him. He is inconsistent. For the personality (therefore soul) survives. His personality, in a sense, is right here, at the present time, and will continue to survive. But he and I did not get to argue religious matters – eclipsing stars and iron multiplets always got in the way. Perhaps it was just as well."

Russell never seemed to interest himself in Milky Way structure, or in the many problems of the star clusters and galaxies, possibly because Shapley talked too fast about them and he had little chance to contribute. Also, he did not get deeply into the field of meteors. But he covered almost all other astronomical fields in lively interest and many of them in original research.

And he enjoyed his researches immensely, especially those investigations where he must calculate the consequences of this or that hypothesis. "One of my clearest pictures of him shows his eager thoughtful gaze at the ceiling or horizon, with a 10-inch slide rule in his hand. He carried the logarithm tables in his phenomenal memory."

In his *Biographical Memoir on Henry Norris Russell,* my father wrote for the National Academy of Sciences: "A few weeks ago I stood alone, with bared head, in the front yard at 79 Alexander Street [the Russell home in Princeton], when his body was carried into the study from which I had so often come out inspired and determined; and I thought: His interval out of infinite time is nobly concluded; it is now our continuing responsibility to pay interest on the investment he made in us."

Many years earlier my father had been in Princeton to pay his last respects to another astronomer and personal friend, Professor Raymond Dugan. He has said that Russell taught him stars, but Dugan had taught him the New Jersey native flora. To Dugan's funeral my father came with a great bunch of New Jersey wildflowers he had gathered to present to the appreciative widow.

Along with inquiries into cosmography come inevitably questions of religion. It is hard for the astronomer to take the Universe for granted without occasionally wondering what was its origin, where is it going, what came before it came, and what, if anything, comes after.

From its beginning in 1940 my father has been associated with the Conference on Science, Philosophy, and Religion. In a lecture he gave for the conference at Columbia University a few years ago, he tells how this came about:

> "Many years ago, a bearded stranger walked right into my office and said: 'Doctor Shapley, I am Rabbi Louis Finkelstein,[2] President of The Jewish Theological Seminary in New York. I've come to ask you to join us in New York in a small meeting to discuss the problems that are ahead of Protestants, Jews, and Catholics.' Now that statement is the version of

the meeting with Rabbi Finkelstein as it was written out for me from his office. I should like to interpolate the true account of that first meeting at the Harvard Observatory. And this truthful account should be off the record. Interesting isn't it, that whenever in this organization we resort to truth we take pains to be off record!

"One or more of you have already heard the truth of this affair. That day when the bearded rabbi barged into my office without warning, either by secretary or telephone or knocking (the way we pagans feel we should do), I chided the young typist for violating my office rules. 'Penny', I said – her name was Penelope Anthon and for reasons the rabbi would not understand we called her Penny Ante. 'Heavens! Penny, I mean Galaxies! You gave me no warning, no time even to get my feet down. It might have been an insurance salesman, or a United States marshal with a summons, or a Harvard Crimson reporter.'

"'I could do nothing,' she said. 'I was sitting here typing and without a sound a shadow fell across the page and a deep voice stated: I have come for Dr. Shapley. I looked up, saw that tall apparition with dark beard, and shining face, and softly penetrating eyes – I was helpless. I could think only of The Second Coming. Obviously, it was a case of mistaken identity.'"

Lyman Bryson, another of the Rabbi's recruits, who was well known for his radio program *Invitation to Learning*, was a personal friend of my father. They had many deep and interesting discussions on philosophy and education. "I once did an experiment in thought for him," my father recalls. In his essay, *A Tribute to Lyman Bryson*, he explains:

"The question was the possibility and usefulness of mass thinking. Might a community thought on a given subject be deeper or higher or richer than the sum of the thoughts by individuals of the community? Might there not be some subtle mental catalyst that would incite a transcendence over the integrated thoughts of the individual thinkers?"

My father turned to the Observatory and with a group of astronomy graduate students – his Full Moonatics – he tried this experiment. A very few bright single ideas came from bright members of the group, but nothing transcendent appeared. The catalyst, if any, was slow acting.

Nevertheless, Catalyst Bryson kept working against the cultural inertia of his radio listeners. He catalyzed them and also his colleagues on the *Invitation* program.

The Conference on Science, Philosophy, and Religion, started by Jews, Catholics, Protestants, and the unchurched, held many meetings and produced several books of essays. But my father felt that it did not get very far – too many words, too few actions. On the other hand, the Institute of Religion in an Age of Science (IRAS), in his estimation has fared better. It had its beginning on Star Island, a rocky and treeless member of the Isles of Shoals a few miles from the shores of Maine and New Hampshire; the island had long been the location of various summer religious conferences. In 1954 a group of New England clergymen from several different denominations, who had become concerned with the possible influence of the scientific method and scientific discoveries on religion as formally exhibited in church, chapel and synagogue, invited a number of leading scientists to Star Island to discuss these matters. Somewhat to everyone's surprise, the scientists accepted the invitations. Apparently, many had been hoping for a rapprochement of modern science and religion, and the two groups have from the first sincerely worked together. For two years my father was president of this organization. It became clear to him very soon that science, in a wide sense, could enrich the holdings of religion, and that we could possibly encourage a proper use of religious myths.

The Star Island group that attends the week-long conference each summer consists of some 200 laymen, clergy, and scientists, who come together to inquire, discuss, answer. A few years ago, some of them put their thoughts on paper and out of the Star Island conference came my father's book, *Science Ponders Religion*. This widely read book presents in 18 essays an account of the way some scientists think about religion. My father mentions in the introduction: "It would be interesting now to hear from the clergy by way of a companion volume on *How Religion Reacts to Science*." That desirable volume, with essays by leading theologians, now appears under the editorship of the Rev. Edwin Booth of Boston University's Divinity School.

Among my father's close friends are Frances and Ralph Burhoe,[3] who, as well as being administrators of the American Academy of Arts and Sciences, are very actively engaged in the Institute of Religion in an Age of Science, and the Star Island programs. And to mention another close friend with religious interests, there was Swami Akhilananda, the Vedanta Society's Hindu pastor of Boston and Providence. They enjoyed discussing psychology, philosophy, and especially liberal religious creeds.

My father has often remarked: "Science is science; Mythology isn't." Continuing in his introduction to *Science Ponders Religion*, he writes:

> *"Before meteorology became a reputable science, the gods handled the lightning; before astronomy, mythical deities managed the planetary motions; before psychology and neurology, the devil inflicted our psychoses. Irrational beliefs arise naturally and persist, and sometimes usefully. But with the present explosive rise of science, primitive beliefs are in retreat. Effective religions must now pay closer attention to reasonableness, and salute more diligently our expanding knowledge of a myriad-starred universe with its probably very rich spread of organic life. The anthropomorphic one-planet Deity now has little appeal."*

In the past, after various delays and resistances, theology learned to live with Galileo, Copernicus, Newton, and more recently Darwin. The general attitude of the conferences was that religious beliefs and teachings should increasingly recognize scientific thinking not as an enemy or threat to religion, but as an ally in the great enterprise of making human living ever more significant and comprehensible.

For six successive years my father has devoted much time and hard work to IRAS. He believes that his book *Of Stars and Men* owes a good deal to the idealism and groping of the Star Island group. The concentrated program of papers, panels, discussions that IRAS offered was no cover-up for island vacationing. Mostly it was very serious business – but there was recreation, of course, and there were some light touches. My father tells of one time when "I was toastmaster at the concluding banquet of the week. We were just adjourning when some ardent and perplexed soul arose and demanded that Dr. Shapley give his definition of God. On the spur of the moment I said, well here is a provisional definition – a short one, a ten-word answer:

All Nature is God,

And all God is Nature."

They scribbled it in their notebooks, and adjourned and scattered, except for the next day's pre-boat breakfast. The Smith College waitress who was dishing out the oatmeal at the breakfast table on that final morning leaned over and whispered, 'Dr. Shapley, you are wrong about the definition of God.' So? I said, it was wrong? 'Yes,' she said, 'it was only nine words!' I thought to myself – I should keep away from theology and Smith girls! But in the nick of time an inspiration came "Ah Mary, I said, didn't you hear that tenth word *Amen?*"

A number of my father's lectures have been given in college chapels, a compliment to one who is and always has been unchurched. Once, a group of Unitarian ministers invited him to a conference. In the course of the discussion, he said, "Maybe you're no more religious than I am. We believe in the same general ethical principles. My interest, like yours, is in man's place in the Universe, the origin of man, his destiny." Before the evening was over one of the ministers said he believed that Dr. Shapley was the most religious man in the room; the others agreed. When people ask him point blank, as people will – do you believe in god? – he answers, "Yes, certainly I believe in you and me and the atoms and the stars – we are all God. I spell it N-A-T-U-R-E." My father admits that they go away rather baffled.

"Most astronomers are agnostics," he goes on to explain, "not atheists – that presumes more conviction than religion does. Scientists cannot accept blind faith. Ours is a perpetual inquiry; any firm acceptance of faith – in a scientific or a metaphysical or an aesthetic sense – brings inquiry to a halt."

In the second chapter of *Of Stars and Men*, he states, "There is no special grandeur in man's position." Many now agree with him. In the *American Rationalist* a reviewer of Shapley's book says:

> "One of Britain's most eminent present-day astronomers, Fred Hoyle, agrees with Harlow Shapley about the probability of life-supporting plan-ets throughout the universe. If these experts are correct, then we have yet another powerful reason for rejecting the traditional Christian theology of an omnipotent God whose primary concern was with the human race, for whom he sacrificed his only son, Jesus, in order to redeem it from sin. To be fair to the other creatures comparable to man throughout the Universe, God would have had to send Jesus to some hundred million planets to save them! Or did God have 100 million sons to do the job?"

But, "we need not be humiliated," says Chapter Two of *Of Stars and Men*:

> "There should be nothing very humiliating about our material incon-sequentiality. Are we debased by the greater speed of the sparrow, the larger size of the hippopotamus, the keener hearing of the dog, the finer detectors of odor possessed by insects? We can easily get adjusted to all of these evidences of our inferiority and maintain a feeling of importance and well-being. We should also take the stars in our stride. We should adjust ourselves to the cosmic facts. It is a magnificent Universe in which to play a part, however humble."

In May of 1962 my father gave an address at the annual convention of the Unitarian Universalists in Washington, attended by delegates from the entire eastern United States. He had a full house – a lot of puzzled and worried elders, but only a few young people. Introduced as the "world leader" in the concern about the fate of religion in an age of science, he reiterated his views on cosmic evolution. As usual when he approaches religion, his comments are a little rough on "the true believers in untruths."

My father has said, "Whether this lecturing is the best service I can give in this decade, I am not sure." However, the students, teachers and general public who have heard him seem to have no doubts. He has lectured since the middle twenties, but sporadically – abundantly only since retirement. Under the auspices of the Association of American Colleges, he has toured (fall and spring in the later years) covering a dozen or more colleges per tour. Although his lectures followed the same themes, each was different in detail. His repertoire included: space probes, galaxies, origin of life, religion in the age of science, poetry, and science (sometimes listed as Lower Criticism of the Higher Poetry), and cosmography. He also gave upon occasion competent illustrated lectures on his life-long hobby of ants.

He has often discussed the Democritan atomic speculations as presented in *De Rerum Natura*. "In my pagan moments," he says, "I like to quote from Lucretius: *Tantum Religio Potuit Suadere Malorum*, which I improperly translate as 'Enough Religion is Plenty.' But of course," he adds, "religion in the Lucretian sense is superstition – and too much superstition can indeed lead to evil – and so I accept the dictum of this writer of the greatest scientific poem of all time."

He notes that various church colleges in the Deep South where he has spoken are not offended by his pantheism or humanism, but "darn it, they go right on praying to their one-planet deities, asking for personal assistance." He feels, however, that perhaps he is slightly liberalizing many of the fundamentalists.

From time to time my father sends out from Sharon carbon-copy letters to offspring and offspring squared. One of them, headed *Some Miscellany from the Woods*, written at the age of 74, had a postscript on the envelope saying, "this letter remained un-mailed for several days – I have two overcoats." After giving a report on things as they seem in Sharon, he writes:

"Last week I did a job to a full house in Columbia University, and the night after at Brandeis University where I argued with faculty and students for three and a half hours. One more difficult lecture ahead – a debate with a nice rabbi on science and religion, in Boston.

"I may have a trip to Honolulu in September and to Star Island in July and maybe a California trip in August for the I.A.U. meetings and a short trip to Nantucket Island for the American Astronomical Society in June – otherwise I am grounded among the pines and maples."

A later letter tells me:

"I am on the road – just now in deep Texas. In St Paul I did ten talks in two days – entertaining a virus all the time; 13,000 teachers heard me in Cleveland – 4 to 5 million (they say) heard and saw me on the Jack Paar Show! Maybe now they have had enough. Numerous requests for talks and committee work – I'm rather pooped."

The inspiration he brings to students and faculties with his lively talks and informal discussions is obvious to anyone who reads his fan mail. Always he is invited back and the best we have heard in years is a common comment. President Francis Horn of the University of Rhode Island wrote, "I can't remember any time in my experience when an individual visiting the campus has made such an impact as you did, both on students and faculty;" and President William Scarborough of Baker University, "The impression he made on student minds will be a lifetime memory for them. His wit and brilliant satire created for us an impression of vitality and strength. Eight hundred individuals had an opportunity to hear, see, and be impressed by this great personality." My father's comment on all this praising is, "I'm still fooling them!"

Fooling them or no, it is evident he has a talent for discussing in simple language the complexities of scientific research. He makes a habit of assembling abundant concrete material and of stating his facts with enthusiasm and whimsical pleasantry. On a discussion panel or as a master of ceremonies he can be counted upon to set a lively pace sprinkled with humor. As a lecturer in some hundred colleges and universities, his aim is to incite more scholarship and more research in science, and in general to encourage his listeners to start thinking along broader lines.

In 1959 he gave the Virginia Educational Association Convention address on *Science and Peace*. The theme was *Homo*'s suicide or survival. He pointed to the fine example of the International Geophysical Year in which 66 nations were involved. "We in the I.G.Y. cooperate. We in the U.N. mostly expostulate." And he paused to curse the diplomats, admitting that the cursing was useless but gave him a bit of relief. He proposed more I.G.Y.-type ventures such as an International Medical Year or an International Culture Exchange Year. "We should all willingly ponder and work for such *Homo* savers – for it is not in our stars, dear Brutus, but in ourselves that we may find salvation."

In another of his talks under the title of *New Horizons in Creative Thinking* he concluded with a list of the ideals needed for these new horizons. Open mindedness with respect to the growth and bearing of knowledge of the material world, according to him, is first. Re-oriented piety is second, and follows naturally. After a particularly long and lively question period following this lecture, he posed a question and answered it himself, "Speaking of ideals – how about ideals for speech-makers? Simple – take an early opportunity and *sit down!*"

Let us now return for a more leisurely visit to the family's home in Sharon, New Hampshire. The large mailbox labeled SHAPLEY stands on Spring Hill Road where a country lane named Cross Road joins the paved highway. Cross seems a rather inappropriate, or at least, ambiguous name for this dirt road, arched with tall trees and bordered with dense woods. A more pleasant country road is hard to imagine. But Cross Road it is, and up this road a short way we come to two entrances spaced a hundred yards or so apart, each marked by rough stone posts half hidden with brambles. From these entrances two narrow driveways wend their separate ways toward the house.

Harlow and Martha in Sharon

One leads up a gentle hill between the meadows and past the twin pines, past the main house site and the old apple tree, and then down to join the other driveway, which has come through the woods, past the abandoned sunken garden, to the front of the barn.

A few months after the Shapleys acquired this property in 1941 the large house burned to the ground, leaving only the chimney and bathtubs and an empty cellar hole. After that, the smaller white frame guest house became *the* house; a potting shed became the guest house or dormitory as it was first called. The barn stayed a barn, but for the Shapleys it served a different purpose than it had for the farmers preceding them. It contained only a little antique hay left by the former owner and an old saddle or two. The only animals that now come in and out are the unwelcome porcupines that seem to like the taste of old wood. In the Shapley barn is a play room, the recreation center, one of the overflow libraries, the tool headquarters, the garage in bad weather for one lucky car; it is also a storage place with a capacity such that nothing the least bit interesting need be thrown away.

My brother Carl, the family architect, with much imagination converted one wing of the barn, consisting of a box stall and several storerooms, into a livable apartment of four roomettes, a shower bath, and a screened sleeping porch which was nicknamed the Snoring Gulch. This apartment became the Studio and is a place where one can play records (particularly the classics) with the volume up to roaring satisfaction without upsetting the household up on the hill. You can also play a small, old, foot-pedal organ there and not be heard, and in the barn, itself, you can play ping pong, the piano, and the radio; a new flagstone floor makes square dancing possible for the energetic. The barn is also good for sudden rained-out picnics and for private music festivals that do not need to attain the perfection of Tanglewood or the close-by MacDowell Music and Art Colony.

For children, the barn has an additional fascination in the cupola, 35 feet above the ground. While adults go up for the 360-degree view which includes Mt. Monadnock, Pack Monadnock, North Pack, Temple Mountain, the twin peaks of Kidder and most of the Temple Range, the small fry (or offspring under eight) climb the stairs and easy ladder with pockets bulging with marbles. In the cupola is the origin of the marble chute. With the help of their grandfather, they had joined together a dozen or so sections of old pipe that had been lying around in the barn for years. The pipes, connected with funnels and other makeshift fittings, run a zig-zag course through the rooms of the barn, always slightly inclined so that the marbles inserted at the top infallibly go clanking zig-zagging down to the ground, making a delightful racket as they fall into a large pail on the barn floor. The cupola also houses a wasps' nest under the roof, but the wasps never seem to complain about the marble enterprise. And if you look carefully you will find a weathered volume of the *Complete Works of Shakespeare* tucked under the cupola eaves!

As the years passed, Sharon began to acquire a personality of its own. There were improvements, of course, and plenty of changes just for the fun of changing. After completing his Studio, Carl turned his talents to the interior of the once guest house and this ordinary seven-room house became something worthy of before and after illustrations in the magazine *House Beautiful*. Next, he worked on the Dormitory which, with a storeroom added to make it L shaped, became the guest house beautiful – a joyful place for family or guests to live in semi-seclusion. Opposite this L he designed a flagstone barbecue area where a gathering too large for inside dining could be fed and where you could burn the dirty dishes afterwards.

The view of the Temple Range across the canyon as seen from the rear porch was my father's responsibility – he kept the maples and birches from growing up too fast and hiding it. The woods soon began to acquire trails leading to the far corners of the property. Willis, Alan, and Lloyd all had a hand in this early woods-work. For arm-chair hikers they made a map of their twisty trails, harder work for them than brush clearing. The map made a pretty network on paper. However, after studying it the trailblazers rushed into the woods to make a new kind of trail – a perfectly straight one!

Exploring and trail-making was fun, but my father was always looking for more unusual activities. This is how the Double Pine Ring came into being. Lloyd and Carl helped him lay out and transplant trees in 60- and 45-foot diameters, respectively. Nursed through the dry summer with pails of water these trees thrived; they grew up and out (now they are 30 feet tall) making a solid double ring that one can penetrate only by forcing the branches apart. In the center of the ring is a small spruce, and at the lowest side of this sloping enclosure is a discarded barn door, placed on the ground as a stage for Greek plays. But nobody has the time to write the tragedies – the stage has waited for ten years. The upper half of the circle waits for spectators to sit on the grass among abundant wild flowers. In the meantime, the children race around between the rings where the ground is covered with slippery pine needles.

Moving small trees about became a favorite pastime. In an open place next to the sunken garden, Lloyd designed and constructed a maze using 600 baby spruce and junipers, mostly hauled up from the banks of the brook. At one point there was an over- and under-pass to the delight of small fry and to the risk of adults. For the old hands who had learned the solution the game was to see how fast you could run through the maze with its 13 dead ends. Early in its life some of the trees had a hard time adapting and there would be an annual summer job of replacing the dead ones, so that people couldn't cheat by going through unintended open spaces.

In later years a four-story tree house was built by the Matthews family in a close cluster of five slim, 75-year-old, pines. Later it was reinforced and improved by other Sharon visitors. From this structure you have a marvelous view of the not-so-marvelous baseball diamond and the little wooded section, which is named Periwinkle Park for its lush green ground covering. Along with the elaborate house there are two tire swings on ropes from a nearby maple.

We moved trees, but also the trees moved by themselves, or at least so it seemed. Always the woods were trying to swallow the meadow. Bushes and small trees would appear each spring and summer. To cope with this problem my father bought what he called a whang-doodle. This was a dangerous toy, a type of power mower that would cut everything that got in its way, and therefore there was much ordering of children stand back when this roaring piece of machinery was put into use and Granddaddy and the whang-doodle went out to retrieve the meadow. Grandmother's electric lawnmower was more tame and sociable. Anyone who was willing to tread lightly and push gently was allowed to operate it on the tender front lawn. The worst that could happen here would be to end up well twisted in the long cord. Around the house were Grandmother's flower beds. Out in the meadow flourished Granddaddy's wildflowers. If the children didn't learn about nature from their grandfather, they missed a fine opportunity. One summer when my June was twelve years old, she and he catalogued the Sharon wildflowers. Several years later her brother, Melvin took up the botanical project and temporarily became a flower expert, finding over forty different varieties.

My father always enjoyed painting, painting with house-painter's paint, that is. The barn painting project was always on the job list. It is a big barn, bigger than both houses put together and over the years we all had a hand in it. Each year someone would tackle a side and some others would finish where the tired tackler left off – and all this was done with care and conservatism. But not so for the little well-house hidden away in the Dark Forest behind the barn. After its paint job was done it was nick-named the Gingerbread House for it got a coat of pink and yellow on one side and red, white, and blue stripes on another. What a gorgeous sight it was when the painter and the painter's helpers finished. The years have done little to tone it down! The Dark Forest is one of our favorite playgrounds. Here there is a deck tennis court, stakes for pitching horseshoes, a rope swing, and plenty of picnic benches.

There is an ancient but well-preserved buggy, a topless surrey waiting in the corner of the barn for a horse that never came. This, the Shapleys pulled out into the sunlight and washed and oiled. Fortunately, there was some paint nearby. The body got a new coat of black, the wheel spokes turned pink and the under springs became a bright yellow. Probably no horse after this gay transformation would be seen dead hitched to it – but we had willing two-legged horses – fathers and grandfather who would pull a load of gleeful children down the driveways.

Porcupine trouble is common in New Hampshire and if you care to produce the ears of your catch, you can collect 50 cents a pair from the Governor or someone. Each spring they attack the weeping willow by the wishing well near the old house site; each year it becomes sadder, but it never quite dies. Little by little a porch at the back of the barn where some salt once was stored is disappearing, via porcupines. One summer when the marauders began making frequent nocturnal visits to the house, my eldest son Bruce decided to take action. A switch, some wire, and an old telephone he found in the barn were all that were needed. When a porcupine ventured onto the house porch steps, the alarm would sound in the barn bunk room. Bruce and his younger brother Melvin would jump out of their beds and in their bare feet and pajamas armed with flash lights and clubs, they would go rushing up to the house after the embarrassed animals. For some reason they didn't bag as many of these destroyers as they expected to, but they earned eight dollars for their hunting ability from the Granddaddy who was satisfied.

Harlow in 1942 with grandchildren Bruce (L) and June (C) Matthews and Sarah Shapley (R)

There were two series of grandchildren; my brother Willis's Sarah and Deborah, and my three, June, Bruce, and Melvin who grew up simultaneously on opposite coasts but collided during the summers in Sharon; and later there was Alan's Carol, and Lloyd's Peter and Christopher who came along after Series I was pretty much grown up. Or at least, I should say I *thought* they were, and decided they could go alone one summer to Sharon. I even boasted they would need little grandparental supervision – they could relax – I could relax. Almost at once I got back a letter from Bruce (who is the never-write-unless-you-are-provided-with-self-addressed-postcard type) saying, "I'm having a wonderful time learning to fly a Piper Cub and Melvin goes along to take aerial movies of Sharon." Neither boy was old enough to get a common ordinary driver's license for at least two years. I swallowed twice and wrote back for particulars. My brother Carl, it seems, had taken them under his wing; but since Carl was an amateur pilot this under his wing had a thrilling literal meaning. Their air adventures, however, were short-lived, because flying is an expensive hobby for boys with small pocket money. But now we know the Sharon Pine Rings are very impressive from the air. Melvin's movies of them were a great success.

Besides grandchildren Sharon of course also had ants. There were always experiments in progress and frequent inspection trips to the various ant sites. I don't know how many varieties of ants Sharon can boast, but "there are some 3500 kinds of ants known," the Granddaddy has said, "and eventually there will be 10,000 if we remain civilized and curious." He likes to display his ant vocabulary to the small fry in the hopes that a bit of information will stick. "*Liometopum* is the name of a genus," he would begin. "There are several species, one being *Apiculatum* – pretty names, aren't they? Other genera in the sub-family *Dolichoderinea* are *Tapinoma*, *Iridomyrmex*, and *Dolichoderus*. Funny, isn't it – I can remember the first and second names of fifty kinds of ants, but demmed if I know the middle names of my offspring or their birthdays!"

A few years ago, there was an ant tragedy at Sharon. A big nest of *Formica Exsectoides* which my father had watched and played with for a dozen years, moved itself elaborately, carrying eggs and pupae, from the vegetable garden area past the dormitory to cracks in the foundation wall of the house porch ten feet from the kitchen door. They were prospering. My father set up a speed trap to measure their activity as a function of the air temperature – the same as he had done forty years ago in California. "I did not plan to publish any new results," he says. "I did not want to spoil a good hobby by turning into a bad semi-pro. The curtain pole that was to serve as the runway for the ants seeking sweet moisture was inserted in the ground alongside of the stone wall nest. It stuck up a foot above the porch floor and was baited with cantaloupe. The trap was marked off in 30-centimeter sections – all was set for a happy summer of telling accurately the temperature not by the thermometer on the nearby wall, but by the speed of the ants. It was a fine set-up right at my back door. Then catastrophe! Twenty feet away, concealed in the same wall, was a nest of another ant – another species, black and bigger than my *Exsectoides*. A war ensued. For two days the fight went on. I could do nothing about it. It was a dramatic case of genocide – the complete wipe-out of a nest; my research was finished, for the *Exsectoides* is rare in this latitude. I see only a few around now and then, and many of the black murderers. The latter will not climb rods and cooperate in the advance of science. So that is that."

In the same vicinity, on the kitchen window shutter, there was another natural exhibit that took his mind off his various formicine sorrows. A big paper nest of *Vespa Maculate* appeared, menacingly for anti-wasp enthusiasts. The milk man, for one, refused to make his delivery to the back door; and my father defended the rights of the wasps. The nest was nothing insignificant. It measured two feet long and one foot thick. In his lectures on social insects he often refers to this nest, and the grandeur and antiquity of its civilization. "For 30 million years the wasp has been making nests in trees and the ground, and, when eventually man showed up, on his barn and house sides; it was making waterproof paper millions of years before the ancient and highly praised Chinese discovered the art of making paper from wood pulp. Furthermore, the wasp, and also the ants, knew and practiced altruism, civic duty, birth control, food conservation, loyalty and other noble virtues that man has only recently introduced into his culture."

While my father's hobby goes on with as much enthusiasm as in the old days, he hasn't done any recent serious research on ants. But his old work has not been forgotten. In 1959 some scientists at Brookhaven National Laboratory were working on certain properties of tendons and muscle fibers. They found an old paper of Shapley's on the *Thermokinetics of Dolichoderine Ants* and discovered that his formulae of 1920 could be successfully applied.

If my mother thought her social duties would taper off when she left the director's residence in Cambridge, she missed her guess. While no one kept any records, friends sprinkled with family came and come and keep coming so that Sharon is a lively rather than a restful place in the summer. My father writes about her activities when she is too busy to write. "Gretchen had a tea and a dinner for 22 people – important friends – the executive board of the IRAS – elegant and expensive but appreciated – and a lot of leftovers! She hopes to catch up enough with running this too big establishment to do some gardening, but it seems as soon as she finishes with one wave of guests and social obligations another comes."

Even in this rather isolated spot in New Hampshire some sixty miles northwest of Cambridge, people manage to find the Shapleys. Sometimes they telephoned first, sometimes they arrived unannounced. A reporter showed up recently with his photographer in tow and luckily for him found my father at home with time to talk. The interview began with the usual questions for which my father, accustomed to interviews, had quick answers.

"Dr. Shapley, what do you think of astrology?"

"It's superstition."

"Are you superstitious?"

"No – but demmed if I will sleep 13 in a bed on a Friday night!"

"Then there is nothing at all in astrology?"

"Sure, there's something in it. Here's a story that might interest you: The Second World War had been going bitterly for a couple of years. Hitler was winning on all fronts. There was much talk or gossip in Washington about the Czech astrologer whom Hitler consulted. One of the prominent Washington officials – a link between the scientists and the military – was apparently touched by this situation, or was it his wife? In any case, from the scientific administration came the request that I examine and report on a New York astrologer who claimed great success. In fact, he insisted that by his astrological research, using all nine major planets, he had predicted the Pearl Harbor disaster. He had to make heavy calculations, he claimed, and therefore he did not finish his prediction until December 8, 1941. The blow fell, you remember on December 7, 1941. If the government had given him money for assistance, he could have saved hundreds of lives. Now he wanted money to help in future work. He claimed he had cast the Horoscope of Wall Street, of the Battle of Lexington, of the Japanese emperor, F.D.R. and so forth – a truly wonderful man! A City College of New York professor of psychology and I met in New York on a quiet Sunday morning, and by appointment we went to the astrologer's apartment. Now, a part of the moral code of investigating operators in the black arts is that one is kind, does not violate the ground rules, does not blow up and challenge the operator. We played the code – listened to his claims, said we would report to Washington, which pleased this sixty-year old fraud – for he was a complete fraud. He showed pages of numbers, strangely labeled. He used a slide rule for god knows what. My interest faded when he showed his major tabulation, the study of which was basic in solving all future mysteries. A quick glance at this major horoscope table showed that he had simply copied out of the back of a schoolbook the table of natural sines and cosines – he had not expected an astronomer to know that table! For his Pearl Harbor prediction, he had tied together Pluto the god of darkness, ant mounds, Fujiyama, Japanese, Bang! Some of the miraculous steps I don't remember – but you can see how it's done. I made my report to Dr. Vannevar Bush the President's chief scientific advisor, and nothing more was heard of the astrologer, or the Washington foolishness. Dr. Bush, of course, knew and argued that astrology is all bunkum; but it is a rather profitable business for the charlatans who practice astrology on the dupes. I have been told that there is about $30,000,000 a year in the business: so, when I am asked by a glassy-eyed believer if I think there is something in astrology I say yes indeed there are millions in it!"

"Dr. Shapley, what about the repeated stories of flying saucers observed by so many persons – can't we believe in them either?"

"It's all nonsense. I'm convinced there is no verifiable truth in the reports. People see something, but not vehicles from outer space. All the reports of UFOs – Unidentified Flying Objects – have been investigated in detail by competent people. In nearly every case the saucers have been explained beyond question as natural phenomena or as experiences with which we are fully familiar. A very tiny percentage of reports have not been explained. The reason for this is simply that the reporter didn't provide enough evidence to let us form a convincing judgment. The UFOs are good stuff for science fiction and that's about all."

Another reporter at another time, trying to match my father's humor, reacted to Shapley's announcement that there may be a hundred million planetary systems supporting life, in this manner:

"Ever since reading Dr. Shapley's estimate I have been dreaming, not of seeing flying saucers but whole flying pantries. If, as Shapley says a hundred million planets may have different kinds of life in a hundred million different stages, we can imagine they whirl through space with such diversions as children, mortgages, bingo and war. Some may have people who have lost the art of locomotion altogether, but developed two heads so they can think through their problems better; and mammals that grow weary and put down roots and trees that get tired of the view and learn to walk? There may be some real dillies up there in space, so Shapley says, but if there are some forms of life so much smarter than Homo sapiens up there in space, then why haven't they been down to see us, instead of waiting for us to figure out the means of getting up to see them?"

When asked by a reporter what he thought of our program and the race to send a man to the Moon and back, he replied: "I won't say it's possible or impossible to send a man to the Moon and get him back, but if I had ten billion dollars I would sooner spend it on humanity here on Earth than on one of these stunts."

Another time, interviewed after his recent trip to Russia, he spoke of the friendliness of the Russian people in general. "The Russian intelligentsia have all studied English, which I feel is much to their credit. It is not to our credit, on the other hand, that the Americans have little knowledge of Russia, and none of their language."

Discussing Russia further, he said: "The difference between Russian and American education in science is mainly one of method. In straight technical education the Russians are definitely ahead. But I happen to be strongly in favor of our liberal education – certainly it won't be easy – but all that matters, is that we remain good. I don't believe we have to be first in everything."

Asked at the same time about his trip to Australia, he said: "I spent four weeks there early in 1961. I flew from New York via Moscow and Delhi to Sydney, and returned from Sydney via Fiji, Honolulu to Los Angeles thereby testing the hypothesis that has long been bruited about – namely, that the planet is spherical. I did the usual things expected of a tourist, such as being photographed scratching the throat of a mother kangaroo."

He stayed in Canberra most of the time. It is the federal capital and has a new and rather outstanding university. A few miles out of town is the Mount Stromlo Observatory with about eight telescopes and a beautiful view of distant mountains. It is here that Professor Bok is stationed as director; he is one of the half dozen best known scientists in Australia. As a guest of Dr. Bok and the government of Australia, he lectured and conferred with graduate students, took part in meetings, went on various long drives to see the rivers and woods in this part of the country. From Sydney he took an air trip into the hinterland to visit the site where the world's best radio telescope is now situated. The second largest in the world at that time, it is located at Parkes, far from electrical disturbances. He also found time to visit some Australian entomologists and their experiments.

But to return to the reporter who invited himself to Sharon, his final query was: "Do you have sons also in the field of astronomy?"

"No – Willis is with the Bureau of the Budget in Washington; Alan is with the Radio Physics Laboratory of the National Bureau of Standards; Lloyd is with the Rand Corporation, a mathematician of much ability; Carl is in the field of Education and the Fine Arts. No astronomers, but I am naturally pleased that in the recent edition of *American Men of Science*, my write up is bracketed by the citing of two scientific sons – for Alan comes alphabetically before Harlow, and Harlow before Lloyd. I wonder if there are many such trios."

My father notes that he is accumulating scientific progeny in the second generation as well. In April 1962 he went to Washington to attend meetings of the National Academy of Sciences, which happened to be scheduled simultaneously with the spring meeting of the American Physical Society. His granddaughter, June Matthews, arriving in Washington and learning of this coincidence, asked him: "As long as you're in town, would you like to come and hear me give my first scientific paper?" He went to the Physical Society session, and later reported with pardonable pride, "June's fifteen-minute report of her work on an experiment in nuclear physics was excellently done!"

When world news is discouraging my father easily becomes depressed. Being optimistic, he doesn't allow this mood to last very long, but he remains impatient that man has so much trouble living with man on this planet. In one such sober mood I asked him if he would reflect on his personal troubles in the past – passed disappointments and errors.

"Errors and faults – that's easy," he said. "Once I offered to give a paper at the Examiner Club on my blunders, but they allowed me only a half hour for the job, so it wasn't worthwhile. As to faults, I can rattle off a few in fast succession; a) too ambitious for the comfort of others; b) too anxious for the Harvard College Observatory to go to the top; c) too many white lies; d) too superficial in my studies; e) not enough playing with the offspring; and others to the end of the alphabet.

"My few disappointments are harder to remember. One or two are better not talked about. In attempting to raise money for the Harvard

Observatory I naturally had many financial disappointments – everybody does. There were disappointments, at times, in connection with the family. None of that is very interesting. There was one perhaps that is. When I finished with the Observatory and started my lectures on cosmography, I hoped that the Harvard Corporation would make me an honor-filled University Professor – but they didn't. The President's excuse was that the public might surmise that the University agreed with my so-called liberal political views. That was at the time when liberal politics was identified with radicalism, even with communism. The fact that I have never met but one or two communists in America in all my life, never had any truck with communists, never have been asked to join up with them – all this does not count among the suspicious. Percy Bridgman,[4] Zechariah Chafee, Werner Jaeger, Roscoe Pound all were University Professors and because of my wide scholastic ranging many thought I should be. But President Conant claimed he took the matter to the Corporation and that it said *no*. I don't know why we dig up old irritations. I have plenty of work and problems ahead of me. Too many. Sometimes it's a nuisance being conspicuous."

Another question my father is frequently asked is: "What do you consider your most substantial contributions in the field of astronomy?" For this he has compiled a list of eleven:

1. *Calibration of the period-luminosity relation for Cepheid variable stars as a measuring device for the Universe.*

2. *Discovery that the center of the Galaxy is some 25,000 light years distant from the Earth in the direction of Sagittarius, thus showing the eccentric position of Earth and Sun in the Milky Way.*

3. *The proposal of the pulsation theory of Cepheid variables, and the demonstration of the associated variability of the Cepheid spectra.*

4. *Measurement of the diameter (100,000 light years) of the Milky Way as a galaxy through determination of the distances of outlying globular star clusters and cluster-type variables.*

5. *Discovery of a kind of galaxy (the Sculptor type) hitherto unknown, which turns out to be a low-population dwarf spheroidal galaxy, and very common in neighboring space.*

6. *Survey of the opacity of the interstellar dust clouds of the southern Milky Way.*

7. *The discovery in 1915 of the characteristic color-luminosity relation for the bright stars in globular clusters. This pioneering work has recently been much extended by Alan Sandage, Halton Arp, and others using the Hale 200-inch Palomar telescope.*

8. *Derivation from faint variable stars in high latitudes of the evidence of a low-density spherical corona or halo of stars surrounding the discoidal galactic system.*

9. *The proof (with an accuracy of one part in 20,000,000,000) of the equal velocity of blue and yellow light, through the timing of variable stars in globular clusters.*

10. *The discovery and exploration of the peculiar distribution of period lengths of Cepheid variables in the Magellanic Clouds.*

11. *The writing of a small volume Of Stars and Men, which has emphasized the importance of modern astrophysics to the other sciences and to religious philosophy.*

The late Dr. Nicholson of Mt. Wilson, speaking of the old Pasadena days, once told me that Shapley, having just undergone the ordeal of making his first public speech, received a fee, and remarked, "Now I can buy my baby daughter some shoes – so *no more speech-making!*" Now, some thousand speeches later, his daughter has shoes – I'm even buying my own – but my father is still lecturing. "I do try to be the best science lecturer in the country," he says, "and I almost make it, thanks to the fast pace I set and my lovely subject."

Dr. Payne-Gaposchkin has said, "He is the outstanding exponent of the inter-relation of science and society and possesses the alert, direct, realistic response to the Universe as it is, and the rare power to realize it and describe it."

"It's pleasant to know that people think you are OK" my father says, "and I suppose praise and flattery are all right if you don't inhale. But frankly I'm a little tired of me – maybe I should have talked less and tried to push further into the unknown than I did. But if through my lecturing I have incited fresh new inquirers who will continue the assault on the unknown, all this speech-making may be justified. I hope so. The revolutions of the planet are beginning to creep up on me. Let us enjoy the sunset over Mt. Monadnock, the asters and goldenrod in the meadow, and salute the Perseids that will shoot into our atmosphere tonight."

Harlow Shapley enjoying his cigar in Sharon

AFTERWORD

Mildred Louise Shapley was born on February 15, 1915 to Harlow and Martha Betz Shapley, their first child, in Pasadena, California. She would eventually have four younger brothers. In 1921 the family moved to Cambridge, MA, when Harlow Shapley became the Director of the Harvard College Observatory. Mildred inherited a passion for science, particularly astronomy, from her parents. She attended the University of Michigan, received a B.S. in Physical Science, and was elected to the honor society Phi Beta Kappa.

She married her college sweetheart, Ralph Matthews, a music education major, in 1937; her daughter June was born in 1939; her son Bruce in 1941. The family moved to Altadena, CA in 1945, where son Melvin was born and which was their residence for about 20 years. During this time Mildred pursued a scientific career as a research assistant to Professor Jesse Greenstein, an astrophysicist at Caltech, but her life was strongly centered on her family. She once said that, despite everything else she had done, she felt that raising her children was her most important vocation. When June, Bruce, and Melvin were essentially grown up, she and Ralph adopted their fourth child, Martha, as a baby in 1963.

The Matthews family was close and did many things together. Road trips were a frequent activity, including travels all over southern California and beyond, seeing the sights and exploring the environment. The family traveled across the country to spend summers with the Shapley grandparents in Sharon, New Hampshire, often making stops at national parks or to visit other relatives along the way.

Mildred loved science and loved to travel, was particularly drawn to Italy, perhaps as a result of her love for Italian opera. She set out to learn Italian, and took several trips on her own to Italy. Her favorite place in the world was Venice, to which she returned many times, including several visits while she was in her 90s, accompanied by family members.

One of her early trips to Italy led to an association with two Italian astronomers, Margherita Hack and her husband Aldo De Rosa. Margherita, who would become director of the *Osservatorio Astronomico* in Trieste, offered Mildred a job. Young Martha spent her early years in Trieste, attending a Montessori School, before returning to the United States in 1970, when Mildred was offered a position at the Lunar and Planetary Laboratory at the University of Arizona in Tucson. She became the Editor of a series of reference books on Space Sciences which eventually extended to 30 volumes, and held this position until she retired in 1996 at age 81. For this work she received the Harold Masursky Award for meritorious service to planetary science from the American Astronomical Society in 1993.

After Mildred's retirement she set off the see the world in earnest. She traveled adventurously to every continent except Antarctica. She climbed the pyramids of Egypt, the Great Wall of China, and the Harbor Bridge in Sydney, Australia. She rode on practically every conveyance imaginable: small aircraft, boats, camels, elephants, mules, dogsleds, ziplines. And whenever there was an opera being performed in town, she'd take that in. In December, 2012, at age 97, she traveled to Stockholm, Sweden as a guest of her brother Lloyd Shapley who was being awarded the Nobel Prize in Economics. She had a front-row seat for many of the festivities.

When she was interviewed at her 100th birthday party, in February 2015, she said that she was "still having fun in this beautiful world." And indeed, until just a few months shy of her 101st birthday, she was having fun, and living life to the fullest. And wondering whether she would be able to make one more "farewell trip" to her favorite city, Venice. Sadly, that was not to be.

All good things must come to an end, and in mid-August of 2015, Mildred's health began to fail. She had abdominal surgery, from which she recovered, but the recovery took a long time. The problem recurred in January of 2016, and she was perfectly clear that she didn't want another surgery. She said that she had lived a long life, and was ready to take leave of the world, but she wanted to do so at home. My sister Martha and I brought her home from the hospital, after the doctors and nurses had gathered in her room and sung "Happy Birthday" and presented her with a bouquet of red roses. We had no idea how much longer she would have, but she spent a pretty good ten days, spending some time outside in the garden and watching the birds at her feeder. Martha and I were with her continuously, and our brother Melvin and his wife Donna came to visit. Our other brother, Bruce, at his home in New Hampshire, was in touch by telephone. At the end she was in some pain, but was strong enough to say goodbye to each of us. She died on February 11, 2016, just four days shy of her 101st birthday. She is survived by her four children, seven grandchildren, twelve great-grandchildren, and numerous loving nieces and nephews.

Mildred's father, Harlow Shapley, known to all as "HS," loomed large in her life, from her youth to her old age. She idolized him. She had an excellent memory and was continually regaling us with stories of her childhood and young womanhood. (Many of these found their way into her book.) It took me some time to recognize how special these lives – hers and HS's – really were. Even before I realized the importance of HS's scientific work I was struck with his ebullient personality and wide range of interests. This made the summers that we spent with the grandparents in Sharon really special – woods, trails, ants, gardens, wildflowers, trees, brooks, construction and painting projects, conversation, his sense of humor, etc. And the lucky child who got to light his after-dinner cigar, which was always accompanied by exciting spurts of flame coming out the end!

In my childhood I mainly recall Martha Betz Shapley (MBS)'s role as that of providing sumptuous meals in Sharon. I especially remember corn on the cob fresh from a nearby farm stand, and the large chest freezer in the basement that held at least a dozen flavors of locally made ice cream in gallon containers. And a constant supply of home-made toll-house cookies. At that point MBS was simply "Grandmother." Later I came to know and appreciate other aspects of her personality.

Those were magical times for my brothers Bruce and Melvin and me in Sharon. HS managed to provide an environment full of inquiry, creativity, and just plain fun. We learned about ants and collected wildflowers; I recall having identified over a hundred different ones which I pressed into a note-book (the flowers, not the ants, of course). Maybe strangely, there was no telescope on the property, though we did a fair amount of naked-eye star-gazing. Once HS took me fishing in one of the two brooks – he looked very professional in his waders. I think that we caught only one 6-inch trout, which MBS dutifully cooked for supper. He planted a vegetable garden, with some success; I recall eating what he called the "rabbit lettuce," because "the rabbit let us…" We learned the rules of baseball, as HS was a devoted follower of the Boston Red Sox. MBS, too, with her prodigious memory, could recite the batting averages of most of the players. There was no television, so we spent many lazy afternoons listening to the games on the radio. I still remember our jubilation when Ted Williams, who was our hero, hit a home run, which of course he did frequently.

The Matthews family were the most frequent summer visitors to Sharon, although occasionally Mildred's oldest brother Willis appeared with his wife Virginia and their two daughters, Sarah and Deborah. Mildred's youngest brother, Carl, was pretty much a permanent resident. I don't recall either of the two middle brothers, Alan and Lloyd, spending much time there. They were pretty well ensconced in their homes in Boulder, CO and Santa Monica, CA, respectively, and busy with their careers. Also, they were both bachelors until the mid-1950s.

I eventually became aware of MBS as more than "simply" a wonderful grandmother. She was a complex person with many talents and a formi-dable intellect, whose achievements were, understandably but regrettably, overshadowed by HS's. As HS recounts in his quasi-autobiography *Through Rugged Ways to the Stars*, he first met Martha Betz in a mathematics class at the U. of Missouri; "she sat in the front row and knew all the answers." She has been acknowledged as the better mathematician of the pair, and applied her skills to assisting HS in the completion of his Ph.D. thesis at Princeton. (She was a graduate student at Bryn Mawr at the time, where she had received a scholarship in philology!) Following their marriage, she continued her research in astronomy, despite the demands of a growing family, and published a number of papers, both before and after their move from Mt. Wilson to Harvard. This work inevitably diminished as her duties as the "First Lady of Harvard College Observatory" burgeoned. I am sure that the entire Observatory family – astronomers, students, and visitors – appreciated and admired her principally as the most gracious of hostesses. She appeared to relish this role, inspired by HS's boundless enthusiasm for people and for entertaining. Did her lack of a parallel scientific career cause her disappointment or frustration? I wish that I had been able to talk about this with her. I recall occasionally seeing cracks in her cheerful demeanor, but on the whole she seemed contented with her life, and was deeply devoted to HS and to her children and grandchildren.

HS continued lecturing at colleges and universities until he was in his early 80s. But in the late 1960s age began catching up with him at an accelerating pace – he had developed Parkinson's disease and his eyesight had begun to fail. He had always been a voracious reader and had accumulated an enormous library. One of my fondest memories of Sharon was the profusion of books in practically every room, on every conceivable topic from scientific works to classic fiction and nonfiction to detective stories. Whenever I visited I could always count on finding something interesting to pore through. It was very sad when he could no longer read, neither for pleasure nor to keep up with the literature in his field. I'm not sure which bothered him the most. Once he saw me reading a Perry Mason novel and asked if I would mind reading it aloud to him – of course I didn't mind. And he would ask me questions about new developments in physics and astronomy. I could do pretty well with the former (*e.g.* neutrinos) but not so well with the latter (*e.g.* quasars).

Despite his deteriorating health he struggled to retain his good humor, and sparks of his brilliant personality would occasionally burst through. Mildred and her daughter Martha had returned to the US from Italy in 1970, and I know that he enjoyed seeing and interacting with his youngest grandchild.

After a Christmas visit in 1971 with their son Alan and his family, HS and MBS decided to remain in Boulder, CO rather than return to the harsh New England winter. They rented an apartment near Alan's home, but after a few months his needs became too great for her to manage, and he moved to a nursing home.

I still recall the day in October, 1972 – I had a position at Rutgers University at the time – when my cousin Deborah Shapley telephoned to tell me that HS had passed away. I was numbed by the news, but not grief-stricken, as I felt that I had already gone through a period of mourning him. Later, speaking with Mildred, I learned that she felt the same way.

MBS moved to Tucson to live with Mildred and her daughter. Although MBS's health was failing by this time, she was able, with the assistance of the nurse who was caring for her, to make a three-week "farewell visit" to Sharon one summer in the late 1970s. I was living in Cambridge at the time, and was delighted when visiting her to see how much "at home" in Sharon she appeared to be. She knew exactly where she was, and where everything in the house was. She passed away peacefully in Tucson in 1981 at age 91.

A granddaughter of Carol Shapley Etter, Alan Shapley's daughter, was born on June 5, 2016 and was named Harlow Emerson Etter in honor of her illustrious great-great-grandfather.

June L. Matthews (2020)

NOTES

CHAPTER ONE

1. In 1915 the Mt. Wilson Observatory, high in the San Gabriel Mountains overlooking Pasadena, was the world's leading astronomical observatory, with superb year-round seeing conditions. It operated a 60-inch reflecting telescope – the largest in the world – and was in the process of fielding a 100-inch reflecting telescope (the Hooker Telescope) that would be commissioned in 1918. The Harvard College Observatory had an extraordinary collection of photographic plates of the skies, but its telescopes were more modest, and the astronomical climate less favorable, than Mt. Wilson's.

2. Asteroid 878 *Mildred* was discovered by Harlow Shapley [HS] and his colleague Seth Nicholson on 6 September 1916 using the 60-inch reflector on Mt. Wilson. They continued to observe the minor planet through October 18th of that year, but it was then subsequently lost for nearly 75 years until it was rediscovered on 10 April 1991. Located in the asteroid belt between the orbits of Mars and Jupiter, 878 *Mildred* takes 3.63 years to orbit the sun.

3. Willis Harlow Shapley, the second child of HS and Martha Betz Shapley was born in Pasadena on 2 March 1917, and died in Washington, on 24 October 2005. He attended Harvard for two years before transferring to the University of Chicago, where he graduated in 1938. He enjoyed a distinguished civil service career as both a budget analyst and a science administrator. He joined NASA in 1965 where he had oversight for

MILDRED SHAPLEY MATTHEWS | *SHAPLEY'S ROUND TABLE*

budgetary, legislative, and international affairs. He played a pivotal role in shaping America's space program and ensuring the success of the Apollo missions.

4. Alan Horace Shapley, their third child, was born in Pasadena on 23 March 1919, and died in Boulder, Colorado on 20 October 2006. He graduated from Harvard in 1940 and pursued a long and highly decorated career as a geophysicist/space scientist, beginning with the Department of Terrestrial Magnetism at the Carnegie Institution of Washington and concluding with the National Oceanic and Atmospheric Administration. He was a noted authority on solar-terrestrial interactions and one of the principal organizers of the International Geophysical Year Program (1957 – 1958). He was also an accomplished cellist and a generous patron of the arts.

5. Martha Betz was born 3 August 1890, in Kansas City, Missouri to Louise Wittig (*Grossmama*) and Carl Betz. She married HS on 14 April 1914. She passed away in Tucson, Arizona on 24 January 1981. Martha had three sisters who lived with their mother in Kansas City. *Tante* Annette or Nettie (1886 – 1987) and *Tante* Alma (1888 – 1978) did not marry. The youngest sister, *Tante* Louise Julia Betz Woods (1898 – 1988) was born just after the tragic and premature death of her father.

6. Edward Charles Pickering (1846 – 1919) was the fourth director of the Harvard College Observatory [HCO] from 1 February 1877 until his death 42 years later. He created the world's largest program in photometric, photographic, and spectroscopic stellar research. After the death of Henry Draper, Pickering secured the interest and financial support of Draper's widow, Mary Ann Palmer Draper, for the Observatory to continue and greatly extend the work that her husband had begun. Pickering initiated the practice of employing a cadre of talented women to analyze the copious amounts of data gleaned from the extensive photographic plate collection. Their story is the subject of Dava Sobel's *The*

254

Glass Universe: How the Ladies of the Harvard Observatory Took the Measure of the Stars.

7. Annie Jump Cannon (1863 – 1941) is credited with classifying the spectra of over a quarter-million stars based on a system of her own devising. She attended Wellesley College from 1880 to 1884 and was appointed to the HCO staff by Pickering in 1896. She learned to use a hearing aid and to lip-read to deal with her progressive loss of hearing. It is believed that her deafness resulted from exposure to harsh winter cold during her first year at Wellesley. Cannon won many honors for her work: She was the first woman to be awarded an honorary doctorate from Oxford University in its 600-year history, and the first woman to be awarded the prestigious Henry Draper Medal. A biography and an account of her accomplishments is long overdue.

8. Henry Norris Russell (1877 – 1957) was the most distinguished and influential American astrophysicist of his generation. He pioneered the use of the new developments in quantum mechanics and atomic spectroscopy to decipher the physical nature, composition, and ultimately the evolutionary behavior of the stars. Along with George Ellery Hale he championed problem-oriented research based upon physical questions. Russell had a phenomenal memory and a prodigious capacity to tackle complex problems. A deeply religious man, he knew the Bible by heart. He could also spend hours on end reciting limericks. More on his life can be found in David DeVorkin's *Henry Norris Russell: The Dean of American Astronomers.*

9. George Ellery Hale (1868 – 1938) was an extraordinary scientific visionary, organizer, and entrepreneur. The son of a wealthy Chicago elevator manufacturer, Hale used his affluence to pursue his scientific dreams. He had an unrivaled ability to separate wealthy patrons (including his father, the Chicago financier Charles Tyson Yerkes, the steel magnate Andrew Carnegie, and the hardware-store mogul John Hooker) from

their fortunes in the name of the advancement of science. He founded the Yerkes, the Mt. Wilson and the Mt. Palomar observatories and financed their superb telescopes. Hale's own astrophysical research in solar physics revolutionized our understanding of our nearest star. Despite his phenomenal accomplishments, he was troubled by deep insecurities and recurring bouts of mental instability.

10. George Russell Agassiz (1861 – 1951) was perhaps the least well-known member of the celebrated Boston family of natural scientists and philosophers. His grandfather, the biologist Louis Agassiz, moved the family to the U.S. from Switzerland, and his father Alexander was a chemist and the President of the National Academy of Sciences. George was a Professor of Zoology at Harvard; he took a great interest in the welfare and success of the HCO under both Pickering and HS.

11. Theodore Lyman IV (1874 – 1954) was an American physicist and spectroscopist who was associated with Harvard University throughout his entire career. His father was a student of marine biologist and ardent Harvard supporter Louis Agassiz. Lyman's research focused on the ultraviolet portion of the spectrum. The transitions between excited states and the ground state of the hydrogen atom are named in his honor. Lyman's unwillingness to accept Cecilia Payne as a female candidate for the Harvard Physics Ph.D. prompted HS to begin his own graduate program in astronomy.

CHAPTER TWO

1. Arville Dodge Walker (1883 – 1963) joined the HCO staff in 1906 after graduating from Radcliffe College where she specialized in mathematics. She was one of the legion of women "computers" who worked under the direction of Henrietta Leavitt and Annie Jump Cannon. On his appointment as Director, she was appointed as HS's executive assistant. Beginning in 1946, she became for several years, unknown to HS,

a confidential informant on her boss for the Federal Bureau of Investigation. The motives remain obscure, but she may have disapproved of the growing predominance of political over astronomical matters in the director's office.

2. Mildred's maternal great-grandmother was Annette Wittig (1840 – 1945); her maternal grandmother was Louise Wittig Betz (1865 – 1956). The third, fourth, and fifth generations are Martha, Mildred, and her daughter June Matthews (1939 –).

3. The merry-go-round desk was originally built for Edward Pickering and was inherited by HS when he succeeded to the directorship. When Donald Menzel succeeded HS, he had the desk summarily removed and tossed on a scrap heap. James G. Baker rescued it from destruction. It was subsequently transported to Boulder Colorado, where Alan Shapley built his home around it. When Alan and his wife Kay sold their home in 1995, University of Colorado astrophysicist Thomas Ayres was tapped to drive the dismantled desk back to Cambridge. It remained there in storage for some number of years until Harvard historian Sara J. Schechner and her husband Ken had the desk refurbished and installed in their home.

4. Lloyd Stowell Shapley was the Shapleys' fourth child. He was born in Cambridge on 2 June 1923 and died in Tucson, AZ on 12 March 2016. Attending Princeton University like his father, he obtained his Ph.D. in mathematics in 1953. He was a colleague and contemporary of John Forbes Nash, Jr., the subject of the popular book and film *A Beautiful Mind*. Author Sylvia Nasar credits the title to a remark made by Lloyd Shapley. Lloyd spent most of his career in southern California with the RAND Corporation and later joined the faculty of the University of California at Los Angeles in 1981. He is widely acknowledged to be one of the principal architects of modern game theory, for which he was awarded the 2012 Nobel Prize in Economics jointly with Alvin Roth.

5. The theory of stellar evolution was not well understood in 1926 when HS gave his impromptu ship-board lecture armed with balloons, fruits, and vegetables. Mildred's recollection of this lecture may also have tarnished with the passing years. In any event, the content of this paragraph is at odds with our current understanding of stellar evolution. Most stars spend most of their existence as red or yellow dwarf stars, and then they evolve rapidly into red giants for a brief period near the very end of their lives. Our Sun is currently in this normal dwarf phase of its life and will remain there for several billion more years. Depending upon its mass, a star will subsequently emerge from the brief red giant phase and conclude its life fading away peacefully as planetary nebulae and white dwarf, or it will die cataclysmically in a supernova explosion which leaves behind a neutron star or perhaps a black hole in its wake.

6. According to a printed program, the Observatory Philharmonic Orchestra (Founder, F. Woodworth Wright) presented its First Season in 1949. The orchestra personnel included names of several of those, and their relatives, who appear elsewhere in this story. In the violin section were Cecilia Payne-Gaposhkin (concertmaster), David Layzer (1925-2019, cosmologist, student of Donald Menzel), and Frances Wright. Elizabeth Menzel (daughter of Donald) played cello. An undergraduate at the time, astronomer William Liller (1927-2021) played bass (George?), and also contributed an original composition ("Première Performance") to the program. In an obituary is the story of his "set[ting] up in the Observatory's carpenter shop and construct[ing] a standup bass out of two-by-fours and plywood, which he subsequently played in the orchestra's maiden concert … [which] Fred Whipple and his wife Babette attended in tuxedo and evening gown." Edward Gaposhkin (son of Cecilia and Sergei) played trumpet, and Bart Bok played the mandolin. Among the percussionists required for the Toy Symphony were Dora Shapley (daughter of John and Fern Shapley), Katherine Gaposhkin (daughter of Cecilia and Sergei), and Dora's future husband Uco van Wijk, who also served as Orchestra Manager. Dr. and Mrs. Harlow Shapley are listed as Patrons.

7. Bartholomeus "Bart" Jan Bok (1906–1983) was a noted Dutch astrono-
    mer. He studied at Groningen under Pieter Johannes van Rijn. He left in
    1929 before completing his Ph.D. (awarded in 1933) to come to the U.S.
    and marry his sweetheart Priscilla Fairfield, a professor at Smith College
    and a frequent visitor at the HCO. They met at the 1928 meeting of the
    International Astronomical Union in Leiden. Bok remained at Harvard
    until 1957 as HS's protégé. He rose rapidly through the ranks, but he
    was passed over as HS's successor in favor of Donald Menzel. Eventually
    disenchanted with Menzel's leadership, Bok left Harvard in 1957 for Mt.
    Stromlo Observatory in Australia. He finished his career as the Director
    of the Steward Observatory from 1966 to 1970. He is best known for his
    pioneering studies of the Milky Way. For more on the Boks, see David
    Levy's *The Man Who Sold the Milky Way: A Biography of Bart Bok*.

8. Fred Lawrence Whipple (1906 – 2004) grew up on a farm in Iowa before
    the family moved to Long Beach, California. He obtained his bachelor's
    degree at UCLA in 1927 and his Ph.D. (1931) under Armin Otto Leus-
    chner at the University of California at Berkeley and the Lick Obser-
    vatory. He joined the Observatory staff in 1932 and remained there
    throughout his career. In 1955 he was named Director of the Smithso-
    nian Astrophysical Observatory, when it moved from Washington to
    Cambridge. Whipple was an authority on meteors and comets. Unlike
    Bok, HS, and Menzel to a lesser degree, he eschewed politics. The defin-
    itive treatment of his life is David DeVorkin's *Fred Whipple's Empire: The
    Smithsonian Astrophysical Observatory, 1955–1973*.

9. Carl Betz Shapley was the Shapleys' fifth child, born on 11 October 1927
    in Cambridge. At an early age he became involved with the Christian
    Science Church which was a large influence throughout his life. He was
    gifted in the fine arts – painting, architectural design, and music – and he
    was deeply interested in education, philosophy, and religion. He estab-
    lished a preparatory school, the Shapley School, in Ridgefield, Connecti-

cut and pursued a wide variety of endeavors across the globe. He died in the Republic of Moldova on 14 August 2012 and is buried in Chişinău.

10. Frank Bunker Gilbreth (1868 – 1924) and his wife Lillian Evelyn Moller Gilbreth (1878 – 1972) were pioneering industrial/organizational psychologists famous for their time and motion efficiency studies. Between 1902 and 1922 they had 13 children of whom 11 survived beyond childhood. In 1921 they purchased property on Nantucket and made it their summer residence. During their seaside summers, Lillian became close friends with Margaret Harwood, the Director of the Maria Mitchell Observatory, and a frequent visitor to the HCO. In 1948, two of the children, Frank, Jr. and Ernestine, wrote a popular autobiographical story about their family life titled *Cheaper by the Dozen*, which was made into a movie by 20th Century Fox in 1950, starring Myrna Loy and Clifton Webb, and was subsequently remade by Fox in 2003 with Steve Martin and Bonnie Hunt.

11. John Shapley was HS's youngest brother. He was born on the family farm near Nashville on 7 August 1890, and he shared in many of HS's early adventures around the homestead in southwestern Missouri. He obtained his bachelor's degree from the University of Missouri (1912) and, like HS, went to Princeton, where he obtained a master's degree (1914). His Ph.D., in art history, was secured at the University of Vienna. He held professorships at several outstanding universities and specialized in Byzantine and early Christian art and archaeology. In 1918 he married fellow Missouri alum and art historian Fern Rusk, who became a scholar of Italian painting and curator at the National Gallery of Art in Washington, DC. They had two daughters, Ellen and Dora, the younger of whom married astronomer Uco Van Wijk who founded the astronomy program at the University of Maryland. John Shapley died in Washington DC on 8 September 1978.

CHAPTER THREE

1. Lillian Shapley, HS's sister, was born on the family farm near Nashville, on 7 October 1880. She was a lifelong educator, teaching first in a one-room schoolhouse near the family homestead, and subsequently in the states of Oregon, Washington, and Montana, before returning to southwestern Missouri. Not only did she encourage her brothers Harlow and John to attend college, but she also took courses at the University of Missouri between 1915 and 1917. In 1920 she married Willard Willis Golladay in Montana. The couple returned to Barton County, Missouri where Lillian passed away on 19 January 1960. Asteroid *756 Lilliana*, found by Joel Metcalf in 1908, was named in her honor in 1926 thanks to HS's influence.

2. Horace Shapley was HS's twin brother. Unlike his academically inclined siblings, he elected – or perhaps was left – to stay and farm on the family homestead in Arkansas and Missouri. His two marriages ended tragically with the premature deaths of his wives. He was bitter during his later years, claiming to have gone for 29 years without speaking to his brother Harlow. Near the very end of his life, he decided to obtain a college degree, and he was the President of the Octogenarian Club at Missouri Southern College. He passed away on 17 June 1980.

3. *S Andromedae* was the first, and still the brightest, supernova to be observed in another galaxy – in this case M31, the nearby Andromeda Nebula. The discovery was announced, however, as early as 31 August 1885. In fact, the discoverer, Ernst Hartwig of the Dorpat Observatory, had first observed the supernova already on August 20. By early November of 1885, when HS was born, the supernova had dimmed considerably from its peak brightness back in August. It appears that several observers across Europe stumbled upon, but were perhaps unaware of the implication of, the unprecedented brightening in the Andromeda Nebula a week or so before Hartwig's correct identification. The two events – HS's

birth and the supernova – were therefore close in time, but not quite as close as Mildred suggests.

4. Frederick Hanley Seares (1873 – 1964) was an American astronomer noted for his seminal contributions to photometry. He received his bachelor's degree from the University of California at Berkeley in 1895 and continued his studies for several more years there as well as in Europe. In 1901 he accepted the Directorship of the Laws Observatory at the University of Missouri. In 1909 he was called to Mt. Wilson by George Ellery Hale, where he remained until 1946. A careful, methodical and a patient craftsman, he was in many ways the antithesis of the young HS.

5. Carl Betz was born to German parents in Belleville, Illinois on 1 June 1854. In 1876 he completed his course work at the Seminary of the Turnerbund in Milwaukee, Wisconsin, enabling him to teach physical education at the gymnasiums of the Turner Societies located across the United States (the Turnverein, founded by Friedrich Ludwig Jahn in early 19th century Germany). He married Louise Wittig of Terre Haute, Indiana in 1885, and in 1886 was appointed director of physical training for the Kansas City school system. Carl was also an accomplished musician who sang and played the piano and cello. He published an instructional songbook for children, *Gems of School Song* (American Book Company, New York, 1896), a copy of which was given to his daughter Martha and can still be found in the Matthews family's piano bench. Carl Betz died on 28 April 1898. In addition to his four daughters he also had two sons, Carl Egmont and Carl William. Carl William's son, Carl Lawrence Betz, was a well-known stage, film, and television actor. Carl Betz the elder greatly revered Goethe, who inspired his first son's middle name, Egmont. This admiration extended to his daughter Martha, and may in fact account for HS's nickname for her, Gretchen.

CHAPTER FOUR

1. Arthur Stanley Eddington (1882 – 1944) was the most distinguished astrophysicist of his generation. Born to a Quaker family of modest means, he was fortunate to obtain a scholarship to study at Trinity College, Cambridge, where he was awarded his bachelor's (1905) and master's (1909) degrees. After a brief stint at the Royal Greenwich Observatory (1906 to 1913), he was recalled to Cambridge, where he spent the remainder of his career. Eddington was the first to work out the physical processes responsible for the light variation of the Cepheids. He also coined the term "main sequence" for the dwarf stars of the H-R Diagram. He played a seminal role in the solar eclipse expedition of 1919, which confirmed one of the key predictions of Einstein's theory of relativity.

2. Solon Irving Bailey (1854 – 1931) was an American astronomer who spent his entire scientific career with the HCO. He obtained master's degrees from both Boston College (1884) and the HCO (1889). Edward Pickering sent him to find a site for a southern observing station in the Andes. After much adventure, Bailey settled on Arequipa, Peru, where he directed operations between 1893 and 1909. Upon his return to Cambridge, he served as the acting director between Pickering's death and HS's appointment in December 1921. Disappointed over being passed over in favor of HS, Bailey nevertheless was loyal to the new director and served under him in an exemplary fashion.

3. Henrietta Swan Leavitt (1868 – 1921) attended Oberlin College from 1885 to 1887 before matriculating at Radcliffe. After obtaining her degree in 1892 she spent several years as a volunteer before departing in 1896 on a two-year trip to Europe. On her return she joined her family in Beloit, Wisconsin, but eventually asked Pickering if she could return to work at the HCO, which she did in 1902. It was during this period that she carried out her investigations of Cepheid variables in the Large and Small Magellanic Clouds, which resulted in her discovery of the celebrated

period-luminosity relationship, published in a 1908 Harvard Circular. She suffered several debilitating illnesses throughout her life and she died just as HS was officially named to the directorship. For more on her life and work, consult George Johnson's *Miss Leavitt's Stars.*

4. Jacobus Cornelius Kapteyn (1851 – 1922) carried out a careful and detailed statistical analysis of the proper motions and distribution of stars in the night sky. He obtained his Ph.D. at Utrecht in 1875 and spent the remainder of his career at the university in Groningen. Based on his painstaking labors, he constructed one of the first models of the galaxy, the so-called Kapteyn universe: a stellar disk about 5000 light years thick and 30,000 light years in lateral extent. He placed the Sun at the center of this disk owing to the observational fact that the neighboring star density did not show a preferential enhancement in any direction. Later, HS showed that the Sun was displaced significantly away from the disk center, in the direction of the constellation Sagittarius. Kapteyn's overall structure for the Milky Way galaxy was essentially correct, though a factor of three too small in its size.

5. This account of the evening meeting of the National Academy of Sciences on 26 April 1920, which has subsequently been christened the Great Debate by the astronomical community, must be taken with some measure of caution. Mildred wrote this in the early 1960s based in part on inputs from her father and possibly Bart Bok. The only published material on the debate available to her was a pair of articles written by Shapley and Curtis after the meeting (from which she borrows heavily), published by the National Research Council in their May 1921 Bulletin (volume 2, part 3, number 11). These articles are not a verbatim summary of the talks. By her own admission, Mildred was not an astronomer, and so the detailed analysis she presents of the pros and cons of the arguments developed by Curtis and Shapley probably traces back to her father, Bok, and this 1921 publication. In his subsequent autobiography *Through Rugged Ways to the Stars*, Shapley edited and revised her narra-

tive significantly in his retelling of the events surrounding the debate. Shapley spoke first, followed by Curtis, not the other way around as it is portrayed here. Beginning in 1970, this event began to attract serious interest from historians and much has subsequently been written, carefully researched, and hypothesized about the event, the arguments presented, and the motives of the two protagonists.

A further complication is that Mildred (as well as HS in *Rugged Ways*) has confused this meeting with a *different* meeting of the National Academy held almost a year later on 25 April 1921 where Albert Einstein was present, an evening dinner was held, and the hookworm story originates. By this time, Shapley certainly would have made the acquaintance of his Harvard colleague Winthrop Osterhout. Osterhout and Pearl were present at both the 1920 and the 1921 meetings. Einstein was not present at the April 1920 meeting; he was in Europe at the time. The debate began at 8:15 p.m. and was followed by an open discussion commencing at 9:30 p.m., making a follow-on dinner on 26 April 1920 out of the question.

There is no evidence to support the statement that Charles St. John presented a paper at either of the two Academy meetings on his solar observations bearing upon Einstein's theory of relativity. This event occurred during January 1931 when Einstein was visiting the California Institute of Technology and the Mt. Wilson Observatory where St. John worked. Numerous tours, seminars, and lavish dinners were staged to commemorate Einstein's visit, including one hosted at the home of the Hollywood mogul Charlie Chaplin. HS was present at some of these events and probably witnessed Einstein's reaction to St. John's talk at this time.

CHAPTER FIVE

1. At the end of the 19th century, the desire to extend the systematic charting of the northern celestial hemisphere to the southern skies led numerous observatories to establish stations south of the equator. Under Edward

Pickering's leadership, and Solon Bailey's efforts, Harvard selected and developed a site near Arequipa, Peru in 1889. It was called the Boyden Station after Uriah Boyden, whose bequest to Harvard helped fund the observatory. From this site, the Magellanic Clouds are visible, providing a wealth of valuable information on cosmic distances.

2. Cecilia Helena Payne-Gaposchkin (1900 – 1979) was a distinguished British-American astrophysicist who spent her entire career from 1923 to 1979 at Harvard. After obtaining her undergraduate degree at Cambridge University, she came to the Observatory where she was awarded the first Ph.D. in astronomy in 1925. Her thesis was a highly original and influential study, which suggested that stars were composed mostly of hydrogen. Otto Struve called it the most brilliant Ph.D. thesis ever written in astronomy. A complex and oftentimes complicated individual, her reminiscences are to be found in daughter Katharine Haramundanis's *Cecilia Payne-Gaposchkin: An Autobiography and Other Recollections*. In vivid and eloquent prose, Donovan Moore celebrates Cecilia's life in his recent (2020) biography *What Stars Are Made Of*.

3. Sergei Illarionovich Gaposchkin (1898 – 1984) was a Russian-American astrophysicist who endured significant hardship until he met Cecilia Payne in Germany, and came to the U.S. in 1934 at her invitation. Sergei and Cecilia eloped to New York City where they were married on 5 March 1935, with the assistance of Winthrop John Van Leuven Osterhout and his wife. Sergei invariably lived in the intellectual shadow of his more accomplished spouse. Sylvia Boyd's magnificent *Portrait of a Binary: The Lives of Cecilia Payne and Sergei Gaposchkin* recounts their tangled lives and their turbulent relationships with HS.

4. Gerard Swope (1872 – 1957) and his better-known brother Herbert Bayard Swope (1882 – 1958) rose from modest immigrant means to prominent positions in American society and politics. Gerard was trained in engineering at M.I.T. and rose through the ranks to become the

President of General Electric in 1922. Gerard, his wife, and their young daughter Henrietta also spent a few years living at Jane Addams's Hull House in Chicago. Herbert was a Pulitzer Prize-winning journalist and noted editor of the *New York World*. Together the brothers Swope exercised considerable influence on American political and economic events.

5. In 1873 HS's paternal grandfather, Calvin Harlow Shapley Jr., was married for a second time to Kate Stowell. Two half-uncles, Lloyd Stowell Shapley and Walter Shapley were born of this marriage. HS's paternal grandmother Melissa Carmichael had died in 1871. In 1877, HS's father, Willis Harlow Shapley, was married to Kate's younger sister, HS's mother, Sarah Stowell. This meant that Lloyd and Walter were also HS's first cousins as well as his half-uncles. Walter was three years older than HS. Lloyd had a distinguished career in the U.S. Navy and served as the Governor of Guam. It also meant, as HS was particularly fond of saying, that he was his own father.

    The diagram drawn, presumably from memory, by HS and reproduced by Mildred, is not entirely accurate. Calvin Harlow and Kate Stowell Shapley's daughter was named Edith Anne (not Ruth); she died at age 6 in 1884. Although Calvin Shapley is credited as "my grandfather," note that he and Horace Stowell were both HS's grandfathers. Also, Sarah Stowell and Willis Harlow Shapley had a daughter, Bertha, before Lillian, who died at age 3 in 1880 a month after Lillian was born. Edith Anne and Bertha are buried together in the Lamar, MO cemetery.

6. See Chapter Two, Note 4

7. Venetia Katharine Douglas Burney (1918 – 2009) was one of thousands of people from around the globe who wrote to the Lowell Observatory in the excitement that ensued after the announcement of the discovery of Planet X. Her suggestion for its name, Pluto, the Roman god of the underworld, was adopted on 1 May 1930. The symbol for Pluto, , is a monogram formed from the letters P and L. As time passed, it became

increasingly obvious that the mass of Pluto was insufficient to cause any effect on the orbits of Neptune and Uranus. In 1992, the International Astronomical Union officially demoted Pluto from its position as the 9th planet to its current classification as a dwarf planet.

CHAPTER SIX

1. Donald Howard Menzel (1901 – 1976) was an American astrophysicist. He grew up in Leadville, Colorado and earned his undergraduate degree under Herbert Alonzo Howe at the University of Denver. He obtained his Ph.D. at Princeton with Henry Norris Russell, and he spent the summers of 1923 and 1924 working at the HCO. After a productive stay at the Lick Observatory, Menzel was called to Harvard by HS to replace Harry Plaskett. Menzel made important contributions in a wide variety of areas – especially solar physics – and wrote a number of technical books and monographs. He succeeded HS as Director in 1954 and guided the HCO on a new course, until he stepped down in 1966. He had many extracurricular talents and accomplishments, including successes as a science fiction writer, cryptographer, cartoonist, and a debunker of UFOs. His amazing life has yet to find a biographer.

2. Georges Henri Joseph Édouard LeMaître (1894 – 1966) was a Belgian mathematician and cosmologist. He pursued both his academic (B.A., 1920; Ph.D., 1927) and religious (ordination, 1923) training in Louvain. He secured the title of Monseigneur after his election to the Pontifical Academy of Sciences in 1936. He spent the period between 1924 and 1926 at the HCO. LeMaître is best known for his contributions to relativistic cosmology and the expansion of the Universe. He was the originator of the Big Bang Theory of the beginning of the universe. In 1927 he was the first to estimate the so-called Hubble Constant, relating the velocity of objects in the sky to their distance, as 600 km/sec/Mpc. The currently accepted value is a more modest 70 km/sec/Mpc.

3. Ellen Dorrit Hoffleit (1907 – 2007) was an iconic American astronomer who was active in a variety of endeavors from variable stars to meteoritics. Dorrit and her brother Herbert, a noted Latin scholar, overcame modest means to achieve greatness in their respective endeavors. After earning a B.A. from Radcliffe in 1928, Dorrit joined the HCO staff where she spent many happy hours mining the photographic plate collection for new discoveries. She obtained her M.A. in 1932 and earned a Ph.D. in 1938. During World War II she joined Ted Sterne at the Aberdeen Proving Ground where she worked on ballistics. She returned to the HCO when the war ended, despite more lucrative offers elsewhere. After HS retired, she left for Yale University, where she was a research astronomer from 1956 to 1975. She succeeded Margaret Harwood as Director of the Maria Mitchell Observatory on Nantucket (1957 – 1978). Dorrit's charming autobiography is called *Misfortunes as Blessings in Disguise*.

4. Alice Victoria Hodson Watson (1910 – 2002) was born in Reading, Massachusetts and graduated from Radcliffe in 1932. After interviewing successfully with Martha Shapley, she was hired as an *au pair* for the family. In 1935, she married Fletcher Guard Watson (1912 – 1997) who had come to the Harvard to study astronomy after securing an undergraduate degree from Pomona College in 1933. He obtained his M.A. (1935) and Ph.D. (1938) from Harvard and was eventually appointed executive secretary to HS.

5. Boaz Piller (1887 – 1964) was the contra-bassoonist from the Boston Symphony whom Jenka Mohr persuaded to substitute for the reticent first cellist, Jean Bedetti (1883–1973).

6. Henrietta Hill Swope (1902 – 1980) was the daughter of Gerald Swope. She earned a B.A. at Barnard College in 1925 and was set to pursue business studies at the University of Chicago when Swope family friend Margaret Harwood, then Director of the Maria Mitchell Observatory on Nantucket, got her connected with the HCO, where she started her

work in 1926. She obtained an M.A. at Radcliffe in 1928 and continued her research activities at the observatory until 1942, when she moved to M.I.T. to contribute to the war effort. Between 1947 and 1952 she taught briefly at Barnard College and Connecticut College. In 1952, she was invited by Walter Baade to work on observations of variable stars in the Andromeda galaxy using the new 200-inch telescope atop Mt. Palomar. She was a frequent guest of Mildred and Ralph Matthews in Pasadena, whose children were fond of saying that they were "having Miss Swope for dinner."

7.   Alvan Clark (1804 – 1887) and his sons were the premier American telescope makers of the 19th century. Alvan began his career as an engraver and subsequently took up portrait painting on which he concentrated until 1860. It was his son George Bassett Clark (1827 – 1891), who first tried to make a reflecting telescope after the excitement created by the great comet of 1843, and who started the telescope making company around 1850. The second son, Alvan Graham Clark (1832 – 1897), and their father eventually joined the firm, which initially specialized in reflecting telescopes but eventually moved on to fashioning exquisite glass lenses for refractors. Several times during the late 1800s Alvan Clark & Sons held the distinction of having constructed the world's largest telescope. The peak of their artistry is the 40-inch refractor at Yerkes Observatory.

CHAPTER SEVEN

1.   On 10 August 2017 Harvard entomologist Edward O. Wilson wrote to June Matthews:

"During 1951 – 56 I was a Ph.D. student, about to become a member of the Society of Fellows, and then new assistant professor of biology. Once each week, students in entomology and special guests would meet for late

*afternoon tea in the office of Frank M. Carpenter, professor of entomol-
ogy and my Ph.D. advisor.*

*"One of the frequent guests during 1951 – 53, and the most remarkable
in every way, was the famous astronomer Harlow Shapley. Ants were his
hobby (at least one of them), and I enjoyed a great deal of conversation
with him about these insects, and broader issues concerning them (such
as how can they walk on walls and ceilings).*

*"I learned how Shapley traveled around the world, representing scientific
policy for the U.S. It was his habit to collect a few ants from each destination and preserve them in the strongest spirits served in the country.*

*"One such adventure was dinner in the Kremlin with Stalin and other
notables from the U.S. and U.S.S.R. He spotted ants on the table and
bottled two of them in vodka.*

*"On hearing about these specimens, I asked to see them, and identified
them as the common Eurasian species Lasius niger. It happened that I
was studying the genus Lasius and would be delighted to have a Russian
locality record — and Stalin's residence, no less. I asked to borrow one
of the two specimens and lodged it (dried out) in Harvard's collection. I
never got around to returning the loan.*

*"When he wrote me later, he'd forgotten the Lasius loaned me and
expressed puzzlement: when he checked his collection, he said, he could
find only one Kremlin specimen. What happened to the other one he
wondered? I never had the chance to tell him.*

*"One day toward the end of his life, when I was a young faculty member
with widening interests, I found I had a real friend in the great astronomer. He stopped me in the Faculty Club and said, 'I've just told Mr.*

*Pusey that you are the most important assistant professor at Harvard.'
I've never received a compliment that meant more."*

2. Archibald MacLeish (1892 – 1982) was an American writer and states-
    man. He pursued his undergraduate studies at Yale University and
    studied law at Harvard, graduating in 1919. He practiced law with the
    prestigious Boston firm of Choate, Hall & Stewart for three years before
    leaving for Paris (1923), where he honed his literary skills. With the help
    of Supreme Court Justice and Roosevelt confidante Felix Frankfurter,
    MacLeish became the 9th Librarian of Congress in 1939. He subsequently
    served as a high-ranking official in the Department of State and led the
    U.S. National Commission for UNESCO. In 1949 he joined the faculty
    of Harvard University and remained there until his retirement in 1962.

3. Martha Alice Ingham Dickie Sharp-Cogan (1905 – 1999) was an Amer-
    ican missionary, social worker, Zionist, and Unitarian. She was born in
    Providence, Rhode Island, graduated from Pembroke College in 1926,
    and carried out social work at Jane Addams's Hull House in Chicago.
    She married a Unitarian Pastor, Waitstill Hastings Sharp, in 1927, and
    they spent the next ten years ministering in Pennsylvania and Massachu-
    setts. In early 1939, they went to Prague and later to Lisbon to aid in the
    relief of Jewish refugees. Martha became active in the endeavors of the
    Hadassah Women's Zionist Organization of America. Martha's grandson,
    Artemis Joukowsky III, and Ken Burns co-directed a PBS documentary
    in 2016 on the mission to Czechoslovakia and Portugal titled: *Defying
    the Nazis: The Sharps' War.*

4. Joseph William Martin, Jr. (1884 – 1968) was an American conservative
    politician, who served as the Republican congressman from the district
    surrounding North Attleborough, Massachusetts from 1925 to 1967.
    He was Speaker of the House of Representatives from 1947 to 1949, and
    again from 1953 to 1955. He was an ardent opponent of Roosevelt's New
    Deal policies.

5. John Elliott Rankin (1882 – 1960) was an American politician. He served as a Democratic congressman from Mississippi's 1st district (Tupelo) from 1920 until 1952. Rankin helped to establish the House Un-American Activities Committee (HUAC) as a standing committee of Congress in 1945. Although a supporter of the New Deal, Rankin was a vociferous demagogue and bigot, who held and espoused racist opinions of Jews, African Americans, and Japanese Americans.

6. John Parnell Thomas (1895 – 1970) was a conservative American politician. He served as a Republican congressman from New Jersey's 7th district from 1937 until 1950. In 1947 when the Republicans gained control of the House of Representatives, Thomas was tapped to lead the HUAC. He was forced to resign in 1950 when he was investigated by a grand jury for a salary kick-back scheme. Ironically, Thomas invoked his Fifth Amendment Right in refusing to cooperate with the grand jury investigation, and, after he was convicted, he spent nine months at the same Danbury, Connecticut prison where Lester Cole and Ring Lardner Jr. of the Hollywood Ten were serving time for contempt of Congress stemming from their HUAC interrogations.

7. Zdeněk Kopal (1914 – 1993) was a Czech American British astrophysicist. He obtained his Ph.D. in 1937 at the Charles University in Prague. After studying at Cambridge with Eddington, he came to the Observatory in 1938, remaining in the U.S. until he joined the faculty at the University of Manchester in 1951. He made seminal contributions in a wide variety of areas, particularly the study of close eclipsing binary stars. During World War II, Kopal worked on ballistics and eventually moved across Cambridge to join the M.I.T. faculty. Kopal was a great admirer of the Shapleys. His 1986 autobiography, *Of Stars and Men – Reminiscences of an Astronomer,* provides a vivid and opinionated account of his years at Harvard.

8. Charles Sydney Hopkinson (1869 – 1962) was a noted American painter. After studying in Paris, he returned to the U.S., where he maintained a workshop in the Fenway Studios in Boston. He specialized in portraits and watercolor landscapes. He was commissioned to paint portraits of Calvin Coolidge, Oliver Wendell Holmes, and E.E. Cummings.

9. Ernestine "Enit" Zerner Kaufman (1908 – 1961) was an Austrian American portrait painter. When World War II interrupted her successful career, she fled in 1939 with her husband to New York. She has the distinction of having painted portraits of four American Presidents, Hoover, Roosevelt, Truman, and Eisenhower, as well as scientist Arthur Holly Compton, and Secretary of Labor Frances Perkins.

10. Dorothea Frances Canfield Fisher (1879 – 1958) was an American educator, writer, and social activist. She obtained her undergraduate degree from the Ohio State University (1899) and her doctorate from Columbia University (1904). She focused on childhood education and helped to introduce the Montessori method into America. Eleanor Roosevelt called her one of the ten most influential women in America. She married John Redwood Fisher in 1907. She was a forceful and outspoken proponent of women's rights and racial equality. She supplied the text that accompanied Enit Kaufman's portraits in *American Portraits*.

CHAPTER EIGHT

1. Faith Elliot Chestman Hubley (1924 – 2001) was an American film producer, born in New York to Jewish immigrants. She left home at age fifteen to work in the theatre, she met her future husband, John, while employed at Columbia Studios. John Hubley (1914 – 1977) was an American animation artist and film director. From 1935 to 1952 he worked in Hollywood for a variety of firms, including Walt Disney Studios, Screen Gems, and United Production Artists. He developed training films for the U.S. Army in World War II. In 1949 he created the character Mr.

Magoo, based on one of his uncles, which featured the voice-over of actor Jim Backus. John was a victim of the 1952 HUAC investigations and left Hollywood to form an independent film production company, Storyboard Studios, with his second wife, Faith, whom he married in 1955. They worked on a variety of film projects including *Moonbird*, which won them an Oscar for the best short subject in 1959. John died in 1977 during the filming of *A Doonesbury Special*, and Gary Trudeau dedicated the film to John's memory.

2. Louis Eliezer Finkelstein (1895 – 1991) was a conservative rabbi and Talmudic scholar. After graduating from the City College of New York (1915), he studied at, and eventually rose to be Chancellor (from 1940 to 1972) of, the Jewish Theological Seminary of America. He was a leading proponent of the Conservative Judaism (Masorti) movement. Finkelstein founded the Institute for Religious and Social Studies, which, after his death, was renamed the Finkelstein Institute in his honor.

3. Ralph Wendell Burhoe (1911 – 1997) began his career as a meteorologist and retired as an eminent theologian. Between these occupational bookends, he served from 1947 to 1964 as the executive director of the American Academy of Arts and Sciences. He met HS, Kirtley Mather, Hudson Hoagland, and other Boston-area intellectuals through this appointment. His discussions with these savants honed his preoccupation with the role of religion in a scientific society, and it motivated them to establish the journal *Dædalus*. He was called to a professorship at the Meadville/Lombard Theological Seminary in Hyde Park, Chicago. In 1966 he founded the journal *Zygon: Journal of Religion and Science*. He was the first American to win the prestigious Templeton Prize for Progress in Religion.

4. Percy Williams Bridgman (1882 – 1961) was a noted American physicist and 1946 Nobel Laureate. He entered Harvard in 1900, was awarded his Ph.D. in 1910, and he served on the faculty until his death in 1961. He

made many contributions to thermodynamics, the physics of high-pressure phenomena, and the philosophy of science. He was one of the 11 signatories on the Russell-Einstein Manifesto (1955), which highlighted the dangers of nuclear weapons in the Cold War environment. Bridgman became an icon for proponents of legal euthanasia when he ended his life by gunshot while suffering from metastatic cancer, writing "It isn't decent for a society to make a man do this thing himself. Probably this is the last day I will be able to do it myself."

Prepared by Thomas J. Bogdan, November 2020; edited by June L. Matthews, 2020-2021.

SELECTED PUBLICATIONS BY HARLOW SHAPLEY

Starlight. The Humanizing of Knowledge Series. (New York, NY: George H. Doran Company), --+143. [1926]

The Universe of Stars. Radio Talks from the Harvard Observatory. Edited by Harlow Shapley *with* Cecilia H. Payne. (Cambridge, MA: Harvard College Observatory), ix+205. [1926]

Flights from Chaos. A Survey of Material Systems from Atoms to Galaxies. (New York, NY: Whittlesey House), vii+168. [1930]

A Treasury of Science. 1st Edition. Edited by Harlow Shapley *with* Samuel Rapport & Helen Wright. (New York, NY: Harper & Brothers), xi+716. [1943; revised editions in 1946, 1954, 1958, 1963, 1965]

Galaxies. (Philadelphia, PA: Blakiston Company), vii+229. [1943; revised edition in 1961]

Climatic Change. Evidence, Causes, and Effects. Edited by Harlow Shapley. (Cambridge, MA: Harvard University Press), xii+318. [1953]

The Inner Metagalaxy. (New Haven, CT: Yale University Press), xiii+204. [1957]

Of Stars and Men. Human Response to an Expanding Universe. (Boston, MA: Beacon Press), vi+157. [1958]

Science Ponders Religion. Edited by Harlow Shapley. (New York, NY: Apple-ton-Century-Crofts, Inc.), x+308. [1960]

The View from a Distant Star. Man's Future in the Universe. (New York, NY: Basic Books, Inc.), ix+212. [1963]

Of Stars and Men. The Human Response to an Expanding Universe. Revised & Illustrated Edition. (Boston, MA: Beacon Press), iii+134. [1964]

Beyond the Observatory. (New York, NY: Charles Scribner's Sons), --+223. [1967]

Through Rugged Ways to the Stars. Ad astra per aspera. (New York, NY: Charles Scribner's Sons), vii+180. [1969]

With Paul W. Hodge. Galaxies. 3rd Edition. (Cambridge, MA: Harvard University Press), x+232. [1972]

APPENDIX

Harlow Shapley's Impact

Owen Gingerich, *Harvard-Smithsonian Center for Astrophysics*

Presented at the International Astronomical Union "Harlow-Shapley Symposium on Globular Cluster Systems in Galaxies," August 25-29, 1986[**]

I t was almost four decades ago that I came to work as a summer assistant for Harlow Shapley, an event destined to turn me toward professional astronomy. Thus perhaps even I can be considered a minor example of Shapley's impact. However, this doesn't make it much easier for me to summarize Shapley's influence in a few pages. On the other hand, the fact that I helped him prepare his memoirs, *Through Rugged Ways to the Stars*, does help. At the time I suspected that Shapley subscribed to the old adage that one must not let truth stand in the way of a good story, and so I took some trouble to check out those tales that loomed larger than life in his account. To my surprise, I could verify one story after another. Yes, he really was the man who almost single-handedly put the S into UNESCO. Yes, he really did find academic places for numerous refugees from Nazi and Fascist tyranny

[**] ©1988 by the International Astronomical Union. Used by permission.

in Europe. And yes, he did pickle in vodka an ant collected from Joseph Stalin's banquet table.

To probe into Harlow Shapley's legacy, I think we must briefly explore three aspects: his scientific contributions, the institutions he built, and his astonishingly wide reputation as a spokesman for astronomy. These areas blend seamlessly into each other, but let me try to separate them. I shall begin with a few remarks on his scientific achievements.

The Period-Luminosity relation was neither Shapley's discovery, nor was he the first to apply it. Yet, by the dramatic results he achieved with it, he effectively made it his own. Thus, when Edwin Hubble found the light curves for several M31 Cepheid variables, it was to Shapley at Harvard that he turned for the most up-to-date calibration of the Period-Luminosity relation. On February 2, 1924, Shapley responded to Hubble saying:

> *Your letter telling of the crop of novae and of the two variable stars in the direction of the Andromeda nebula is the most entertaining piece of literature I have seen for a long time.*

Note that Shapley didn't say "*in* the Andromeda nebula" but "in *the direction of* the Andromeda nebula." Shapley must have realized that his debating position of just a few years earlier was crumbling, and he made one final parry of resistance. Even though Shapley had in 1917 found one of the novae in M31 and had suggested a distance of a million light years, he had hastily back-pedaled after devising his new model of our galaxy. Without interstellar absorption our Milky Way seemed so enormous compared to the spirals that it appeared to be a cosmic unit of altogether different proportions. In the 1920s Shapley thought of the Kapteyn universe as one cloud of an enormous flattened assemblage, a supergalaxy as he called it. The familiar cross section with the globular clusters in their halo-like array was *not* the model Shapley had in mind then – the familiar old picture is from J. S. Plaskett's Halley Lecture of 1935. Even after Trumpler's discovery of interstellar absorption in 1930, the anomaly persisted; and I shall return to this question at the end of my paper.

Meanwhile, let me remark on Shapley's own scientific work at Harvard. Here he was hampered both by weather and by the lack of the big telescopes that he had used so effectively at Mount Wilson. Hence he followed in Pickering's footsteps as an astronomical administrator, organizing large scale surveys – of spectral classes, of variable stars, of stellar magnitudes; for himself, he chose galaxies. The Shapley-Ames catalog of bright galaxies was one result. Another was his forceful demonstration of the inhomogeneity of galaxy distributions.

A result of these investigations, in 1937, was the discovery of the Sculptor and Fornax dwarf galaxies. One of the women who counted galaxies for him on the large A plates from the South African station noticed a peculiar peppering of fine stars, almost like a thumbprint, and called Shapley's attention to it. He soon recognized that it was a new class of objects, unlike any galaxies that had been seen before. In such a case we might well ask who really discovered the Sculptor system: Was it the person who master-minded the investigation, who raised the funds and set the survey into motion, or Sylvia Mussells, who went beyond her immediate instructions of marking galaxies and who noticed the smudge? Was it the person who found the smudge or the one who figured out its significance? These are questions that, in their many guises, historians of science must struggle with, but in general the historical interest lies not with the person who first saw an object or who first grasped a theoretical idea, but with the one who recognized and exploited its significance.

In our era of big science, such questions have increasing poignancy when one plants and another reaps. Harlow Shapley lived in a transitional age, already inherited from Pickering and even from George Ellery Hale, when an effective scientist-administrator could marshal forces beyond a single person's capacity, bringing not only to himself but to his colleagues or assistants resources that they might not otherwise have. Such was to a large extent Shapley's role at Harvard, and if he himself made no discoveries as grand at Harvard as he had in those heady days at Mount Wilson, we should hesitate to judge that it was a mistake for him to leave the clear skies of southern California. To very few is given the chance to change our conception of sidereal structure as much as Shapley once did, and to have asked him to do it again at Harvard is demanding rather much. And we must ask as well, did he not play a key role here as a catalyst for his colleagues' discoveries? Surely the answer is yes! So this brings me to the second aspect of Shapley's legacy, his role as builder of institutions.

In four decades as director, Edward Pickering had turned the Harvard College Observatory into a world-class research establishment. But astronomy education at Harvard took place not on Observatory Hill, but with an entirely different staff in the astronomical laboratory, a frame building that stood just north of the Harvard Yard. Once in an undergraduate career there was an opportunity to see the real observatory, when seniors lined up two abreast to march up Garden Street to visit Pickering's domain. As for graduate students, there may have been some apprenticeships, but surely no formal degrees. Shapley's approach was obviously different, and not many years after his arrival he seized an opportunity to work toward an astronomy graduate program.

In May of 1922 Shapley had gone to the Rome IAU meeting, and later in the month he spoke briefly about the spectrographic work at the Harvard College Observatory at the centenary meeting of the Royal Astronomical Society in London. Among his fascinated listeners was Cecilia Payne, then a Cambridge undergraduate, who boldly told him after his lecture that "I should like to come and work under you." Shapley cheerfully agreed; but it undoubtedly surprised him when she eventually turned up in the American Cambridge.

After about a year Shapley suggested that Miss Payne turn in a thesis for a Ph.D. at Radcliffe College. There was, however, no provision for advanced degrees in astronomy, and Theodore Lyman, chairman of the Harvard physics department, was adamantly opposed to a woman candidate in physics. How Shapley managed to have Payne's doctorate awarded in astronomy is not known, but this event in 1925 marked the birth of the graduate school in astronomy. Soon there were other graduate students, and doctorates including Helen Sawyer Hogg's. As the program expanded, Shapley recruited Harry H. Plaskett from Victoria to teach astrophysics, and on October 18, 1928 he included in a letter to Edwin Hubble the following typically light-hearted note:

> Curiously enough I find that H. H. Plaskett has grave doubts about the large distances for extra-galactic nebulae. He is sufficiently serious about it that he and Miss Payne are to debate the subject at a colloquium two weeks from today. If he convinces me, I shall cable you.

One of the educational innovations Shapley established, beginning in 1935, was the Harvard Summer School in Astronomy, which was deliberately designed to bring together physicists and astronomers. For this he used the famous and influential Michigan summer school in theoretical physics as his model. The Harvard program, the first of its kind in America, introduced graduate students such as Jesse Greenstein, Leo Goldberg, James Baker, and Lawrence Aller to scientists such as Jan Oort, Ira Bowen, Meghnad Saha, Bengt Edlen, H. P. Robertson, John Slater, Robert Marshak, and George Shortley.

Shapley was particularly proud that he had assembled such an international group at Harvard Observatory, and he delighted in showing a picture taken around 1940 with students or staff from 13 foreign countries. This sort of enthusiastic internationalism, which is so essential to the International

Astronomical Union, was eventually to get him in trouble with the House Un-American Activities Committee and with Senator McCarthy, episodes that are also part of Shapley's impact.

I could mention also his role in reforming the American Academy of Arts and Sciences, or the long hours he spent reviewing funding proposals for the American Philosophical Society and for Sigma Xi. These and many more topics you can find in his autobiography, *Through Rugged Ways to the Stars.* If you knew Shapley, you can hear him talking in the book, a raconteur with a splendid combination of vanity and a sly facetiousness that enabled him to poke fun at himself. I always thought he carried a continual air of amazement that a farm boy from Missouri could become a celebrity and meet presidents and dictators and even the Pope.

Something of that quality carried over to the public platform, where Shapley eventually became an engaging speaker and also enough of a journalist to know what made good headlines. He frequently spoke of his own most brilliant achievement, from heliocentric to galactocentric, and I often heard him say that in the old days at Mount Wilson he had no idea of the *philosophical* implications of his research. In fact, that was patently false, as the following letter to George Ellery Hale, written on January 19, 1918, shows:

> So the center has shifted: egocentric, lococentric, geocentric, heliocentric.
>
> Now, getting nearer those serious things that the heartless corporation pays me to investigate, we know that for the last few decades some observing and unheeded astronomers have noted that the Milky Way is not a great circle and that it is brighter in some places than in others. But that is not necessarily our fault. We are not responsible for the imperfections of this Universe. We have indeed held on to that heliocentric center doggedly, in spite of increasing doubts when we troubled to think on the subject analytically. If the center got away from us, we feared that Man, the Ultimate Purpose of Creation, would loose [sic] his hold on all things. Instead of MAN and the universe it might become man and The Universe.

Harlow Shapley achieved widespread public fame by speaking artic-ulately and imaginatively about the vastness of space, the peripherality of man, and the industry of ants. The Harvard Archives contains an astonishing number of press clippings, beginning in great quantities with his appointment to Harvard in 1921. Let me select a handful to illustrate the extent of his fame.

Here is a telegram signed "Clarence" from Dayton, Tennessee on July 10, 1925:

> *Distinguished colleagues of yours have suggested you might be willing to come to testify for defense at Dayton Tennessee next week in the case of State of Tennessee versus Professor Scopes STOP We of the defense would be delighted to add you[r] authority to* our *position STOP Your expenses will be paid STOP Will you wire me directly at Dayton and I will let you know what day you will be needed.*

Shapley did not go to Dayton for the famous Scopes trial, but the nature of the invitation is an indicator of his public fame in the 1920s.

In the next decade, we find his picture on the cover of *Time* magazine, on July 29, 1935, in connection with an article on the Paris Congress of the IAU. (Shapley was the second astronomer to gain this distinction, the first having been Arthur Eddington on April 16, 1934.)

In the mid-1940s Shapley's name loomed large in the press on account of his tiff with Congressman Rankin and the House Un-American Activities Committee. Shapley's firmly held internationalism and his stubborn inde-pendence had attracted the attention of congressional witch-hunters, and so he had been called to Washington to testify. He was not allowed to have a lawyer present in the "Star Chamber" hearings before the congressman, but he recorded the session in the shorthand he had picked up as a fledgling reporter in Kansas decades earlier; Rankin left the hearings saying he had never had a witness treat the committee with such contempt. Banner head-lines four centimeters high proclaimed "RANKIN IN ROW WITH SHAP-LEY" – little other identification being needed for the local Boston public.

In the 1950s he not only tangled with Senator McCarthy, but also with Immanuel Velikovsky, the Princeton doctor and author of the best-selling *Worlds in Collision*. Had Macmillan listed the book as science fiction rather than science, they might have avoided trouble from some of the astronomers. Shapley sent a few letters to the publisher about it, complaining that if *Worlds in Collision* were a science book, Macmillan should have had it refereed. Perhaps his harshest but most amusing comments were written to them on January 25, 1950:

> *If I remember correctly, several years ago Dr. Velikovsky met me in a New York hotel. He sought my endorsement of his theory. I was astonished. I looked around to see if he had a keeper with him... I tried, rather futilely, to explain that if the earth could be stopped in such a short period of time, ... [this] would have made [it] impossible that he and I could meet together in a building in New York City less than four thousand years after this tremendous planetary event.*
>
> *Dr. V. seemed very sad. But somehow I felt he was feeling sorry for me and the thousands of other American physical scientists and geologists and historians who have been so, so wrong.*

Velikovsky's fans claimed that Shapley was instrumental in organizing a boycott against Macmillan, but if so, the Archives show no trace of it.

It was only a few years earlier, when the world was at war, that it came time to celebrate the 400th anniversary of the publication of Copernicus' *De Revolutionibus*. Poland was in bondage, but the American Polish community was determined not to let the anniversary pass without notice, so a grand affair was scheduled in New York. It was symbolic of Shapley's public impact that he was the man who read President Roosevelt's greeting to the distinguished guests, and it was to his observatory that a remarkable painting of Copernicus was given. It still hangs in the entrance to Building A, a magnificent gift to the man who took the step from heliocentric to galactocentric.

Today the scientific principle of mediocrity is often called the Copernican principle: we should not expect to be in the center of things, or in the most splendid galaxy. Even Shapley's galactocentric move might today be called a Copernican maneuver. Shapley was clearly troubled by the fact that the Milky Way seemed to be the biggest of them all, and I remember how, in a graduate cosmogony course that he helped to teach in the spring of 1952, he assigned to Frank Orrall the topic of why the globular clusters in M31 were only half the size of those in our own galaxy. Neither Shapley nor any of the students could come up with an answer. I mention this to show what a viselike grip a wrong assumption can have when it seems to fit so coherently into the rest of the picture.

Only a few months later at the Rome IAU meeting Walter Baade announced that two different types of Cepheids had been mixed together in Shapley's Mount Wilson work, and that when these were sorted out, M31 was twice as far as had been supposed, the anomalous globular clusters fell into place, and the Milky Way was no longer the unqualified king of the galaxies. Only in retrospect was it noticed by the overwhelming majority of astronomers that the Copernican principle of mediocrity might have pointed the way.

Baade had the advantage of the world's largest telescopes at his disposal, and he was also one of the pre-eminent observers of our century. Would Shapley have made the discovery if he had stayed on at Mount Wilson? Trying to rewrite history as it might have been is a rather fruitless exercise. Did Shapley lose out in his science by abandoning the giant telescopes of the West? Probably not – as I have noted, few have the chance to make even one discovery as grand – and few have as fine a chance to build astronomy through education, activism, and public appeal. I suspect we all owe much in the public funding of science to this one man's multi-faceted efforts – through the press, through the pioneering Harvard radio talks on astronomy (beginning in the 1920s), through the Harvard books on astronomy, and through his own ubiquitous appearances on the lecture circuit – to arouse in an interested public a curiosity and fascination with topics astronomical.

Thus it is entirely appropriate that the American Astronomical Society has instituted the Shapley lectureships to help in the public understanding of astronomy. Fortunately we are now having the opportunity to commemorate this remarkable man under the auspices of IAU as well as of Harvard with a topic that was always dear to his heart, globular clusters.

I should like to thank the Harvard University Archives for permission to quote from letters in the Shapley collection, and the Shapley family for making many of the materials available to me and to the Archives. Michael Hoskin and Richard Berendzen originally showed me important pieces of the astronomical correspondence related to Shapley's career, which I deeply appreciate.

ACKNOWLEDGMENTS

T he editors gratefully acknowledge the numerous suggestions and the critical guidance generously offered by several individuals. June Matthews enjoyed many conversations with the prolific author Owen Gingerich, Professor of the History of Astronomy at Harvard University, who knew Harlow Shapley intimately and worked with him as a graduate student. We thank him and the International Astronomical Union for permission to reprint his article on Shapley's impact on 20th century astronomy. Science historian David DeVorkin of the Smithsonian Institution read Mildred's manuscript in its entirety. He posed many critical questions, and he made numerous insightful remarks that improved the clarity of the exposition. Science writers Dava Sobel and Marcia Bartusiak provided much encouragement and valuable advice for bringing this project to fruition. Harvard professor and distinguished entomologist E.O. Wilson corresponded with June Matthews on Shapley's fascination with and extracurricular study of ants, and provided the solution to a formicine mystery. Tom Bogdan is especially grateful for the opportunity to have spent several delightful afternoons with Harlow Shapley's son and daughter-in-law, Alan and Kay Shapley, at their Boulder home, listening to recollections of their lives as Shapleys. June Matthews thanks her siblings Bruce, Melvin, and Martha Matthews and her cousin Deborah Shapley, daughter of Harlow Shapley's eldest son Willis Shapley, for their support of this project along the way. Martha Matthews deserves special commendation for re-creating Mildred's hand-drawn illustrations, for proofreading and copy-editing the final manuscript, and for compiling the index.

Finally, we are indebted to Mildred for a sensitive and engaging portrayal of her life as an astronomer's daughter.

ILLUSTRATION CREDITS

Source of all photographs: the Betz and Shapley-Matthews family scrapbooks, Mildred Shapley Matthews, curator

Cover	Courtesy Harvard College Observatory
Frontispiece	Betz collection, unknown photographer
p. 3	Betz collection
p. 4	Betz collection
p. 14	Courtesy Harvard College Observatory
p. 23	Shapley collection
p. 25	Betz collection
p. 26	Courtesy Harvard College Observatory
p. 41	Betz collection
p. 43	Courtesy Harvard College Observatory
p. 59	Betz collection
p. 100	Shapley collection
p. 136	Shapley collection
p. 145	Bachrach Photography, Boston, MA
p. 153	Shapley collection
p. 156	Shapley collection
p. 162	Courtesy Newspictures, New York City
p. 207	Shapley collection
p. 212	Courtesy Harvard College Observatory
p. 220	Courtesy Harvard College Observatory
p. 230	Matthews collection
p. 235	Matthews collection
p. 245	Matthews collection
p. 295	Courtesy University of Arizona

ABOUT THE EDITORS

June Lorraine Matthews, born August 1, 1939 to Mildred and Ralph Matthews, is the eldest granddaughter of Harlow Shapley. Shapley, with his wit, his scientific prowess, and his wide-ranging intellectual interests exerted a profound influence on her life throughout childhood, adolescence, and adulthood. June graduated from Carleton College in 1960 with a major in Physics, and received her Ph.D. from the Massachusetts Institute of Technology in 1967. She held postdoctoral fellowships at the University of Glasgow (Scotland) and Rutgers University before joining the faculty at MIT in 1973, where she remained until her retirement in 2012. From 2000 to 2006 she served as Director of MIT's Laboratory for Nuclear Science. In addition to pursuing her teaching career and research in nuclear physics, June is an avid amateur musician with special passion for the Renaissance and Baroque eras. She lives in semi-rural Lincoln, Massachusetts with her multi-colored tabby cat Daphne.

Thomas Joseph Bogdan was born July 24, 1957 to Margaret Derejko and Leonard Bogdan. He graduated summa cum laude from the State University of New York at Buffalo in 1979 with a joint major in Physics and Mathematics, and received his Ph.D. from the University of Chicago in 1984. He held a postdoctoral fellowship and then a staff position at the High Altitude Observatory of the National Center for Atmospheric Research. From 2006 to 2012 he was the Director of the National Weather Service's Space Weather Prediction Center, and he subsequently served as the 6th President of the University Corporation for Atmospheric Research. He lives in Boulder, Colorado with his wife Barbara Cardell and their black labrador Yeti.

ABOUT THE AUTHOR

Mildred Louise Shapley Matthews was born in Pasadena, CA on February 15, 1915, the eldest child of Harlow (1885-1972) and Martha Betz (1890-1981) Shapley. She graduated Phi Beta Kappa from the University of Michigan in 1936 with a major in Physical Science. In 1937 she married Ralph Vernon Matthews (1914-2002). They had four children: June (b. 1939), Bruce (b. 1941), Melvin (b. 1945), and Martha (b. 1963). During a long career Mildred worked in several areas of astronomy, at the California Institute of Technology, the *Osservatorio Astronomico* in Trieste, Italy, and the University of Arizona. From 1970 to 1996 she was Scientific Editor of the *Space Science Series* at the University of Arizona's Lunar and Planetary Laboratory. For this work she won the Harold Masursky Award given by the American Astronomical Society for meritorious service to planetary science in 1993 (see photograph below). Her major interests outside science were grand opera and world travel. She passed away on February 11, 2016.

INDEX